MODERN BUSINESS

A Series of Texts prepared as Part of the

Modern Business Program

Registered Trade Mark
United States and Great Britain
Marca Registrada, M. de F.

ALEXANDER HAMILTON INSTITUTE

BANKING

by

Raymond Rodgers, A.B., M.B.A.

PROFESSOR OF BANKING,
GRADUATE SCHOOL OF BUSINESS ADMINISTRATION,
NEW YORK UNIVERSITY

Alexander Hamilton Institute, New York

Preface

Banking is indispensable in our modern economy with its specialization and division of labor. Today, more than ever before, banking serves government and business, and, in addition, serves the consumer directly as well as indirectly. In fact, it is not too much to say that continuous and adequate access to the banking mechanism is prerequisite to success in business.

Banking, in so far as its basic functions of credit extension, transferring of values and safekeeping are concerned, is almost as old as recorded history; but, in recent years, a new dimension of great importance has been given the banking process. This new aspect of banking is the conscious, purposeful *management* of money and credit to accomplish specific government objectives, such as financing war and moderating the swings of the business cycle. In other words, banking is used today as an instrument of social policy as well as a handmaiden of business.

Our national policy of using money and credit management to influence business activity, employment levels, and economic expansion makes it imperative for business men to understand what can, and what *cannot*, be done with this comparatively new and increasingly powerful mechanism. In other words, since credit management by our monetary authorities largely determines short-term interest rates and the availability of credit for business, it follows that successful business men must understand the principles and aims of such management.

To explain the principles of the banking and money management of today, and tomorrow, the Institute engaged Professor Raymond Rodgers, an authority well-known to banking and business groups throughout the country and Canada as a teacher, writer, and convention speaker for more than thirty years.

Professor Rodgers, a Kentuckian by birth, became a member of the faculty of New York University in 1925, and has been for many years Professor of Banking in its Graduate School of Business Administration.

He is also a member of the faculty of the Graduate School of Credit and Financial Management of the National Association of Credit Men at Dartmouth College, and of the Graduate School of Banking of the American Bankers Association at Rutgers University.

Professor Rodgers is co-author of "Money and Banking," a standard text in the field of banking since 1936, and a contributing author of the recent text, "American Financial Institutions." Also, he is one of the principal contributing editors of the "Financial Handbook"; and he wrote the sections on "Currency" and "Money" for the "Encyclopedia Americana." He is Special Contributing Editor of "Bankers Monthly," and is a frequent contributor to other magazines and periodicals in the field of banking and finance.

He is well-known as a consulting economist, having served such outstanding organizations as Savings Banks Trust Company (New York), State Street Trust Company (Boston), Mobil Oil Corporation, and Magnolia Petroleum Company. For many years he has been a frequent speaker before state banking association conventions and national conventions in finance and industry.

It is the author's wish that special acknowledgment be given to Mr. G. Arnold Hart, President, Bank of Montreal, whose speech "This Business of Banking" before the Canadian Club, Montreal, February 22, 1960, was a veritable gold mine of inspiration and information in the preparation of Chapter XX; and also to the staff, Bank of Montreal, New York agency, for their assistance and cooperation with respect to factual content.

EDITOR-IN-CHIEF

Table of Contents

CHAPTER I

The First 5,000 Years

SECTION   PAGE

1. The Lessons of History   1
2. Temple Banking   2
3. Private Banking Emerges   3
4. Banking Under Roman Rule   3
5. The Money Lenders of the Dark Ages   4
6. The Bank of Venice   5
7. The Bank of Amsterdam   6
8. Contribution of the Goldsmiths of London   8
9. John Law—Gambler and Banker   9
10. John Law's Bank   10
11. Law's Scheme   11
12. Why the "System" Failed   12
13. Another French Experiment   14
14. The Bank of England   15
15. Contributions of the Past   16

CHAPTER II

American Trial and Error

1. The Evolution of American Banking   19
2. Banking in the Colonies   20
3. Colonial Banks   21
4. The First Bank of the United States   22
5. The Second Bank of the United States   23

SECTION   PAGE
   6. Unsound and Scandalous Practices of the Second
        Bank of the United States   *   25
   7. The Bank War   27
   8. Lessons of the Banks of the United States   29
   9. The Era of State-Chartered Banks   30
  10. "Wildcat" Banks   31
  11. Bank Notes Unlimited   32
  12. The Hard Way   34

CHAPTER III

Development of Our Banking System

   1. Our Banking System   36
   2. Mobilizing Banking Resources   37
   3. Dedication to "Independent" Banking   38
   4. Reasons for the Suffolk "System"   39
   5. The Suffolk System   39
   6. The Safety Fund System   41
   7. Free Banking System of New York   43
   8. The Independent Treasury System   44
   9. The Civil War "Greenbacks"   47
  10. Reasons for the National Bank Act   48
  11. Lessons of the National Banking System   50
  12. Gradual Improvement   51

CHAPTER IV

Commercial Banks—Source of Our Modern Money

   1. A Bookkeeping Mechanism   53
   2. Banking Credit Differentiated from Other Credit   54
   3. Monetary Credit, a Social Product   55
   4. Recognition of the Right to Credit   56
   5. Establishing the Right to Credit   58

SECTION | PAGE

6. Substitution of Bank's Credit for Borrower's Credit   59
7. The Transferring of Values   60
8. How Loans Create Money   60
9. All Deposits Are Derivative So Far As the Banking System Is Concerned   62
10. Double Entry Bookkeeping Tells the Tale   63
11. Repayment Reduces the Money Supply   66
12. Our Money Must Be Defended   67

CHAPTER V

Where the Bank Gets Its "Money"

1. Sources of Bank Funds   70
2. Functions of Bank Capital   70
3. Present Capital Situation   72
4. Amount of Capital Needed   75
5. Relation of Capital to Deposits   76
6. Relation of Capital to Assets   77
7. Responsibility for Adequate Capital   78
8. Relation of Capital to Profits   80
9. Relation of Capital to Growth   81
10. Difficulty of Sale of New Stock   82
11. Primary Deposits   83
12. Reserves Created by the Federal Reserve Banks   84
13. Borrowing by Banks   85

CHAPTER VI

Loan Services of Banks

1. Wide Range of Loan Services   87
2. Revival of Bank Lending   88
3. Adequacy of Bank Credit   89
4. Loan-Deposit Ratios   91

SECTION   PAGE

 5. Concept of Loanable Funds   92
 6. Relation of Loans to Character of Deposits   93
 7. Relation of Loans to the Business Cycle   95
 8. Self-Liquidity vs. Shiftability   96
 9. Loans Classified as to Purpose   98
10. Further Classification of Loans   100
11. Protection on Interest Rates   102

CHAPTER VII

Open Market and Other Short-Term Borrowing

1. Use of the Term "Open Market"   104
2. Disadvantages of Open-Market Borrowing   105
3. Advantages of Open-Market Borrowing   106
4. Bankers Acceptances   107
5. Trade Acceptances   110
6. Commercial Paper   112
7. Sales-Finance Companies   113
8. Factors   118
9. Accounts Receivable Financing   122

CHAPTER VIII

Bank-Deposit Services

1. Countless Services of Banks   126
 2. Bank Investments   127
 3. Why Banks Buy Securities   127
 4. The Deposit Services of Banks   128
 5. Checking Accounts   130
 6. Service Charges   132
 7. Savings Services   134
 8. Reasons for Regulation of Interest Payments   137
 9. Government Deposits   139
10. Treasury Tax and Loan Accounts   140

Contents

CHAPTER IX

Deposit Protection

SECTION	PAGE
1. Guaranty and Insurance of Deposits	144
2. Federal Deposit Insurance	146
3. The Federal Deposit Insurance Corporation	147
4. Management of the Federal Deposit Insurance Corporation	148
5. Termination of Insurance	148
6. Method of Protecting Depositors	149
7. Costs of Deposit Insurance	151
8. Relation of the FDIC to the Money Supply	151
9. Contribution of Banking Education to Deposit Protection	153
10. Banking Schools	154
11. Banking "Commissions"	156
12. Bank Publications	156
13. Banking Magazines	157
14. Publications of Alexander Hamilton Institute	158
15. More Knowledge Means Better Banking	158

CHAPTER X

Clearing and Collections

1. Transferring of Values	161
2. The Clearing Principle	161
3. The Clearing House	162
4. Method of Clearing	163
5. Other Clearing House Functions	165
6. City Collection	166
7. Transit	167
8. The Universal Numerical System	168

SECTION	PAGE
9. Automation	169
10. Country Collection	171
11. Par Collection	171
12. Mechanics of Out-of-Town Collection	174
13. Interdistrict Settlement Fund	175
14. Observations on Clearing and Collections	176

CHAPTER XI

Commercial Banking Structure

1. Licensed and Regulated	180
2. Number of Banks	182
3. National vs. State Charter	183
4. The National Banks	185
5. The State Banks	185
6. Our Dual Banking System	186
7. Unit Banking	187
8. Outlook for Independent Unit Banking	189
9. Branch Banking	193
10. Arguments for Branch Banking	194
11. Arguments Against Branch Banking	196
12. Holding-Company Banking	197
13. Importance of Holding-Company Banking	199
14. Summary on Banking Structure	200

CHAPTER XII

Savings Banks and Savings and Loan Associations

1. Financial Intermediaries	202
2. Nature of Savings Banking	203
3. Economic Need for Promotion of Saving	205
4. The Savings Banks	206

SECTION	PAGE
5. Savings Bank Investments	209
6. Efficiency of Operation	210
7. Mutual Form of Organization	212
8. Taxation of Mutual Savings Banks	213
9. Importance of Management	214
10. Savings and Loan Associations	216
11. Liquidity of Shares vs. That of Deposits	218
12. Difference Between FDIC and FSLIC (Federal Savings and Loan Insurance Corporation)	219
13. The Home Loan Bank System	220

CHAPTER XIII

The Federal Reserve System

1. A Central Banking System	222
2. The "Independence" of the Federal Reserve System	223
3. Board of Governors of the Federal Reserve System	225
4. Functions of the Board of Governors	226
5. Structure of the Federal Reserve System	228
6. The Federal Open Market Committee	230
7. The Federal Advisory Council	231
8. Regulations of the Board of Governors	232
9. Supervisory Functions of the Federal Reserve	237
10. Earning Assets and Liabilities of the Federal Reserve Banks	238
11. Contributions of Federal Reserve System	240

CHAPTER XIV

The Money Market

1. The Money Market	243
2. Why Wall Street?	244
3. Services of the Money Market	246

SECTION   PAGE
4. Major Institutions in the Money Market   248
5. Five Markets for Money   252

CHAPTER XV

The Money Market (Continued)

1. The Commercial Paper Market   254
2. The Bankers Acceptance Market   256
3. Loans to Brokers and Dealers   258
4. The Federal Funds Market   259
5. The Short-Term Government Securities Market   261
6. Money Market Rates   263
7. Relation of the Money Market to the Economy   264

CHAPTER XVI

Credit and Money Management

1. Credit and Money Management   266
2. Definition of Money Management   266
3. Goals of Money Management   268
4. Determinants of Monetary Policy   269
5. Two Aspects of Monetary Policy   271
6. Techniques of Quantitative Credit Control   275
7. Results Achieved by Money Management   279
8. Problems of Money Management   280
9. Dangers Faced by Money Management   282

CHAPTER XVII

Meet Your Bank

1. Importance of a Good Banking Connection   284
2. Selecting a Bank   285
3. Head Office or Branch?   286

Contents

SECTION   PAGE

 4. Opening an Account   287
 5. Kind of Deposit Account   290
 6. The Receiving Tellers   292
 7. The Paying Teller   293
 8. Endorsement   294
 9. Certification of Checks   297
10. Stop-Payment Orders   299

CHAPTER XVIII

How to Get the Most from Your Banking Connection

1. Banking Service   302
2. How to Borrow from Your Bank   304
3. An Important Advantage of Borrowing from Your Bank   307
4. How to Get Maximum Credit Information from Your Bank   308
5. How to Get Faster Banking Service   309
6. In-Plant Banking   315
7. Many Trust Department Services   316
8. Advisory Service   317
9. Rules for Relations with Your Bank   317

CHAPTER XIX

Financing International Trade

1. Special Problems of International Trade   320
2. Differences Between Domestic and International Trade Finance   321
3. Foreign Credit Information   323
4. Information and Advisory Services   324
5. Financing Exports   325
6. Cash-in-Advance Financing   326

SECTION	PAGE
7. Open-Account Financing	328
8. Trade-Draft Financing	328
9. Bank Financing of Exports	330
10. Mechanics of the Commercial Credit	333
11. Traveler's Letter of Credit	337
12. A Word About Foreign Exchange	338

CHAPTER XX

Canadian Banking

1. Similarities and Dissimilarities	340
2. The First Canadian Bank	342
3. Branch Banking	342
4. The Urge to Merge	344
5. Legal Requirements	345
6. Deposits	346
7. Loans	348
8. Investments	350
9. Clearing and Collections	351
10. Bank Personnel	352
11. Banking Supervision	352
12. The Bank of Canada	353
13. Money Management in Canada	356
14. Conclusions	358

List of Illustrations

FIGURE	PAGE
1. Statements Showing Clearing-House Procedure	164
2. Code of Ethics for the Exchange of Information	310
3. Illustration of an MICR Check	313
4. Authority to Purchase	332
5. Confirmed Irrevocable Straight Credit	336

BANKING

CHAPTER I

The First 5,000 Years

1. *The lessons of history.* Santayana, the great modern philosopher, says, "Those who do not remember the past, will be condemned to repeat it." It is in this spirit that considerable reference is made throughout this book, especially in the first three chapters, to the lessons of history in the field of banking. As banking is older than recorded history, it is not surprising to find that there is little in modern currency and banking practice that has not been tried at least once, sometime, somewhere; and there is much that has been tried many times, in many places, in many different eras.

In a field as important as banking is to the individual, to the business enterprise and to the entire economy, full advantage should be taken of this experience of the past. This is not to say that the categorical Biblical pronouncement that ". . . there is no new thing under the sun" [1] is applicable; but it is frank recognition that many civilizations have made contributions—both good and bad—to our modern banking and credit mechanism.

[1] Ecclesiastes 1:9.

Even the failures of the past can be helpful in understanding modern banking, since it is just as important in this field to know what will *not* work as to know what will work. With this firmly in mind, let us start our study of banking with the temples of Babylon, some 2,000 years before Christ.

2. *Temple banking.* Paradoxically, banking developed before there were either banks or bankers. In fact, by the time of the promulgation of the famous Code of Hammurabi around 2000 B.C., the Babylonian temples had developed the basic banking functions of lending and safekeeping as profitable sidelines.

More specifically, they did a flourishing business in *lending* the gold, silver and other wealth that had been left with them for *safekeeping*. Their banking activities were undoubtedly profitable as they charged as much as one-sixtieth of the deposit for the safekeeping, and they charged 20 per cent interest, compounded monthly, for the loans. They, thus, collected twice (coming, and going) on the same money, something no modern banker has been able to do!

The temples of Greece—fifteen hundred years later —were likewise utilized for the safekeeping of the wealth of the community. Although sadly lacking in security by modern standards, the temples, because of the religious scruples of the upper classes and the superstitious fears of the general populace, offered greater security than could be found elsewhere in a country continually torn by war and civil dissension.

While it is not clear whether the Grecian priests loaned the funds left with them for safekeeping, they did lend temple funds at interest; and they did collect fees from their depositors for the safekeeping service.

3. *Private banking emerges.* Evidently, the temple banking of Greece was profitable, as private bankers soon appeared as competitors. These private bankers offered a wide range of banking services, including even foreign exchange. In fact, they brought banking to such a high state of development that in Athens, for example, a special body of law covering banking transactions was formulated and a special court, in which judgment had to be given within thirty days, was established to try banking actions. There was even some state regulation and supervision of banking activities.

Another modern aspect of Greek banking was the widespread practice of government borrowing from the private bankers. One banker even took possession of the citadel of a city as security, and held it until his loan was repaid. It is indeed interesting to note that the public debt found its way into the banks in those far-off days, just as it does today.

4. *Banking under Roman rule.* The vast area of Roman rule, its intricate system of taxation, and its far-reaching and complicated trade and commerce, necessitated a well-developed banking system. The Roman *Argentarii* (dealers in silver) were far more than mere money changers. Citizens of all ranks came to them to borrow,

to sell mortgages, and to obtain letters of credit. These bankers loaned their own capital and, to a much greater extent, the money of their depositors, not only to business men but also to politicians, ambitious wives, courtesans, and even to gamblers. The rates of interest on these non-productive and high-risk loans were naturally high as the losses were great.

These loans, for purposes of *consumption* rather than *production*, and the high rates of interest exacted, brought banking into disrepute. And, even though interest rates eventually, under the Empire, dropped to 2½ per cent per year, banking did not regain respectable standing until many centuries later. In fact, banking completely disappeared during the long years of retrogression of the Dark Ages.

5. *The money lenders of the Dark Ages.* Although banking, as such, disappeared, the banking tradition was kept alive by the Jews who became the money lenders of the Dark Age centuries. The field was left free for them as the Christian Church did not distinguish between interest and usury, and consequently forbade the taking of any payment for the use of money. Although usury (interest) was expressly forbidden for the Jews in both Exodus and Leviticus, these Biblical injunctions were ameliorated in Deuteronomy, Chapter 23, with the provision that "unto a stranger thou mayest lend upon usury." This dispensation made it possible for the Jews many centuries later to specialize in the field of money lending. As interest of 1 per cent

a month was permitted under the laws of the Roman Empire, the Jews were able to gain the experience and accumulate the capital that permitted them to dominate the field of money lending for several centuries.

6. *The Bank of Venice.* The Bank of Venice, founded in A.D. 1171, is considered the first publicly owned bank. Although it did not perform many of the functions of banking; in fact, its services were never as complete as those of the Roman *Argentarii* or even the Greek bankers, it did permit the transfer of credits from account to account. This was made possible by the fact that the bank was originally designed as an officer of record for the public debt incurred by Venice in financing her frequent wars with her neighbors.

This financing, which was in the form of forced loans from its wealthier citizens, was the sole original asset of the bank. The promise of the government to pay 5 per cent interest on these loans gave the credits on the books of the bank such value that the business of transferring them from one owner to another soon developed. After that, it was only a short step for the Venetian merchants to voluntarily deposit their specie in exchange for deposit credit at the bank, even though the specie could be withdrawn only for export and then only under certain conditions.

The important thing to note about the Bank of Venice is that the need for even such limited banking service was so great that it succeeded despite the severe limitations on the withdrawal of funds. In fact, the Bank of Venice was the forerunner of a long series of similar banks, including the Bank of St. George in Genoa, founded in the fourteenth century, the Bank of Barcelona in Spain, started around the same time, the Bank of Amsterdam in 1602, and, even the Bank of England, in 1694.

7. *The Bank of Amsterdam.* The great wave of trade exploration and commerce which made Holland a world power in the seventeenth century caused Amsterdam to become a world trade center. Experiencing increasing difficulty with the widely varying coins of differing weight and fineness that were brought in by foreign traders, a municipal bank of exchange was organized by the city authorities to remedy the situation.

This bank—the Bank of Amsterdam—was essentially a place for the deposit of all kinds of coins at their bullion value. For these deposits, the bank would give standard money or would give deposit credit on its books. Such deposits could be transferred on the books of the bank by written order. (The unit of these orders was the actual physical deposit rather than the individual, as in modern deposit banking.) These orders, known as "bank money," soon became the popular medium of exchange of the day. By law, all bills of exchange were payable in these written orders as they had a standard value. In fact, their convenience and certain value caused them to circulate at a premium of as much as 4 per cent over specie itself!

The substantial charge made on each deposit enabled the bank to make enormous profits for the city and to become so strong that it weathered a serious run in 1672, paying out specie on demand to all who presented "bank money."

Although well-nigh indispensable to the trade of the world, the bank's enormous holding of coins and bullion proved an irresistible temptation to the Dutch politicians. Those responsible for its management betrayed their trust by lending the special deposits for which a *safekeeping* fee had been charged; moreover, the loans, largely to the Dutch East India Company, to Holland, and to the city of Amsterdam itself, were not good loans.

As a result, an investigating committee in 1760 could find only 10,000,000 guilders in the bank's vaults, although its outstanding obligations for deposits supposedly held intact were for 30,000,000 guilders. In view of the substantial safekeeping charge (a charge of 10 guilders—say, $7.00—was made on the initial deposit and about 30 per cent less on each subsequent deposit), this was plain stealing of 66⅔ per cent of the bank assets.

The City of Amsterdam as owner of the bank and guarantor of its deposits assumed the liabilities and eventually paid all depositors in full. Although this had been done by 1802, public confidence had, nonetheless, fallen so low that it became necessary to liquidate the bank in 1819.

Thus, the Dutch learned long ago that constant vigilance is necessary to prevent banks from being looted, even by those supposed to protect them. They also learned the "hard way" that government ownership and government guarantees are no substitute for sound banking and adequate reserves. In short, the sad history of the Bank of Amsterdam demonstrates that public confidence is based on sound banking practices and that such confidence, once lost, is very difficult, if not impossible, to regain, even by government fiat.

8. *Contribution of the goldsmiths of London.* The London goldsmiths of the sixteenth century were the earliest English bankers. Starting with the acceptance of money and valuables for safekeeping, they soon began to make loans and purchase drafts on a discount basis. The proceeds of these discounts were credited to the account of the customer, as were other deposits.

These credits on the books of the goldsmiths were transferred by means of two different types of credit instruments. One type was a written promise of the goldsmith to pay on demand a stated amount to the customer, or to his order, or to bearer. These demand obligations, termed "goldsmith's notes," soon circulated from hand to hand as currency. They were thus the forerunners of the bank notes of today.

The other type of transfer was for the customer to write an order to the goldsmith, directing him to pay on demand the indicated amount to himself, or to order, or to bearer. Such orders were called "cash notes." They bore serial numbers which were recorded for the purposes of authentication in books called "check books." These orders were, thus, an early form of the checks used so widely today.

It did not take the goldsmiths long to discover that the demands for payment were normally only a fraction of their total note and deposit liabilities. They thereupon began to issue notes considerably in excess of the cash they had on hand. As a result of their enterprise, the goldsmiths dominated English banking until 1694 when the financial embarrassment of the Crown was utilized by a Scotsman of perseverance and imagination, named Patterson, to secure authorization for the founding of the Bank of England.

9. *John Law—gambler and banker.* A few years later, another Scotsman, John Law, gave the French a costly lesson in the art of banking. Law, a widely-traveled gentleman, adventurer, gambler and speculator, had observed first-hand the great need for sound credit and currency in the countries he visited. Gifted with outstanding financial ability, it was only natural that he should apply himself to the problem upon his return to Scotland.

Law was unable, however, to convince the Scots of the soundness of his scheme, as it included a currency without any provision for ultimate redemption. After the Scottish Parliament rejected his entire project, he took his scheme to France where the need for sound credit and money was much greater than in Scotland.

10. *John Law's bank.* Although Law found France full of schemers and schemes to relieve the poverty that was almost universal outside of the Royal Court, his fertile brain and social graces soon outstripped those of all others. He first proposed a state bank of issue, the profits of which were to accrue to the state. This was summarily rejected by the Council of Finance.

Law thereupon proposed a privately owned and managed bank of issue subject only to the general control of the government. Through the aggressive intervention of the Regent (ruling in the name of the King, who was only a child), letters of patent were issued on May 2, 1716, for the *General Bank,* despite strenuous opposition.

The General Bank, among other privileges, was permitted to issue bills based on the actual value of the coins or specie on the day of deposit. As these were standard in value and backed 100 per cent by gold or silver, they corresponded to the "bank money" of the Bank of Amsterdam and consequently circulated freely from hand to hand. The bank was also permitted to open accounts, payable in its notes, discount commercial paper and trade in foreign exchange.

Lack of credit facilities and the activities of usurers had driven the prevailing rate of interest in France to more than 30 per cent, but the new bank promptly remedied this. Its initial discount rate was only 6 per cent, and it later reduced its rate to 4 per cent. The need for banking and credit facilities was so great that the bank was highly successful from the start. In fact, it accomplished more than Law had promised the Regent, including substantial profits. (Law had the Regent as a partner in the venture!)

It is indeed sad to observe that the financial history of France would have been much happier if Law had been content with his outstanding success as a banker and discounter; but, unfortunately, his great ambition and fertile imagination caused him to embark on a scheme of "high finance" that led France into one of the wildest and most disastrous orgies of frenzied specu- lation that the world has ever seen.

11. *Law's scheme.* Law's "System," as he called it, included as a first step, on December 4, 1718, the con- version of the General Bank into the Royal Bank, with notes no longer convertible into specie, followed in swift succession by the organization of the *Compagnie d'Occident* (the Mississippi Bubble), ostensibly to colonize the Mississippi Valley, but actually designed to take over the State debt, as only such obligations were accepted in payment for shares. This, in turn, was followed by the organization of the *Compagnie des Indes,* which immediately took over the *Compagnie d'Occident,* the Guinea Company (controlling all trade with Africa), and the China Company, with a monopoly of all trade with the Orient.

Thus, Law's System, through the India Company, had a monopoly of the entire foreign trade of France. Expanding still further, the India Company on July 15,

1719 paid the government 50,000,000 livres for a nine-year monopoly of the issue of coins and management of the mint. And, on August 27, 1719, the India Company, in payment for the tax monopoly, loaned the King the stupendous sum (for those days) of 1,200,000,000 livres to pay off the State debt. The Company also took over the tobacco monopoly.

The most amazing thing about this repayment of the State debt and purchase of the monopolies was that they were financed by the issuance of stock, the par value of which was only 312,000,000 livres, but which was sold to eager "investors" for 1,797,500,000 livres, all of which was paid in bills issued by the Royal Bank. Law's scheme, or "System," had so captured the imagination of the French that frenzied speculation drove the market price of the stock of the *Compagnie des Indes,* for example, to 3,600 per cent of par.

Equally amazing was Law's audacity in refusing gold and accepting only notes of the Royal Bank in payment for the stock issues, with the result that the notes went to a premium of 10 per cent over gold. Irredeemable paper was thus preferred to gold, which certainly is the height of financial insanity. This alone was sufficient indication that a grim, financial reckoning was inevitable and imminent.

12. *Why the "System" failed.* In essence, John Law's System was a conscious effort to create an ever-growing demand for the ever-growing notes of the Royal Bank. This was done through the issuance of more and more

stock by corporations, through feeding the fires of speculation to drive ever higher the market price of stock already issued, and through his monopolies (especially the exclusive right to collect all taxes), which made it possible for him to insist on use of the notes of the Bank for all payments.

Operated solely as business ventures, the various monopolies could hardly have failed to realize a handsome return on the par value of their stock. Their profits, however, were totally inadequate to maintain the inflated market price of 36 times par, to which the stock of the India Company, for example, had been driven (largely to create additional demand for the notes of the Bank).

Finally, when the stock of the Mississippi Company reached a level of 125 times its annual earnings, certain individuals called "realizers," in contempt, began to present the notes of the Bank and demand payment. For a while, the notes were promptly redeemed. Then, in an effort to stem the tide, the Bank, with the support of the government, took various delaying steps, which have become all too familiar in our time. More specifically, the Bank's notes were given preference over specie in the payment of taxes, coins were reduced in weight, specie holdings by individuals were limited, the sale of gold and silver objects was prohibited, and, finally, gold and silver were deprived of legal tender power and confiscated by the state.

In addition, an attempt was made by the government to slow the precipitous drop in the shares of the India Company by setting a definite scale for an orderly reduction in their market price. Inevitably, this plan failed, so trading in the shares was prohibited— notwithstanding, the price continued to fall.

Many other edicts and decrees were issued, but instead of helping, they only caused further alarm. As a result, the notes of the Bank itself dropped to 50 per cent of their face value—and still the "realizers" demanded payment. As the flight from the notes of the Bank gained momentum, commodity prices rose so rapidly that Law was forced to resign as Superintendent of Finance on December 27, 1720, and flee for his life to Brussels. The "System" was then liquidated with enormous losses and the Royal Bank vanished in disgrace.

It is important to remember that all this took place in only three and a half years. In that short period, the "System" had ruined Law and wrecked France financially—such is the power of credit improperly used. And, as for the French people, it took them some fifty years to overcome the unhappy memory of the credit debacle of John Law, for it was that long before another bank was established.

13. *Another French experiment.* Unhappily, the French were fated to suffer on more than one future occasion from prostitution of bank credit by their government. Thus, the Bank of Commercial Discount, chartered in 1776, had its credit weakened to such an

extent by forced loans to the government that it had to be liquidated in 1793.

And immediately thereafter, the French Revolution, with its succeeding Reign of Terror, smothered France in such a welter of blood and fiat money that no private credit institution could be established or survive. To replace the resulting credit vacuum, France again experimented on a grand scale with irredeemable paper money—this time *assignats* instead of bank notes. Although basing them on real property, the authorities were unable to maintain the value of the *assignats*. So, they again sought to bolster the value of their money by stiff laws and penalties; but they again failed miserably under the inexorable force of economic laws. In short, despite Herculean efforts, the value of some 46,000,000,000 *assignats* soon dropped to less than one one-thousandth of their nominal value.

Credit was reborn in France in 1796 under the Directory, and a few banking institutions were established in the three years preceding the rise of Napoleon in 1799. Then, happily, the establishment of the Bank of France in 1800 and the institution of sound fiscal policies enabled Napoleon to maintain a metallic standard, with paper currency at a parity with specie, despite the severe economic and financial strains of his many military campaigns.

14. *The Bank of England.* Even a thumbnail sketch of the evolution of banking would be incomplete without a short reference to the Bank of England.

Although not generally realized, the Bank of England was founded on the public debt of the country. In return for a perpetual loan of £1,200,000 to the government, a charter was granted in 1694 to "The Governor and Company of the Bank of England." As this loan represented all the capital that had been raised, the Bank of England began operations without a pound in the till. This was no great handicap, however, as it had been given the power to issue demand notes; and the need for a credit institution was so great that its notes were in demand from the start. The English being naturally conservative, the Bank was steered clear of the pitfalls which wrecked the French banks, and has survived as a pillar of strength to this day.

15. *Contributions of the past.* As the extremely brief and fragmentary survey of this chapter has shown, modern banking is the beneficiary of practices which have evolved during some five thousand years of trial and error, much of it of the economically heartbreaking variety. It is difficult to comprehend why we, as a people, pay so little heed to the economic and credit fallacies so clearly demonstrated over and over again in the past. In particular, it is indeed discouraging to observe the constantly recurring cycle of slow development of credit along sound lines, followed by a much swifter overthrow through frenzied private speculation and unbridled government spending.

History leaves no room for doubt that bank credit cannot be expanded in unlimited degree without forfeiting public confidence and pulling down the whole credit structure like a house of cards; and that a government cannot continually indulge in unlimited spending and load its obligations upon the banks indefinitely without ultimately ruining the banks, and perhaps itself as well. The fact that most modern nations have disregarded these well-established principles at one time or another during the twentieth century, many of them with disastrous results, clearly demonstrates the need for constant vigilance on our part.

The principles of sound money and credit have been written large in thousands of years of history. They are well known. They have stood the acid test of time. They can be relied upon in the future. Whether we follow them or the primrose path of dalliance and ease promised by false economic Messiahs, is up to us. We *know* the true way—let us have the courage to follow it.

Review

How could banking antedate both banks and bankers?

Specifically, how did the views of the early Christian church on interest affect the development of banking?

Explain the origin of the Bank of Venice. How did the Bank of Amsterdam function?

What was the real object of John Law's "System"?

Why did his "System" fail?

What were the fatal weaknesses of the paper money issues outlined in this chapter?

Why was the Bank of England "the exception which proves the rule"?

Briefly summarize the more important lessons of the past that modern bankers and governments should learn and heed.

Note: The review at the end of each chapter is intended for the personal convenience of the reader in testing his understanding of this chapter. It is not necessary or desirable for the subscriber to submit written answers to the Institute except in a case where he may feel uncertain as to his grasp of the subject under consideration.

CHAPTER II

American Trial and Error

1. *The evolution of American banking.* American banking is indigenous in the sense that it has evolved in response to our needs and that, notwithstanding its vast inheritance from earlier banking in other countries, it has been shaped by our American psychology and philosophy. The total absence of American precedent and legislative restriction combined with the untrammeled pioneer spirit of our forefathers produced a species of banking unlike that anywhere else.

Experiment, innovation, fraud, government participation, and political interference have characterized American financial history from the outset. Our history is studded with a long succession of unsuccessful, and even disastrous, schemes and plans in the field of banking and currency. "Horrible" examples abound on every hand. The fact that a particular plan had failed elsewhere many times in the past did not dissuade us. After all, America was a new country, conditions were different, the people were different, and failure was "for the birds"!

The word "failure" was not in the "bright lexicon" of American progress. Only a country with our enormous natural resources and our unshakable faith (rising even above conviction) that tomorrow will be better than today could have so well survived the heavy economic drain of the poor banking *we inflicted on ourselves.*

2. *Banking in the Colonies.* There was naturally a great shortage of *capital* (the fruits of past production in the form of buildings, roads, machinery, etc.) in the Colonies, but, as the medium through which capital changes hands is *money,* the Colonists mistakenly thought that their need was money, and proceeded to do something about it. And what they did, in their economic ignorance, was, of course, the wrong thing. Specifically, they contrived many plans for creating money by community cooperation, or legislative fiat, or even by private enterprise.

The resulting issues of circulating notes (bills of credit) were in early colonial days known as "banks." Land being by far the most plentiful of the basic economic factors, it was only natural for the Colonists to turn to it as the basis for the security of these note issues. Typically, little or no capital was paid in by the organizers of a "bank"; they merely turned in mortgages and took notes as payment. Still other notes were issued against loans on goods and even for purchase of goods. And, although these early notes rarely carried even a promise (to say nothing of a legally enforceable contract) that they would be redeemed, the need for currency was so great that they circulated freely.

Although, as a practical matter, these notes were irredeemable, since the underlying real estate could not be paid out over the bank's counter in case of difficulty, the even more fatal defect of the notes was the utter certainty of *overissue*. Issued in quantities far in excess of the sustainable needs of the community, only the first holders of the notes received anything approaching their par value in terms of specie. Each succeeding holder received less and less—those who held them the longest lost the most.

Experience with these early "banks" (note-issues) was so uniformly bad that the public eventually would have no part of such a venture, with the result that they would be forced to revert to the delays and inconvenience of barter. As a result, there were no banks worthy of our consideration until after the Revolutionary War.

3. *Colonial banks.* The first real bank in the Colonies was the Bank of North America, established by Robert Morris in Philadelphia in 1781, under a charter granted by the Continental Congress. Most of the capital was subscribed by the Treasury and paid in specie brought in from France. Under the wise guidance of Morris, who had gained much financial wisdom from his experience in almost single-handedly financing the Revolution, a semblance of order was restored to the demoralized and chaotic public and private finances of the Federation. In particular, the bank provided a substantial amount of sound currency through limiting the

issue to the quantity that could be kept at a parity with specie by redemption on demand.

4. *The first Bank of the United States.* As a part of his effort to put the fiscal policies and credit of the United States on a sound basis, Alexander Hamilton induced Congress to charter a national bank of issue, the first Bank of the United States, in 1791. From a banking standpoint, the bank was a success; unfortunately, from a public relations standpoint, it was a failure. The reasons for such schizophrenic consequences are not only interesting but they furnish valuable guidance to bankers, central bankers and citizens today.

First, it should be noted that the bank furnished a circulating medium that was a great step forward for those days, although it would leave much to be desired under present-day standards.

Second, the bank aroused wide hostility by its adamant stand against inflation. This has always been an unpopular course, but in those days of untrammeled expansion, such inflexibility was practically suicidal from a business standpoint.

Third, the bank insisted on punctuality in meeting business engagements, which certainly did not increase its popularity as it was at such wide variance with the free and easy practices of the time.

Fourth, as anticipated by Hamilton, the bank was a great aid to the Treasury in its financing and fiscal operations.

These important services and improvements notwithstanding, the bank was so bitterly opposed that its charter was not renewed upon its expiration at the end of twenty years. Unfortunately, it had aroused the determined antagonism of several states by establishing branches within their borders and insisting on high standards of financial behavior.

Although the foregoing were the real reasons for the opposition to the bank, the most telling charge against it was that it had exercised political influence. Since 18,000 of its 25,000 shares were held in England, this was a very serious charge from a political standpoint, even though only the 7,000 American shares had the right to vote. Desha, a representative from Kentucky, speaking in the House of Representatives, called the bank a "viper in the bosom of our people," and expressed the belief that George III was a heavy shareholder. On such a note ended our first central bank of issue.

5. *The second Bank of the United States.* After the liquidation of the first Bank of the United States in 1811, the only source of note issue became the state chartered banks. With a wide-open field and no regulation or restraining influences, they multiplied in number and overexpanded note issue, individually and collectively.

The ensuing currency inflation and the strains of the War of 1812 forced the suspension of specie payment in 1814. This had a paralyzing effect on business and on the fiscal operations of the government, since the varying discounts on the notes of banks made it very difficult to transfer funds from one section of the country to another. Gallatin lost no opportunity to insist that these unsatisfactory conditions could have been avoided if the charter of the first Bank of the United States had been extended.

To remedy this unhappy state of affairs, several proposals were made for the establishment of another central bank on a national basis. Finally, upon the recommendation of President Madison, the second Bank of the United States was chartered by Congress on January 8, 1816. The bank was to have the large capital for those days of $35,000,000, one-fifth, or $7,000,000, of which was to be subscribed by the government itself. But, in return for this participation, the bank was to pay the government $1,500,000 for its charter, it was to transfer all funds for the government without charge, and the President of the United States received the right to appoint five of its twenty-five directors.

The bank was permitted to deal in bills of exchange, gold or silver bullion, and to sell goods taken over on defaulted loans. It was forbidden to issue circulating notes for less than $5; and all notes and bills for less than $100 were payable on demand; those over $100 were limited to a maximum term of sixty days.

It is particularly interesting to observe that all notes *and deposits* were to be paid in *specie;* and that disability or refusal to pay its obligations in accordance with the foregoing schedule subjected the bank to a

12 per cent per annum interest charge. It is also very interesting to note that the bank was permitted to establish branches; and that, under this provision, it established *twenty-five* branches, which would seem to be an inordinate number for the needs of those days.

6. *Unsound and scandalous practices of the second Bank of the United States.*   Despite the great need for such an institution, the bank was on the verge of insolvency within two years because of improper loans and speculation. For example, it loaned money on the security of its own stock, even though it was only part paid. To compound this unsound practice of lending on its own stock, the bank even loaned on the increased market value caused by speculation in the shares (although they were not fully paid) when other nominal security was pledged.

Adding to the danger of its reckless practices was the unhappy fact that the bank had very little specie. While one-quarter of the $28,000,000 private subscription, or $7,000,000, was supposed to be paid in specie, the bank probably received little more than $2,000,000 from this source. And, of course, the government subscription was in the form of public debt (government bonds), which certainly did not provide the bank with its obligations. Then, to add to its troubles, its Baltimore branch defaulted with a loss of $1,671,221. Drastic action was clearly necessary to save the bank.

Such action came on March 6, 1819, in the form of a new president, Langdon Cheves, of South Carolina, who avoided bankruptcy by borrowing $2,500,000 in Europe and by insisting on repayment of all loans made on the security of the bank's own shares at the rate of 5 per cent every sixty days. The bank was thus put in a solvent condition and it enjoyed public confidence for ten years. During this period, it facilitated the transfer of funds from one part of the country to another; it maintained a uniform circulation, which was equal in value to coins; it materially reduced the rates of exchange which had been abnormally high; and it greatly facilitated and benefited business, especially commerce.

In achieving these results, the bank had inevitably antagonized the state banks. They naturally resented the establishment of a national bank of issue, considering such action an encroachment on the monopoly of note issue which they had previously enjoyed. They also, particularly the border states and, most especially, Tennessee, strongly resented the insistence by the national institution on promptness in meeting obligations.

Unfortunately, the second Bank of the United States insisted on carrying the battle to the state banks. For example, the state banks suspended specie payment because of the War of 1812. This embarrassed the national government which had used them as depositaries after the dissolution of the first Bank of the United States. In consequence, the second Bank of the United States refused to accept the notes of the state banks until they resumed specie payments. This caused such friction that the politicians soon entered the fray.

7. *The bank war.* Although the bank's charter did not expire until 1836, President Andrew Jackson precipitated a violent controversy with his attack on it in his Annual Message of 1829. He charged that the bank had failed to establish a uniform and sound currency, although that was exactly what the bank had done. In fact, the notes of the state banks circulated at a discount of 7 to 25 per cent, whereas the notes of the Bank of the United States circulated at par. Even more damning, the state banks had not resumed specie payment on their notes. In view of this, Jackson's charges were indeed ironic.

Even more ironic, it was the bank's insistence that Jackson's Tennessee neighbors and friends observe the high standards that caused the "Border Captain" to go on the warpath.

In addition to his charge regarding the currency, Jackson also claimed that the bank was unconstitutional. This claim should have been disposed of by Chief Justice Marshall's decision upholding its constitutionality, but Jackson refused to accept the Supreme Court ruling. He likewise refused to accept the clean bill of health given the bank by the Congress which, incidentally, was consistently on the side of the bank in the long controversy. Thus, the stage was set for Jackson's bitter and protracted war on the bank.

The spark that caused the issue to flare up was the refusal of Biddle, the president of the bank, to remove the officer in charge of the branch in Portsmouth, New

Hampshire, on the charge of political favoritism, even though requested to do so by Samuel Ingham, the Secretary of the Treasury. With his characteristic lack of diplomacy, Biddle informed Ingham that the appointment of officers and their political attitude were not under the supervision of the government. In drawing this issue, he overlooked the important fact that Secretary Ingham could withdraw all government funds upon demand. This, of course, gave President Jackson the whiphand.

Thus, leading from strength, Jackson in his 1830 message to the Congress referred to the bank in less hostile terms; and, in his 1831 message, he used still milder terms to the effect that the question could be left to Congress and the people. The Republicans, under the leadership of Henry Clay, their presidential candidate, thought they detected an element of fear in Jackson's more conciliatory attitude, so they decided to make the rechartering of the bank (although still four years distant) one of the chief issues of the presidential campaign of 1832. Jackson, a real fighter, accepted the challenge with alacrity and was reelected by a real landslide of 219 electoral votes to only 67 votes for all other candidates combined. This meant the end of the bank.

Government deposits were withdrawn and deposited in the state banks, known as Jackson's "pets." The $7,000,000 of stock held by the government was redeemed by the bank at 115½ and sold to the public, thus keeping the capital at $35,000,000. And, President Biddle got a charter from Pennsylvania by paying a bonus of $2,000,000 and promising to pay $100,000 annually for twenty years, in addition to agreeing to subscribe to substantial amounts of state, railroad, canal and other local securities.

As the capital of the bank was far more than was needed for operation in only one state (Pennsylvania), the bank began to engage in speculative activities, particularly lending on speculative stocks. It also made other illegal and improper loans, including many to its own directors and officers. As a result, it failed in 1841. Although creditors were paid in full, stockholders lost their entire investment, and Biddle died in 1844, poor and broken-hearted.

8. *Lessons of the Banks of the United States.* The salient facts of the history of the two Banks of the United States have been given in some detail, as they demonstrate several important banking truths. Probably the most important one is that a bank, no matter how indispensable, cannot "beat City Hall." The politicians have the last word, unless the people intervene in defense of the institution.

Another important truth made clear is the unpopularity of any determined stand against cheap money (i.e., inflation). Bankers must have popular support or their position is untenable. This means a better public understanding of the lasting advantages of sound money as opposed to the temporary stimulation of over-expansion. The classic wisdom of *"Vox populi: vox Dei"* (the voice of the people is the voice of God) may apply in political matters, but it does not necessarily apply to economic affairs. In short, their solution requires more than strong emotion and deep conviction.

Still another lesson was that economics also "abhors a vacuum." This was demonstrated by the speed with which the functions of these national banks of issue were taken over by state-chartered institutions. In other words, the services will be continued, the only question being whether they will be done well, or badly.

9. *The era of state-chartered banks.* The difficulties of the second Bank of the United States ushered in an era of great expansion for state-chartered institutions. As regulation and standards were practically non-existent, such banks could be started with little or no capital and thus could be very profitable. Jackson's transfer of the government deposits to state institutions made them even more profitable and greater speculative favorites. People literally fought to subscribe to the stock of such institutions—riots frequently characterized the opening of the subscription books of a new bank.

The state-chartered institutions proliferated at such a rate that 340 banks, with nominal capital of $99,000,000 and with little or no money actually paid in for stock, were opened in the period 1832–1837 alone. Even the Society of Tammany in New York planned to start a bank to get rid of its debt. Another New York entry in the state sweepstakes was the North American Trust and Banking Company, organized in 1838. Although its announced capital was to be $50,000,000, it actually raised only $2,000,000. Since this amount consisted almost entirely of bonds and mortgages, it is not surprising to find that the institution went into receivership only three years later.

10. *"Wildcat" banks.* Typical of this period of unbridled expansion of state-chartered institutions was the experience of the state of Michigan, with its free banking act of 1837. This act permitted any twelve or more freeholders to organize a bank, and issue circulating notes against the deposit of bonds, or mortgages, or even the personal obligations of resident freeholders. Within two years, all but four of the forty banks organized under the law had failed. As many of these banks were located in areas where there were more wildcats than people, they were called "wildcat" banks.

These "wildcat" banks had an advantage highly esteemed in those days. Their location in out-of-the-way places difficult of access made it harder for note holders to present notes for redemption. This enabled the "wildcat" bank to keep more notes in circulation and thus increase profits with less need for specie.

The period between 1830 and 1840 may be summarized by saying that bank expansion was so utterly reckless and wild that it was popularly dubbed the era of wildcat banking, and it is so known to this day.

11. *Bank notes unlimited.* During the period of more or less continuous expansion, from the refusal to extend the charter of the second Bank of the United States to the Civil War, the confusion and profusion of bank note issues reached proportions which can hardly be imagined today. Not only were there hundreds of new banks with note issues; there were also hundreds of banks which had failed, yet their notes continued to circulate. Still other hundreds of banks were organized on paper only for the sole purpose of note issue, and their notes also circulated. And there were still more hundreds of "genuine" counterfeits.

It should also be kept in mind that banks were not the only agencies issuing circulating notes. Railroads, bridge and turnpike companies, fraternal organizations, libraries, schools, orphan academies and other non-banking institutions issued notes which were in circulation at various times in different states.

The confusion was so great that it has been estimated that there were in circulation in the 1850's some 7,000 different kinds of bank notes alone. Of these, 1,700 were issues of banks which existed only on paper, while 3,800, or more than half, were out-and-out counterfeit issues. Every bank had to employ several bank note "reporters" and counterfeit "detectors" to identify and determine the value of the notes offered to it.

The burden placed on business by the unrestrained free enterprise in note issue which characterized the period is dramatically shown in the following record of a traveler's problems with the chaotic currency conditions which he encountered on a trip in 1840:

Started from Virginia with Virginia money; reached the Ohio River, exchanged $20 Virginia note for shinplasters * and a $3 note of the Bank of West Union; paid away the $3 note for a breakfast; reached Tennessee; received a $100 Tennessee note; went back to Kentucky; forced there to exchange the Tennessee note for $88 Kentucky money; started home with the Kentucky money. In Virginia and Maryland compelled, in order to get along, to deposit five times the amount due, and several times detained to be shaved ** at an enormous per cent. At Maysville wanted Virginia money; couldn't get it. At Wheeling exchanged $5 note, Kentucky money, for notes of the Northwestern Bank of Virginia; reached Fredericktown; there neither Virginia nor Kentucky money current; paid a $5 Wheeling note for breakfast and dinner; received in change two $1 notes of some Pennsylvania bank, $1 Baltimore and Ohio Railroad, and balance in Good Intent shinplasters *; 100 yards from the tavern door all notes refused except the Baltimore and Ohio Railroad; reached Harpers Ferry; notes of Northwestern Bank in worse repute there than in Maryland; deposited $10 in hands of agent; in this way reached Winchester; detained there two days in getting shaved **. Kentucky money at 12 per cent, and Northwestern Bank at 10.

* Fractional currency.
** Loss in changing money.

12. *The hard way.* Probably the most insistent lesson of history is the propensity of mankind to do things the most difficult way. This was doubly true with regard to our note issues. Even if we had deliberately set out to do so, it is doubtful that we could have devised a more complicated or less satisfactory currency system than we had prior to the Civil War.

The abuses in connection with redemption, which struck at the very root of the value of our money, were marked and singularly imaginative. For example, banks far distant from one another would arrange to pay out each other's notes, which could not be presented for specie payment until the long trip home was completed. Still other banks would place their head office in an inaccessible place in the country, but would pay out their notes through an agency in the city. Anyone who had the time and the fortitude to present the notes at the head office would receive par, but all others would have to accept a discount, since the agency redeemed only at a discount. "Post notes," which were not payable until one or two months after date, as the case might be, were also issued.

These and countless other schemes to force notes into circulation, and to keep them in circulation, regardless of the needs of business, were a heavy burden on business. Yet, it took more than one hundred years, all told, before anything of consequence was done about it. Such is our infinite capacity to do things the hard way and the slow way.

Review

Why is American banking so different from that of other countries?

Why did the Colonists base the early note issue on land?

Explain the fatal defects of a currency based on land.

Summarize the more important accomplishments of the second Bank of the United States.

Explain the public hostility to the accomplishments of the second Bank of the United States.

Why did Henry Clay decide to make an election issue of President Jackson's hostility to the Bank of the United States?

What were the *real* reasons for Jackson's war on the Bank?

What were the outstanding characteristics of the era of state-chartered banks?

Justify the use of "Bank notes unlimited," as a section heading.

CHAPTER III

Development of Our Banking System

1. *Our banking system.* No bank can stand alone. In the very nature of banking, it must have many and varied relationships with other similar institutions. Born of necessity, these relationships are formalized by law or traditionalized by custom into a *system.*

There are three well-recognized and distinct types of such relationships. They are: (1) the central banking system; (2) the independent charter system; and (3) the "free" banking system. Their difference lies in the conditions under which the banks are chartered, and in the degree of combination of resources and centralization of control. The basic characteristics of these systems are of such importance in understanding banking operations that they will be briefly set forth in the following paragraphs.

The *central banking system* provides an over-all mechanism (in the form of a bank for bankers) for issuing only the coin and currency actually needed, for husbanding currency in time of emergency, for centralizing banking reserves, for granting relief in time of credit stringency through increase in reserves, and for furnishing at all times a dependable market for the credit obligations arising from sound banking operations. In this system, the actual banking operations are left to independent banking institutions which secure varying degrees of unity through the central banking mechanism.

The *independent charter system* is organized on the principle that a limited number of large banks with many branches can satisfactorily perform the services of a central bank and at the same time be of direct service to the public in day-to-day banking operations.

The *free banking system* assumes that each bank is capable of managing its affairs in normal times without outside aid either from a central bank or a distant head-office. It further assumes that, in case of emergency, informal action on the part of the leading members of the banking community will be sufficient to bring concerted action and afford any necessary assistance to an individual bank.

2. *Mobilizing banking resources.* Experience has amply demonstrated that banking safety cannot be achieved unless there is a definite and unfailing method of mobilizing banking resources in times of economic upheaval. The absolute necessity for such mobilization arises from the nature of the banking business, particularly its utter dependence on public confidence, and the equally basic fact that banks can never be in a position to pay their full liabilities *in cash* to all who might, under the stress of fear, demand such payment.

In essence, banking mobilization is concerned with

the principles governing note issue and creation of reserves and the problem of who should hold such reserves. These issues have loomed large in American banking. They were the underlying "casus belli" (cause of war) in President Jackson's war on the second Bank of the United States. They were involved in the founding of our national banks in 1863. They were the basic consideration in the organization of our Federal Reserve System in 1913. They are a bone of contention even today, as evidenced by the activities of the Independent Bankers Association and the refusal of many state banks to accept membership in the Federal Reserve System.

3. *Dedication to "independent" banking.* Independent, local units have always characterized American banking. Fear of undue concentration of economic power through centralized control of banking resources has caused the public to favor unit, or, as it is called, independent banking. As a result, the economic pressures toward branch banking have been countered with restrictive or prohibitory legislation. Also, our federal form of government, with fifty sovereign states, precludes branch banking on a national basis.

Our dedication to independent banking with its thousands of separate, local units has given us special problems of coordination and regulation. In particular, the problem of getting so many fiercely independent local bankers to work together in an efficient "system" and to present a common front in times of economic stress has been a continuous one. The more important efforts to make a banking system out of these separately owned, separately managed, separately situated, separately motivated, and widely varying unit banks warrant special consideration by the serious student of banking.

4. *Reasons for the Suffolk "system."* The Suffolk "system" was one of the earliest efforts to raise banking standards and practices. It arose out of the dilemma in which the Boston banks found themselves. Although they had over one-half of the banking capital of New England, they had only a twenty-fifth of the note issue. The reason for this situation is not hard to understand.

The notes of the country banks circulated at a discount of 1 per cent to 5 per cent in terms of the notes of the Boston banks. Since people could get more for their Boston notes at the banks, they brought them in for redemption and held on to their country bank notes. In consequence, the country banks reaped not only the normal profit from note issue, but also secured extra profits that would have otherwise gone to the Boston banks. Thus, quality was penalized and quantity rewarded. One Boston bank decided to do something about it.

5. *The Suffolk System.* The Suffolk Bank, chartered in 1818, decided to carry the "fight to the enemy" by placing the burden of redemption on the country banks, whose depreciated notes had so severely restricted the circulation of the Boston notes. While the

Suffolk Bank's object was the simple and quite laudable one of increased profits, it accomplished a great deal more.

The Plan, like most truly great things, was the essence of simplicity. The basic feature of the plan was the invitation of the Suffolk Bank, extended to the country banks, to keep a deposit with it of $5,000 plus an additional amount sufficient to redeem such of their notes as reached Boston in the course in trade. (This deposit requirement was soon changed to $2,000, and upward, depending on the country bank's capital.) In return, the Suffolk Bank agreed to redeem at par, or give full deposit credit for, the notes of *any sound* bank when presented by a participating bank.

This was the last thing that the country banks wanted, since it would deprive them of the circulation advantage flowing from their inferior notes. In addition, it added insult to injury by requiring a substantial deposit. The result was that they refused the plan as preposterous.

But the country banks overlooked the club of accelerated redemption which the Suffolk Bank was in a position to wield. So, whether they made a deposit or not, the Suffolk Bank began to redeem their notes and send them home for payment. Located in the wholesale district, the Suffolk Bank was able to secure large quantities of the notes of the country banks, which were not only promptly presented for redemption, but payment in specie was demanded. The fight was bitter and the

Suffolk Bank was forced to wage it alone until 1824, when the other Boston banks saw the light and joined the Suffolk in its efforts to raise the currency standards of the day. With their help, the Suffolk Bank extended its system to cover all of New England.

The combined power of the Boston banks and the pressure of accelerated redemption in specie literally forced the other banks to join; in fact, by 1857, there were 500 banks in the Suffolk System. Because of the quick and certain redemption, their notes circulated all over the United States, and even in Canada. The importance of quick and easy redemption (in Boston) is shown by the fact that such redemptions aggregated the total of all outstanding notes about every five weeks. In other words, the average life, or circulation cycle, of their bank notes was only some *five weeks.*

The Suffolk System's advantages were so manifest and were so appreciated by the public that it flourished until superseded in 1863 by the national banking system, with its requirement that each national bank accept the notes of all other *national* banks at par. The Suffolk System's constant demonstration of the quality of the notes issued by its members did much to establish and maintain the long leadership of the New England banks in the country's financial affairs.

6. *The Safety Fund System.* Whereas the New England method of maintaining the quality of bank notes was through quick and automatic redemption, the efforts in New York were along the lines of mutual

guaranty. This took the form of a "safety fund" into which every new bank and every bank securing an extension of its charter had to make an annual payment of one-half of 1 per cent of its capital until its total contribution reached 3 per cent of its capital funds. The note and *deposit* liabilities of insolvent banks were to be paid from this fund.

The original legislation, the Safety Fund Act of 1829, did not differentiate between note and deposit liabilities. This was obviously unfair to note holders, since the depositor could select his bank whereas the note holder could not, if the notes were to circulate at par. In 1837, this was partially corrected by legislation providing that two-thirds of the Fund be used for redemption of notes and only one-third for deposit liabilities. In 1842, this was fully corrected by a further change in the law so that only the notes were covered.

But the corrections came too late. Although it is generally agreed that the Fund could have paid all *note* liabilities, the deposit liabilities incurred before the changes in the law proved too great a burden. In 1840–1842 alone, eleven banks failed. As a result, the state had to advance some $900,000 to the Fund so that it could meet its liabilities. Although this was eventually repaid with interest and, in addition, $700,000 of notes fraudulently overissued were redeemed, the Safety Fund (mutual guaranty) method of protection had lost public confidence, and so it was superseded by another method in 1838.

7. *Free banking system of New York.* The Free Banking Act of 1838 was a bold forward step in banking by New York. Before its passage, no one could open a bank without a special charter in the form of a specific enactment of the state legislature. This made banking a monopoly specially conformed by the legislature. Political corruption and bribery were the natural consequences. The note and banking difficulties of the 1830's created such public dissatisfaction, however, that the *locofocos* (revolting Democrats), as they were called, joined the Whigs and drove through legislation establishing the principle of free banking.

It was indeed a revolutionary step to throw open the doors to the organization of a new bank by any group with character and capital. Although any group meeting the character requirements could open a bank, they could get notes to issue only by depositing with the comptroller of the State of New York acceptable collateral as security. In the beginning, a fairly broad range of securities and even notes bearing 6 per cent interest and secured by mortgage on unencumbered real estate were accepted.

As might be expected, there was a rush to establish banks—133 had been organized and 76 of them were doing business within a year. The first failure came within another year, and there were 26 more failures by 1844. The system was too "free"—the notes could be redeemed at only 76 cents on the dollar. Thereupon, the law was amended so that only the bonds of the

United States and New York State were acceptable as security for circulation. After this stiffening of the requirements, all insolvent notes were redeemed at par.

It should be noted that the Free Banking system achieved safety at the expense of flexibility of note issue. Whereas under the Safety Fund system notes were elastic and responded quickly to business demands, the Free Banking system required an investment in bonds equivalent to the notes received. Thus, such notes tied up capital. Because of this, the banks secured only enough notes to meet their average requirements and provided no margin for either growth or emergency.

In addition to this lack of elasticity, their notes tended to be inversely elastic; that is, they decreased when they should increase, and *vice versa*. The reason was quite simple. The bankers knew that the rising interest rates which accompany expanding business activity would depress the market value of their bonds, so they retired their circulation and sold their bonds before they dropped in value. This meant that the volume of notes declined when the opposite was needed. This *inverse elasticity* was carried over into the later national bank system of note issue, and was its greatest defect.

8. *The Independent Treasury System.* Although not directly related to the effort to secure a good currency, the so-called Independent Treasury system had a great effect on banking and note issue. This system was, in

essence, an effort of the federal government to be entirely free of the banks in the conduct of its fiscal affairs. The reasons for this effort are not hard to find.

After all government deposits were withdrawn from the second Bank of the United States in President Jackson's war on the bank, they were deposited in selected state-chartered banks, sarcastically known as Jackson's "pets." Many of these depositary banks failed, with heavy losses to the Treasury during the panic of 1837. These failures and wholesale suspensions of payment by the banks so embarrassed the Treasury officials that they decided to act as their own depositary and keep all government funds locked up in the Treasury vaults. Although a law authorizing this policy was enacted in 1840, it was repealed the next year. In 1846, however, a second law authorizing such a policy was passed by the Congress and the Independent Treasury System again came into being. This time, unsound though it was from an economic standpoint, it lasted nearly twenty years.

Although the Independent Treasury method of keeping all government funds in its vaults, either in Washington or in sub-treasuries set up in important centers to facilitate collections and disbursements, was not unsound from the standpoint of safety, it could hardly have been more unsound from the standpoint of the general economy. Since all payments to the government and all disbursements by it were in *specie*, Treasury operations were a continually disrupting influence on economic stability. Thus, when government receipts exceeded expenditures, an increasing amount of cash (in the form of specie) was segregated from the economy, regardless of whether business needed more cash or not. In the same fashion, an excess of government payments would pour money into circulation even though money might already be in excess supply.

Additional difficulties were encountered when the heavy burden of financing the Civil War forced the government to go on a credit basis and resort to the banks again. The resulting National Bank Act authorized the Secretary of the Treasury to designate any national bank as a depositary of the government funds. Under this authority, regular deposit accounts were opened with various national banks, especially in cities where there were no sub-treasuries. In addition, when money became too scarce, the Treasury would place "special deposits" in other national banks as a means of restoring currency to circulation.

It was only natural that such a hit-or-miss system of selection of depositary banks and allocation of government deposits would lead to violent charges of political favoritism. Unhappily, most of these charges were probably warranted; in any event, the methods employed by the Treasury did not give the government a basis for refuting the charges.

The Independent Treasury System thus, long ago, demonstrated the critical impact of governmental fiscal operations on the entire economy. Its complete divorce of the government's fiscal system from the banking system weakened both. Under the stress of war, the system inevitably broke down. Beginning with the Civil War, the fiscal functions performed by the sub-treasuries were slowly transferred to the commercial banks. Finally, the remainder of their fiscal functions were transferred to the Federal Reserve Banks, and the sub-treasuries themselves were abolished in 1920.

9. *The Civil War "greenbacks."* War imposes a heavy strain on the currency and credit of any country, and Civil War brings pressures which are well-nigh insuperable. Suspension of specie payment was one of the early casualties of the great Civil War in the United States. This gave rise to widespread public fear that these banks, no longer under the restraining influence of the necessity of redemption, would issue unlimited and relatively worthless paper money, and lend it to the government.

To encounter this fear and, of course, to help the government finance the war, the Congress passed the Legal Tender Act of February 23, 1862. This euphemistic terminology was simply a sugar-coating for the bitter pill of an irredeemable Treasury-note currency which the bill authorized.

The greenbacks, which was the name popularly applied to the currency issued under the Legal Tender Act, quickly fell to a substantial discount in terms of specie, which, in accordance with immemorial precedent in such matters, began to disappear from circulation. In fact, by July 1864, gold was quoted as 285 in New York, which meant that the greenback dollar had dropped to about 35 cents in terms of gold.

The legal tender aspect of the greenbacks had far-reaching effects on the country's economic and monetary affairs. Because of this attribute, the notes of even the best state-chartered banks declined along with the greenbacks, since they were redeemable in the new legal tender currency. The currency difficulties and further declines in the public credit forced Secretary of the Treasury Chase to warn the Congress that he could not sell additional bonds without seriously compromising the price of all the outstanding government obligations. In typical political fashion, the Congress responded to this warning by authorizing the issuance of still more greenbacks, to pay the army and navy.

In passing, it is significant to note that these greenbacks, although unsound as money and issued as an emergency measure, linger on in reduced quantity today, a hundred years later. Despite many determined efforts, it has been politically impossible to force their complete retirement.

10. *Reasons for the National Bank Act.* The difficulties of financing the Civil War gave rise to our *national* banking system. It is indeed ironic that this great leap forward in American banking was a by-product of war finance, rather than an informed, conscious effort to improve banking and currency conditions. Regardless of the reasons, the national banks, with their higher standards, were a great forward step in banking; and

the national bank notes, with their nation-wide uniformity in appearance and quality, were a real boon.

Salmon P. Chase, Secretary of the Treasury, was the father of the concept of national banking. Familiar with the bond-secured currency system of the Free Banking System of New York, Chase sought to apply the same principle to a national note issue under Congressional control. As early as 1861 (which was even before the Legal Tender Act passed in 1862), he had recommended such an issue, based on government bonds deposited in the Treasury, as a means of enlarging the demand for government securities.

Parenthetically, his expectation that the new system would materially aid in financing the war was not realized, since the process of change from the old system to the new was so slow that there were only $98,896,488 of national bank notes outstanding at the time of General Lee's surrender on April 3, 1865. (This was only 4 per cent of the government's borrowing.)

To speed up the transition to the national system, the National Bank Act, which originally became law February 25, 1863, was completely revised June 3, 1864, along the lines recommended by Hugh McCulloch, the first Comptroller of the Currency. A further and much more powerful step in the effort to force the state banks into the national system was the passage in March 1865 of a bill imposing a tax of 10 per cent per annum on the circulating notes issued by any bank not having a federal charter. Although the law was not effective until

August 1, 1866, the state banks immediately converted almost in a body into the national system.

As is always the case in America, the constitutionality of the new law was challenged. Its legality was upheld by the Supreme Court in the famous constitutional case of Veazie vs. Fenno in 1869, and the issuance of notes by the state-chartered institutions came to an end, since they could not be profitably issued under a 10 per cent annual tax. Since the right to issue circulating notes was considered prerequisite to profitable bank operation, the state banks all but disappeared from the field. In fact, they became so unimportant that for more than thirty years no statistics were kept of their operations.

11. *Lessons of the National Banking System.* As might be expected, especially in view of the circumstances of its birth, and its basic concept of "free" banking, the national banking system evidenced many defects down through the years of its operation. Some of the more important ones prior to the passage of the Federal Reserve Act in 1913 will be briefly mentioned.

One of its most serious defects was the *inverse elasticity* characteristic of any bond-secured currency. This tendency was explained in the discussion of the shortcomings of the notes issued under such a system in New York.

Pyramiding of the bank reserves through deposit of a portion of the legally required minimum reserves against deposits (unless located in the then three cen-

tral reserve cities of New York, Chicago and St. Louis)
in another bank was another serious defect. This practice of considering a demand deposit in another bank
as the equivalent of lawful money held in one's own
vaults practically forced panicky withdrawals of deposits and hoarding of currency in times of emergency.
It was called pyramiding, as the reserve of each higher
bank in the pattern was relied upon by all the lower
banks, as well as by itself.

Still another weakness was the lack of central reserve and rediscount facilities. There was no place to
which the banking system as a whole could turn in case
of pressure on all the banks.

Another defect, more time-and-money-wasting
than dangerous, was the long and circuitous routes
used in the collection of items and the handling of
checks. Since each bank would render such services
free for certain banks (usually on a reciprocal basis)
and would charge all others, the handling of each item
became a sort of game in which it was passed on to a
bank which made no charge even though not in the
direction of the bank which would ultimately pay it.
This practice caused most items to be handled several
times, to travel hundreds of miles, and to take weeks of
time, instead of going directly to the bank in the next
town.

12. *Gradual improvement.* This chapter has briefly
sketched the development of the American banking
system, particularly the evolution of note issue, up to

1913. It outlines only the high lights of those developments which help explain the banking structure of today, and which demonstrate the pitfalls to be avoided
in meeting the currency and credit needs of a dynamic
democratic people.

This recital, however, has also made clear the slow
and torturous nature of real progress in this field. It
has made equally clear many of the ever-present dangers in banking and credit.

The mistakes, the travail and the progress of the
period of nearly one-hundred years covered in this survey culminated in the passage of the Federal Reserve
Act on December 23, 1913. This opened a new era of
central banking and money management, which will be
discussed in the coming chapters.

Review

Why must commercial banks operate as a "system"?

Explain our dedication to "independent" banking.

How did the Suffolk System of New England maintain
the quality of note issue?

How did the Free Banking System of New York maintain the quality of note issue?

What is meant by "inverse elasticity" of notes; and
why is this weakness so serious?

Why was the Legal Tender Act of 1862 unsound?

Give the real reason for the organization of the national banking system.

List the more important weaknesses of the national
banking system prior to 1913.

CHAPTER IV

Commercial Banks—Source of Our Modern Money

1. *A bookkeeping mechanism.* Our commercial banking system is, basically, a vast bookkeeping mechanism which enables goods to be exchanged without the use of currency. In contrast to barter, where goods must be matched against goods, and to currency transactions, where time cannot be a direct factor in the exchanging, modern banking permits, yes, *encourages,* the introduction of time into the exchanging process. In brief, it removes the two great barriers of coincidence of wants and coincidence of ability to pay. It is probably, therefore, the greatest facilitating agency in modern production, distribution and consumption.

It also greatly encourages what the economist calls "division of labor," or what we would call *specialization,* with its manifold advantages in higher average quality and lower cost per unit. Short of extreme regimentation, as in state socialism (erroneously called communism by many), it is not too much to say that mass production and consumption would be impossible without commercial banking.

There are many other services rendered the government, business and individuals by our commercial banks which will be discussed later. In fact, the many services of the banks are what this book is about.

2. *Banking credit differentiated from other credit.* The credit extended by commercial banks differs from all other credit. Whereas other credit effects *one* transfer of goods or resources, banking credit continues to circulate in the economy until it is liquidated. As it passes from deposit account to deposit account in the process of exchanging and transferring of values, it is more properly called *monetary credit*. In other words, it does more than take the place of money—it *is* money.

When commercial banks are viewed as the source of our modern-day money, their importance becomes even more apparent. If commercial bankers extend too little credit, economic growth is retarded and our standard of living does not rise as rapidly as it might. Conversely, the extension of too much of this high-powered monetary credit will result in a rate of growth and a standard of living which cannot be sustained. In everyday language, this is known as "boom and bust"!

It is indeed a nice matter of training, experience and judgment for bankers and business men to arrange for the creation of the precise amount of bank credit appropriate for the circumstances and conditions prevailing (and likely to prevail), so that the delicate balance between inflation and deflation, and between *unsustainable* growth and politically unbearable stagnation, can be maintained.

As creators and custodians of our money supply, commercial bankers touch the lives of all of us all of the time. In the past, and even today in many countries, this function of creation of the money supply is the exclusive prerogative of government. Experience in this country, however, to say nothing of countless other countries, has amply demonstrated the wisdom of entrusting this responsibility to private hands. There is, of course, a large measure of government oversight and, at times, even interference, in our monetary credit process—but, basically, the initiation, creation and liquidation of monetary credit depend on the policies and actions of our bankers and business men.

3. *Monetary credit, a social product.* The use of bank credit as money is a social phenomenon that is the result of many factors. In addition to statutory authorization, business usage slowly evolved through more than a hundred years, public confidence slowly gained through trial and error over a much longer period, and, in particular, a more stable economic and political climate all underlay the general acceptability of bank credit (evidenced by checks) as money.

Putting it in a lighter vein, the commercial banker runs the money machine for us. And it is important for all concerned to understand that he runs it for us— *all of us!* He has responsibilities with regard to prices, interest rates, economic growth, and capital creation which transcend short-run profit considerations, although many bankers do not fully recognize this.

Fortunately, the necessity of operating the individual bank as a member of the banking system and the powers of the Federal Reserve banks (particularly with respect to credit control), to say nothing of those of the other supervisory authorities, go far in keeping over-all performance in line with economic realities. However, as in other fields, "perfection is not of this earth."

4. *Recognition of the right to credit.* It is in the exercise of the most basic of all commercial banking functions, namely, *recognition of the right to credit,* that most of the banking errors of too much or too little, and too early or too late, arise. As operator of the monetary credit pool of the entire economy, the commercial banker's function is akin to that of the watermaster in an irrigated community.

It is the responsibility of the watermaster to allocate the water, which is always in limited supply relative to the demand, to those users who can realize the greatest individual *and* community return from it. This precludes automatic allocation to the highest bidder. It involves careful consideration of long-run consequences as well as more immediate objectives. It is based on the goal of well-rounded community development by the most efficient users of the vital and limited community resource, water.

In similar fashion, the commercial banker must select those enterprises and individuals able to use the social joint-product, monetary credit, most productively, and thus make the greatest contribution to our national goal of an ever-higher standard of living for everybody, everywhere. This is virtually the power of economic life and death with regard to the individual business man, or even a particular industry or geographic area.

For example, suppose a banker in a one-bank town arbitrarily refuses to lend on the left side of town, but concentrates all lending on the right side. The left side will wither and atrophy; the right side will experience a luxuriant growth which will collapse under the pressure of any consequential adversity. This would not only be unfair to both groups of borrowers, it would be financially disastrous to many of them, with the attendant community and over-all social losses.

Since modern business cannot operate without access to the banking system, it follows that the banker should go to maximum lengths in determining the monetary credit worthiness of those seeking such access.

Selection solely on the basis of whim, prejudice, or "the old school tie" would obviously be an economic crime, as it would put the great productive power of credit in the hands of those who might lose it, waste it, or use it for purposes which would not contribute to our standard of living. (Speculative raids, market monopolization, and similar anti-social activities would be examples of uses which would not contribute to the American dream of more and more, for less and less.)

Instead, the banker must use the tools of analysis,

the wisdom of experience and the art of banking judgment in helping the business man establish his right to credit on a high and lasting basis.

5. *Establishing the right to credit.* The right to banking credit is not automatic. It must be earned by past performance, present position, and future potentiality established by adequate presentation of these and other relevant criteria to the banker. The skill of the banker in separating the real from the spurious, in distinguishing between wishful thinking and hard capability, in evaluating profit opportunities in the field involved, in weighing the character risk, and in exercising the imagination and vision necessary for all progress, will determine the amount of credit that will be created in each instance.

To aid in this determination, the banker maintains a considerable volume of records in a credit department (and still other records in operating departments) and participates widely in credit interchange and credit-education efforts. In view of this, it is well for the business man to remember that "the eyes of the banker are upon you," and act accordingly. In these days of business cooperation and rapid communication, practically every financial act of any consequence is not only recorded, it is communicated—to others.

In addition to a good record, training and experience commensurate with the purpose for which the financing is sought must be a part of any successful presentation to the banker. The applicant must also demonstrate to the satisfaction of the banker that capital and other balance-sheet items, as well as income-statement items, are appropriate for the type of business and the time of the year.

When these factors have been established so indisputably that they are accepted without consequential reservation, the banker weighs them against his estimate of the conditions which are likely to prevail during the period of the loan, and arrives at a decision.

The banker naturally wants to arrive at a favorable decision. No one knows better than he that he makes his living by lending. But he also knows that he must have a record which will stand up even though the loan may not. Any good banker really tries to make every possible loan, but he must be given the necessary material to validate his decision. Every business man should understand how anxious the banker is to loan, and make every effort to establish his "right to credit" in such positive fashion that the banker can "recognize" it for the maximum amount without question.

6. *Substitution of bank's credit for borrower's credit.* After a favorable decision, the next step is a credit of the amount to the deposit account of the borrower. In this way, the bank substitutes its own credit, which is well known and generally acceptable, for the lesser-known but equally valid credit of the borrower. The increase in the borrower's deposit account is, of course, an increase in the money supply. Thereafter, by means of transfer orders known as checks, it circulates freely

throughout the economy, as does currency. This transferability makes it freely acceptable so that it can perform its function as our modern money. In fact, it might better be called *money-plus,* as it has safety and record aspects that are not possessed by any other kind of money.

7. *The transferring of values.* As the transferring of values makes possible the use of demand deposits as money, such transferring is obviously an important function of banking. This third function is not as important as the basic banking function of "recognition of the right to credit." Nor would it be so important if it were not for the second function of banking which is "the substitution of the bank's credit for the borrower's credit."

Nonetheless, and even though largely mechanical and an internal operating matter in the banking system, it is very important not only because of its contribution to the utilization of demand deposits as money, but also because of the services it makes possible for banks to offer business in the field of collections and other areas.

8. *How loans create money.* The common experience of going to the bank to make a deposit has caused considerable misunderstanding as to the origin of deposits. The deposits which are taken to the bank are either checks on other deposit accounts or currency. If checks, they do not "create" a deposit so far as the banking system is concerned; they merely move it from a deposit account which is already in existence to an-

other deposit account—in short, it is only a transfer.

If currency, it is likewise merely a transfer from the account from which the money was withdrawn (perhaps a considerable time before), to the account in which it is deposited. This can be said categorically, since *all our currency is issued through the banks.* In other words, there is no way for a dollar to get into circulation without a deposit account being reduced. This means the deposit of currency merely restores the deposit total to the amount which existed before the currency withdrawal.

The deposits arising from such transfers are called *primary* deposits. While they are welcomed by the receiving bank and constitute a problem for the paying bank, they do not affect the over-all deposit total except in so far as the total of money in circulation and in hoarding goes up or down.

Deposits credited to an account as the result of a loan or an investment are called *derivative,* or *secondary,* deposits, as they are made possible by reserves in the form of deposits at the Federal Reserve Banks. In contrast to primary deposits, derivative deposits increase the money supply; and, instead of supplying reserves from the reserve accounts of other banks, they require supporting reserves which are created by the Reserve Banks in the same fashion as the derivative deposits are created by the commercial banks, namely through investments, discounts, loans and advances.

The *derivative* deposits made possible by these reserves constitute our money supply. As these deposits arise from the proceeds of loans credited to borrowers' accounts and from payments for securities purchased by the banks, it is clear that loans and investments determine our money supply. Instead of *reducing* the available money, loans and investments made by commercial banks actually *increase* the money supply.

9. *All deposits are derivative so far as the banking system is concerned.* A little reflection on the preceding paragraphs will make it clear that so far as the banking system is concerned, all deposits are *derivative*, that is, created. This means that the money supply is "made to order," as such deposits are the result of investment action by the banker or loan action by the banker upon the initiative of a borrower. A clear understanding of this aspect of our monetary credit system will be of great help in understanding price behavior, inflationary pressures and similar phenomena of the free market.

Reviewing some of the actual procedure in the deposit-creation process will give a better idea of cause and effect, as well as probable impact on the rest of the economy. In establishing the amount of the loan, the borrower first justifies the number of units, or the scale of the venture, and then applies to that the prevailing price level. Prices thus determine the quantity of money that is created and not the opposite, as is so frequently asserted by those who misread the quantity theory of money.

Moreover, it would not be the whole story if we stopped weighing the impact at this point. This is true because it is beyond question that, after the creation process of the first step, the quantity thereafter does affect prices as it moves from account to account in the process of exchanging goods and services. But, even here, the further limitation of the velocity (turnover) with which it moves from account to account impinges on the quantity. So, the impact of the money supply upon prices, employment, and business activity is far more than a simple quantitative one, as will be explained at some length in later chapters.

10. *Double entry bookkeeping tells the tale.* The stylized entries called T accounts (because of the T form used) will help in visualizing and understanding the banking miracle which turns the debt of the individual borrower into purchasing power for all; and, in similar fashion, turns a federal deficit represented by a government obligation into purchasing power for all so long as the security is on the books of the banks. It is hard, indeed, for the mind to accept the paradox of debt becoming money, or the obvious contradiction in the nonetheless true fact that the more the government spends, the more we all will have to spend if the securities issued by the government are purchased by the commercial banks.

Careful consideration of the following T accounts will show that double-entry bookkeeping, which gives the two sides of every transaction, underlies the paradox. Thus, the obligation of the government is an asset of the bank, which is offset by the deposit liability of the bank to the general public (since the government promptly spends the proceeds of the borrowing!).

The following set of T accounts shows how loans and discounts create * deposits:

Assumption: a loan of $4,000 to buy an automobile
Original Bank

First National Bank

Assets	Liabilities
Loans & Discounts + $4,000 (asset: Note of Raymond Rodgers)	Deposits + $4,000 (deposit: in account of Raymond Rodgers)

Note: Increase of deposits must match increase in loans.

Banking System (when Rodgers spends the "money"!)

First National Bank		Detroit Trust Company	
Loans & Discounts + $4,000	Deposit of RR + $4,000	Reserve at FRB + $4,000	Deposits of Motors, Inc. + $4,000
Reserve at FRB − $4,000	Deposit of RR − $4,000		

* But not out of "whole cloth"; credit determination, membership in banking system, adequate capital and *reserves* of both borrower and bank, purpose, policy, etc., are conditions precedent.

Banking System

Loans and discounts + $4,000	Deposits of RR + $4,000 (*First National Bank*)
Reserve at FRB − $4,000	Deposits of RR − $4,000 (*First National Bank*)
Reserve at FRB + $4,000	Deposit of Motors Inc. + $4,000 (*Detroit Trust Company*)

Note: So far as the banking system is concerned, there is an increase in deposits (liabilities) equivalent to the increase in assets, whether in one bank, or all banks. Original bank in system illustration has, *so far*, merely an increase in earning assets (loans and discounts) and a decrease in its reserve balance at the Federal Reserve Bank, *but* it will receive offsetting deposits created by expansion at other banks, as such probability is the very basis of banking.

As the following T accounts demonstrate, *investment* by commercial banks also creates deposits *:

A. If seller has an account at buying bank:

Buying Bank

Investment + $1,000	Cashier's (treasurer's) checks + $1,000
	Cashier's checks − $1,000
	Deposit account of seller + $1,000

Note: Deposit increase matches investment increase.

* Even though an individual bank buys securities for cash by exchanging the asset, reserves at the Federal Reserve Bank, for another asset, investments, as in B above, there is nonetheless an increase in deposits in the banking system, unless the securities come from another commercial bank or a Federal Reserve Bank. In the latter event, the deposit increase came earlier when the securities first entered the banking system.

B. *If seller does not have an account at buying bank:*

Buying Bank		Seller's Bank	
Investment + $1,000	Cashier's checks + $1,000	Reserve at FRB + $1,000	Seller's deposit account + $1,000
Reserve at FRB − $1,000	Cashier's checks − $1,000		

Banking System

Investments + $1,000 (Buying Bank)	Cashier's checks + $1,000 (Buying Bank)
Reserve at FRB − $1,000 (Buying Bank)	Cashier's checks − $1,000 (Buying Bank)
Reserve at FRB + $1,000 (Seller's Bank)	Deposits (of seller) + $1,000 (Seller's Bank)

Note: Deposit increase is inevitable when a bank *buys*, but the increase may show up in another bank. In short, when securities come on the balance sheets of the banking system as assets, they must also appear on the other side as liabilities, i.e., deposits.

11. *Repayment reduces the money supply.* If increase of loans and investments increases the money supply, it necessarily follows that decrease reduces it. That *repayment* of a loan to a bank should *decrease* the money supply is hard for the mind to accept, but it is nonetheless true. As this process of creation and extinguishment of money has not only an immediate effect on the borrower involved but on the entire economy, its importance is obvious.

In view of its monetary aspect, the total of such bank credit should not be thought of as something abnormal which ought to be extirpated as soon as possible. On the contrary, it is not only normal, it is absolutely necessary, to have a large volume of such credit in existence at all times to maintain our high levels of business activity.

Moreover, prices, interest rates, monetary turnover and business anticipations adjust to the volume of such credit; and, thereafter, any consequential changes in the total affect them as well as the other factors in the economy. In fact, money management in this country is focused on controlling the costs and *availability* of bank credit, which is to say, the money supply.

Even though an individual borrower repays his loan and thus decreases the money supply, another borrower secures a loan which increases the money supply, with the result that the total money supply is not greatly affected by normal operations except for a slow secular increase due to growth in population and business volume. It is only under the impact of such abnormal influences as government financing through the banks, or continued inflation, or excessive speculation, that there are radical changes in the money supply. And these, of course, should be guarded against in every possible way.

12. *Our money must be defended.* Marvelous as is our money process, it is nonetheless extremely vulnerable to pressure groups. There are limits to the confi-

dence which makes such a system possible. As no one can know what those limits are until it is too late, our money must be carefully guarded at all times. Every action of government, every broad change in methods of business operation, and, above all, every change in commercial banking should be weighed against its impact on our money. Even such continuous vigilance may not be enough to preserve the integrity of our dollar in these days of world-wide responsibilities and high-level government spending; but we must make every effort to do so.

Too many people view only their own spending program and disregard the over-all effect. The social responsibilities assumed by government must be kept within the limits of our earning and taxing power, if the purchasing power of our dollar is to be preserved. Giving every pressure group all it wants through the too-easy process of inflating the money supply is the road to economic ruin. As was trenchantly observed by a high official of the Federal Reserve System, "If we can afford these things, why don't we pay for them?"

When voters understand that unwise government spending, chronic budget deficits, and unwarranted increases in prices, wages and costs can only further reduce the value of *their dollar,* they will insist on fiscal responsibility in government, in labor, and in management. In the meantime, the problem of preventing inflation will be the task of those who understand the process of deposit creation and the dangers involved

when purchasing power is increased faster than goods
are produced and distributed.

Review

Specifically, how is banking a great facilitating agency
in today's business life?

In what basic respect does bank credit differ from
other credit?

Why is "recognition of the right to credit" the basic
function of commercial banking?

How do loans create money?

Indicate the possible adverse effects on the economy if
the banker functions poorly.

What must the business man do to help the banker
recognize his credit?

Distinguish between primary deposits and derivative
deposits.

Explain the statement: So far as the banking system is
concerned, all deposits are derivative deposits.

Why is it normal for a certain amount of bank credit
to be outstanding?

Why must our money be continually defended?

CHAPTER V

Where the Bank Gets Its "Money"

1. *Sources of bank funds.* A bank secures the funds with which it operates from four sources—invested capital, primary deposits, reserves created by the Federal Reserve Banks, and borrowings. While all four are important, the first is both a legal and economic prerequisite. After all, it seems reasonable to expect that those who organize an institution to lend to others, and to serve as the repository of the most liquid funds of the community, should be recommended and validated by funds of their own.

The bank's own funds constitute its capital. In addition to original invested capital, banks have secured a substantial part of their capital by leaving earnings in the business. They have been able to do this because of extremely conservative dividend policies, and not because of excessive earnings. As a matter of fact, down through the years, bank earnings have lagged behind earnings in manufacturing and business.

2. *Functions of bank capital.* Just as in any other business, capital has many functions in banking. But, in addition, banking has special characteristics which give bank capital special responsibilities. For example,

banking is indispensable in our modern economy, since no other agency has its power of credit expansion and contraction. Since our economy is a growing one, subject, of course, to shorter-term upward and downward swings, it follows that given sufficient time, reasonably competent management, and the aid of the business cycle, a bank can work off its losses through earnings.

In view of this, the primary function of bank capital is not, as in other lines of business, that of a cushion to absorb losses. On the contrary, its primary function is to inspire such confidence on the part of the public and the supervisory authorities that the bank will be able to remain open, and offset the lean years with the fat years. In other words, the true function of bank capital is to keep the bank open so that time and earnings can absorb the losses which it is bound to have if it fully meets its responsibilities for the credit function in our cyclical economy.

Since no way has yet been devised to eliminate risk, even in a business as conservative as banking, a bank which does not accept its share of bankable risks simply retards the growth of its customers and the economy. With the modern view that economic growth is a categorical imperative, it is easy to see that if the bank does not function to the extent of its capabilities, other agencies, including the government, will supply the necessary credit. This clearly indicates the second function of capital, which is closely related to the first.

The second important function of capital, then, is

to enable the bank to function in a countercyclical manner. In plain words, a bank should not only have enough capital to survive, it should have enough so that it can combat serious declines in business activity by boldly extending credit and creating new purchasing power to offset declines in other quarters. As custodians and creators of our money supply, banks bear a basic responsibility in our efforts to minimize the "boom and bust" tendencies of our economy. And, as Gaylord A. Freeman, Vice Chairman, First National Bank of Chicago, put it, "To move against the ebb tide of depression takes great courage; it also takes capital."

The third important function of bank capital is to represent ownership. The widely spread, private ownership of our banks is an important and unique characteristic of the American banking system. It is a strong defense against concentration of financial power. It enables the reward for supplying our money to be distributed among all our people through purchase of bank stock. And, it permits continuity of the banking enterprise through passing the ownership, represented by the stock, from one generation to the next.

While still other functions of bank capital could be listed, the foregoing, with their implications, constitute the ones to keep in mind from a business standpoint. 3. *Present capital situation.* The long-time downward trend in the capital position of the banks has given rise to a great deal of discussion in recent years. This is certainly justified, since the ratio of total capital accounts to assets of the commerical banks has shown a marked downward trend for more than eighty-five years. This ratio, which was around 35 per cent in 1875, had dropped to 20 per cent by 1900 and to 10 per cent by 1940, from which it declined still further to its recent levels of some 7 per cent.

Before drawing any alarming conclusions from this great change, however, consideration should be given to the even greater changes in banking assets. Today's assets are of much higher quality. And, finally, a substantial portion of banking assets today are government bonds and, thus, considered non-risk assets. (While there may be loss on other than the shortest-term issues in case of forced sale, there can be no loss on any government obligation if held to maturity.)

Deposit insurance also lessens capital requirements, as it preserves public confidence and thus gives the banks a much better opportunity to "work off" (orderly liquidation) loans which have become "sticky," and to hold securities until they can be sold without loss.

Then, too, the capital accounts of today are more conservatively stated than in earlier years. There is a much larger proportion of banks in the better bank categories; their valuation of assets is more conservative; and their hidden reserves are greater.

It should be emphasized that all of the capital resources of a bank do not appear on the balance sheet. In addition to the conventional capital and surplus of other corporations, banks have an undivided-profits ac-

count (similar to earned surplus in non-bank corporations), and they have substantial reserve accounts
which appear on their balance sheets in addition to the
hidden reserves mentioned in the last paragraph.

The relation of surplus to undivided-profits account
warrants special mention. The surplus of a bank is considered a capital surplus and may not be reduced without permission of the supervisory authorities. Dividends
are paid, and ordinary capital adjustments are made,
through this undivided-profits account and not through
surplus.

When the assets of a bank drop to a point where
their value does not exceed the liabilities by an amount
equal to the par value of its outstanding shares, its capital is said to be *impaired*. The supervisory authorities
will insist that such impairment be promptly corrected. If the bank does not have hidden reserves which
can be brought on the balance sheet, it will have to
make up the impairment by assessing its stockholders.

Going a step further, when the value of the assets
of the bank falls below that of its liabilities, it is said to
be *insolvent*. This, of course, brings immediate action.
Until recent years, such a bank was simply closed and
the creditors were paid whatever the assets realized.
This took time, was painful, and destroyed public
confidence. Nowadays, instead of closing the bank with
its attendant bad publicity, a merger with a stronger
institution is generally arranged. If the bank is insured,
the absorbing bank is customarily guaranteed against

loss on the acquired assets by the Federal Deposit Insurance Corporation, and the whole thing is done so quietly and expeditiously that the general public never realizes it is a "shotgun wedding."

4. *Amount of capital needed.* Minimum capital requirements are established by law for new banks. These legal minimums in the case of a national bank vary from $50,000 for cities up to 6,000 in population, to $200,000 for cities with more than 50,000. With a few notable exceptions, the minimum requirements for state-chartered institutions are much lower than those for national banks. It should be kept in mind that these are the legal minimums for starting a bank. They are, by no means, the amount which a bank will actually need in carrying on its business.

The amount of capital needed will depend primarily on the amount of the bank's assets subject to risk (i.e., the proportion of risk assets to nonrisk assets such as government securities), and the degree of risk in those risk assets. There can be no hard and fast rule on this, since only the banker himself is in a position to know the risks he has assumed. This means that the public and the supervisory authorities must rely on the character, ability and experience of the banker as much as, or even more than, on balance sheet capital.

Certainly, the bank should have enough capital to take care of the needs of its customers. Many banking operations are tied to the amount of capital. For example, the maximum unsecured loans which can be made to one interest cannot exceed 10 per cent of a national bank's paid-up and unimpaired capital and surplus. This means that big business requires big banks. As a matter of fact, banks are under continuous study by corporate treasurers on this point, and, of course, on safety.

The whole question of the amount of capital needed can be put in a nutshell by saying that it must have enough to satisfy the banker, enough to satisfy the general public, enough to satisfy the corporate treasurer, and enough to satisfy the supervisory authorities.
5. *Relation of capital to deposits.* Many states have statutes which tie the capital requirements of their banks to deposits. There is a common tendency on the part of the supervisory authorities, as well as the general public, to measure capital needs by deposit totals. This is a sort of accounting shorthand which can easily mislead a business man trying to select a bank. It is an oversimplification which can contribute to bad banking and thus be dangerous to all.

While it is true that there is a relationship between capital needs and deposits, it is not properly of the ratio type, i.e., quantity to quantity. The true relation is that of the *quantity* of the capital to the *character* of the deposits—time, or demand; large, or small; volatile, or stable, etc.

That there is no direct quantitative relationship between capital needs and deposits is easily demonstrated by the following facts:

(a) The degree of risk in relation to deposits is not uniform. This is true because of the nature of deposits, as mentioned above. It is even more true on the assets side, since all banks do not invest the same proportion of their funds in the same type of assets; moreover, there is not the same degree of risk in all assets of the same type.

(b) Capital is not a substitute for liquidity. If the capital and deposits are tied up in unmarketable assets, the bank is in a "frozen" (non-liquid) condition, no matter how much capital it has. In the same fashion, liquidity is no substitute for capital. Even though a bank's assets consist solely of cash due from banks and the shortest-term government securities and it is thus 100 per cent liquid, it is still insolvent if its liabilities exceed its assets.

(c) The need for capital does not necessarily increase with an increase in deposits. In fact, the new deposits are almost certain to be invested in more liquid assets than the older deposits. Moreover, banks relate their holdings of risk assets to their capital rather than to their deposits. So, an increase in deposits in a well-run bank means an increase in non-risk assets rather than risk assets, and thus over-all risk is increased but little, if any.

6. *Relation of capital to assets.* A good banker measures his risks against his capital, surplus, undivided

profits and reserves. He knows that all assets have some degree of risk. Even cash can be stolen or misplaced. (One of the large New York banks misplaced a million-dollar bond not long ago and no trace of it had been found three years later!) So, the banker carries insurance against the insurable risks on his assets and relies on his capital for protection on the non-insurable risks.

In looking to his capital in this respect, a banker weighs the amount of his risk assets and their degree of risk. To do this more accurately, he divides his assets into categories ranging from non-risk (although there is always some risk, the term non-risk is used for the most riskless) to those in which the risk is almost complete. If the maximum potential loss shown by this calculation does not fall well within the total of his capital accounts, he takes steps to improve his assets or increase his capital. Thus, bank capital in a very real sense is related to bank assets and the elements of loss they contain.

7. *Responsibility for adequate capital.* It is the banker's responsibility to see that his bank has adequate capital to absorb such losses as are bound to occur and still remain strong enough to not only remain in business but to grow with the community and the economy. He is paid by the stockholders to protect their investment, and he is entrusted by the depositors to protect their interests. He cannot "pass the buck" on this responsibility to the supervisory authorities as they do not have the direct authority to compel a bank to

increase its capital—only the banker has the legal authority to increase his capital.

The supervisory authorities, however, do have broad powers under which they can bring pressure on a bank to increase its stock or otherwise conform to their views.

The Comptroller of the Currency, for example, has several things he can do to embarrass or punish a national bank which does not comply with his suggestions. Thus, he is authorized by law to publish his report of examination of any national bank which does not comply with his "recommendations or suggestions." Or, he can examine the bank *quarterly,* and, in states with branch banking, he can withhold permission to establish a new branch.

In addition, he can legally remove officers or directors of a national bank if they "have continued unsafe and unsound practices . . . after having been warned by the Comptroller to discontinue . . . such . . . practices." But, to use this weapon, he would have to prove that the bank's capital was so low that it made the bank unsound. Such a proceeding is so drastic, as it would seriously affect public confidence, that it is practically never invoked. In short, the remedy is worse than the cure.

The Federal Reserve authorities are authorized to consider the adequacy of the capital of a bank applying for membership; but once a bank is admitted, they have no further legal authority in this respect.

The Federal Deposit Insurance Corporation has the power to consider the adequacy of a bank's capital only in connection with its request to: (1) reduce its capital stock; (2) establish a new branch; (3) merge or consolidate; or (4) move its main office to another location. But, as long as a bank does not request any of these four permissions, the Corporation does not have the legal authority to require an increase in capital.

So, although the supervisory authorities make many suggestions for capital increases, they must rely on persuasion and indirect methods for compliance. This leaves the problem up to the banker. His dual responsibility to stockholders and depositors and his actual power to increase the capital place the responsibility squarely on his shoulders.

As the foregoing paragraphs clearly indicate, the business man in selecting his bank must rely on bank management for adequacy of capital rather than on outside agencies.

8. *Relation of capital to profits.* Bank shares were the original "growth" stocks as banks paid small, conservative dividends and used the remainder of their earnings to build up their capital. Even today, retention of earnings continues to be the major source of additions to bank capital. But, since World War II, the banks have been faced with two very important pressures which make the capital additions derived from this source inadequate for their needs.

Although the banks have more than doubled their

capital accounts since the end of the War, the great growth of loans and other risk assets has cut their ratio of capital to risk assets from 26 per cent to approximately one-half that percentage—and this, despite the sale of substantial amounts of stock for new capital.

Bank earnings, even with conservative dividend policies, have not been large enough to supply their traditional share of the capital needed to support the rapid growth of risk assets. This is obscured by the practice of relating bank earnings to capital. On this basis, earnings have been close to historical levels, but, since risk assets have far outpaced capital growth, earnings in relation to growth of risk assets have been totally inadequate.

For example, in recent years, it has taken more than $100 of risk assets to produce $1 of annual addition to capital. If the generally held view that an absolute minimum of $15 of capital is needed for each $100 of risk assets is accepted, the inadequacy of profits as a source of capital becomes painfully apparent. In other words, present-day competitive conditions and heavy taxes have undermined the historic role of bank earnings as an adequate source of bank capital.

9. *Relation of capital to growth.* As a growth industry in a growing economy, banks need constant additions to capital funds. There is reason to believe that the steady growth in demand for bank credit and other banking services from business, individuals and government will continue.

In this connection, Mr. Jesse P. Wolcott, former Chairman of the Federal Deposit Insurance Corp., expressed the view that, if national output continues to grow at a yearly rate of around 4 per cent, bank deposits by 1983 will reach the $600 billion level. This would require a capital growth of $30 billion merely to maintain the present ratio of capital to loans and other risk assets. Even this enormous increase, he felt, was not good enough, as prevailing capital levels were not sufficient and likely to become even less so as the years rolled by.

The political platforms and pronouncements of recent years leave no room for doubt that the government will step in, or take over, if the banks do not make what the politicians consider a proper contribution to the ever-expanding economy. They will be given no choice where economic growth is concerned. Their role is clear-cut: they can either march, or be marched.

10. *Difficulty of sale of new stock.* It is beyond question that banks will need enormous amounts of new capital to finance our economic growth. Earnings, the traditional source of bank capital, can no longer do the job, as pointed out earlier. This leaves banks faced with the hard necessity of selling additional stock for new capital. This is a hard necessity because of the difficulty of selling new bank stock under conditions which sometimes exist.

At times, no class of securities of comparable size has such a limited marketability as bank stock. In addition, the price-earnings ratio is frequently low. Whereas a bank's stock might sell for only 7 or 8 times earnings, the stock of a typical industrial corporation might sell for 15 to 20 times earnings, or more than twice as high. This often gives rise to the lament that many banks are worth more dead than alive, since stockholders can get more for their stock in a merger than on the open market.

Banks are doing many things to increase their earnings and make their stock more attractive to investors. To cut costs, they are "automating" with electronic "brains" and magnetic inks. To increase their income, they are offering many new services and more aggressively mechandising their old services to meet the competition of the finance companies, the savings and loan associations, and other financial intermediaries.

What the ultimate solution will be, no man can say. But two things are certain: banking will grow and capital must grow. The only question is whether this will be done privately, or by the government. But, it will be done!

11. *Primary deposits.* Another important source of banking funds is *primary deposits*. These are deposits transferred *from* other banks. Since such transfers are settled through the medium of the respective banks' reserve accounts at the Federal Reserve Banks, an incoming balance increases a bank's reserves. In similar fashion, cash received by the bank is either sent to the Reserve Bank and increases reserves, or it is paid out

and thereby prevents a reduction in reserves, since banks otherwise have to secure such cash from the Federal Reserve Bank.

So, regardless of form, primary deposits give a bank an equivalent amount of reserves which can be used as a basis for credit expansion. The exact opposite is true of transfers made to other banks, since such transfers are primary deposits for them. This primary deposit factor explains why banks compete so aggressively for deposits, since any deposit lured away from another bank becomes the raw material (reserves) for a multiple expansion of credit.

12. *Reserves created by the Federal Reserve Banks.* Another, and far more important source of banking "wherewithal" than is generally realized is the Federal Reserve Banks themselves. Many bankers honestly do not understand this; and still others profess not to understand it. But the plain fact is that when the Federal Reserve Banks buy securities, the reserve account of some member bank is increased.

The ability of the Reserve Banks to create reserves and deposits was dramatically demonstrated in World War II. More specifically, during the period from December 31, 1941 to December 31, 1945, the twelve Federal Reserve Banks increased their holdings of government securities by $22 billion, thereby creating the reserves to support the financing of the war. In other words, the banks of the United States received that great volume of reserves without incurring any direct obligation on their part—it was, so to speak, "on the house."

13. *Borrowing by banks.* Another important source of banking funds is that of borrowing by the banks; but they never use that term for the obligations they incur. Borrowing, in the banking *metier*, is strictly for the customers. The banks use much more soothing terms, such as rediscounting, advances, repurchase agreements, negotiated deposits and similar euphemisms.

Regardless of terminology used, banks run short, even as you and I. And, when they do, they have to turn to other banks or the central bank (the Federal Reserve Bank in the United States) for help. This help may be in the form of a temporary sale of assets, or a temporary deposit of primary funds, or an out-and-out borrowing under some other name, but it is a necessary and commonplace feature of our banking system.

Review

From what sources does a bank get its "money"?

Why has bank capital become a special problem since World War II?

Explain the long-term trend of the ratio of capital to assets.

List the more important factors which reduce the need for bank capital today.

Indicate the shortcomings of the capital-deposits ratio as a measure of banking safety.

Why are corporate treasurers especially interested in the capital-assets ratio of a bank?

How does a new *primary* deposit increase a bank's lending power?

Give some of the methods whereby banks, as a practical matter, borrow, but a different terminology is used.

CHAPTER VI

Loan Services of Banks

1. *Wide range of loan services.* The loan and discount function of the commercial bank is of paramount importance to the business man. Through this access to bank credit, he is able to bridge the seasonal and temporary gap between cash inflow and outflow. Through it, he is able to cushion the impact of emergencies and take advantage of opportunities. In fact, ability to command such services in full measure is undoubtedly the most valuable tool any business man can have.

A thorough understanding of the wide range of loan services available to American business, the relative desirability of these various loan services for a particular need, and the best method of securing maximum credit with minimum risk to all concerned, is of inestimable value in business. Unfortunately, most business men tend to get into a rut in their borrowing from a bank. Instead of utilizing all of the avenues of borrowing, they *overuse* one. This is more expensive for them and more risky for the bank—moreover, the total credit which can be secured is severely circumscribed by such a provincial approach.

Bank loans and discounts today cover practically

the whole gamut of human activities. Production, storage, distribution and consumption are all financed in varying degrees with bank credit. Even the government borrows heavily at the commercial banks. But, since it does so through the medium of securities, the credit extension falls in the investment, rather than the loan and discount, category.

2. *Revival of bank lending.*   During the great depression of the 1930's, bank loans declined to such an extent, it was confidently asserted in many quarters that bank lending would never regain its former importance. Banks were urged to concentrate on the investment of their idle funds in securities, rather than waste their efforts in the dying field of loans.

During World War II, loan conditions were little better, since the government largely financed war production and there was practically no civilian distribution or consumption that needed bank financing.

After the war, however, the enormous backlog of pent-up demand and the rapid expansion of our economy required a greater volume of bank loans than had ever been dreamed of before. Since then, levels that would have been considered fantastic and impossible even in the roaring 1920's, have been reached throughout the field, particularly in consumer credit.

Quantifying these swings, bank loans and discounts, which had dropped to $16.2 billion by 1933, and had only recovered to $26.6 billion by December 1941 at the beginning of World War II, increased so rapidly after the war that they reached $287 billion by 1967.

The growth of consumer credit was even more striking, since it rose in the postwar period alone from a $5.7 billion level at the end of 1945 to $99 billion in 1967. These totals include the consumer loans made by sales finance companies, credit unions, consumer finance companies and others, as well as those made by banks. The commercial banks' proportion of this credit showed an even more spectacular increase, since it increased from $0.7 billion at the end of 1945 to $34.0 billion in 1967. (This consumer credit total of the banks should not be counted twice—it is included in their loan and discount totals.)

This revival of bank lending has been so massive in recent years that some bankers and a considerably lesser number of students of banking fear that our present banking system will not be able to meet all of the justifiable demands for future credit extension. Such fears are not warranted, as the following brief analysis clearly shows.

3. *Adequacy of bank credit.* The ability of our commercial banks to expand their credit (loans, discounts and investments) depends on four basic factors. The following thumbnail and categoric (since some terms have not yet been covered in this text) sketches of the status of each of these limiting factors indicate that there is no danger of the "money running out":

(a) The *monetary gold stock* is the most basic limiting factor, as it is required for the expansion of the central bank credit of the Reserve Banks themselves. While it is true that the United States is subject, at times, to large outflows of gold, the fact remains that we have so much excess (free) gold and such economic power to counteract outflows and to command future gold that it is not likely to be a serious limiting factor in the foreseeable future.

(b) The *reserves,* which the member banks must maintain with the Reserve Banks, are another limiting factor, but they can be created at will by the Federal Reserve Banks (so long as they have the necessary underlying gold) through open market operations or through rediscounting for the member banks. Moreover, the present reserve requirements, which are higher than in most other free countries, can be further reduced by the Federal Reserve Board, giving the member banks excess reserves they can utilize for further credit expansion.

(c) The *capital resources* of the banks, which must bear a proper relation to their risk assets, are another limiting factor. But this can easily be solved when banking profits are adequate, through plowing back earnings and through the sale of additional stock. Obviously, the higher interest rates flowing from the need for additional loans would give the profits needed to increase the capital structure.

(d) The *ability of bank management* to lend freely and wisely is another limiting factor. But the

banks are improving this factor every day with
their banking schools, their in-service training,
their special conferences, and their ever higher
requirements for *banking* personnel. Thus, the
professional competence of the loan officers is
being constantly improved; and there is no
reason to think that they will not have the
vision and confidence necessary for full utilization of this increased competence.

As the foregoing summarization demonstrates, business men need have no fear that there will not be
enough bank credit to support any level of business
activity our monetary authorities consider a *sustainable*
one. No, a much greater danger under our system of
fractional reserve banking is that too much credit may
be extended, causing inflationary price increases and
costly fluctuations of the "boom and bust" variety in
business activity.

4. *Loan-deposit ratios.* Good bankers keep a watchful
eye on the relation of their loans to their deposits. They
consider loans as *risk* assets, so they want a varying
percentage, depending on business conditions and outlook, of high-grade investments which they can sell to
meet any shrinkage in deposits or increase in loan demands. This loan-deposit ratio varies somewhat from
bank to bank, but it is characteristically higher for city
banks than country banks, and for larger banks than
smaller banks.

When the ratio of loans to deposits of the large city

bank approaches 70 per cent, the bank begins to put the brakes on further loan expansion through higher loan requirements, and even through credit rationing, at times. While the exact loan-deposit ratio which will start such action is a matter of individual bank policy, borrowers should keep in mind that it is much lower than the above percentage for most banks, and that it is a very important factor in a bank's determination of the amount of credit it will be willing to extend in a particular case.

In other words, when bankers begin to talk about being "loaned up," they mean their loan-deposit ratio is beginning to give them concern. This is fair warning to the business man to have a plain talk with his banker to find out just what can be expected in the way of loan accommodation during the credit squeeze.

5. *Concept of loanable funds.* When the banks have more reserve deposits at the Federal Reserve Bank than required by law, they are said to have loanable funds. This is somewhat misleading to those who are not in the banking business. It does not mean that they have any actual funds on hand. It simply means that they are in a position to expand their credit, i.e., make loans or investments.

This credit-expansion power is ordinarily closely related to its loan-deposit ratio, as the heavy loan demands which cause high loan-deposit ratios generally use up the available reserves the bank has at its Federal Reserve Bank. In addition, high loan-deposit ratios cause the Federal Reserve Banks to bring pressure on the reserves of the member banks to slow credit expansion.

The term loanable funds, as applied to a commercial bank, thus defines its ability to meet additional credit needs. Although its ability to lend depends on its reserve position at the Reserve Bank, its willingness to do so depends on its loan-deposit ratio. Business men, therefore, should keep a more than casual eye on both of these factors.

6. *Relation of loans to character of deposits.* In establishing its loan policy, a bank naturally considers many factors. One of the most important factors is the character of its deposits. If it has a heavy proportion of time deposits, payable at a definite time in the future or upon stipulated notice, it can safely have more long-term assets.

But such a generalization should not be carried too far. The time deposits, instead of being true savings, may merely be temporarily idle funds that may be reactivated at any time. They may be in fact, if not in form, much closer to demand deposits than true long-term deposits.

The demand deposits themselves also vary greatly in their activity from bank to bank. The deposit turnover in a Wall Street bank will, obviously, be much greater than in, say, a Hanover, New Hampshire, bank. Even in the Wall Street bank itself, there are almost unbelievable extremes in activity. For example, one study has shown that, in the contrast to a typical New York City turnover of some fifty times a year, the deposit account of a government bond dealer may turn over more than 10,000 times a year. (This means the checks drawn on the account each year aggregate more than 10,000 times its average balance.) No argument is needed to show that such active deposits should not be invested in long-term mortgages or, for that matter, in anything longer than *demand*.

The banker must also keep in mind the psychology of depositors with respect to his bank. Does it have the public confidence born of triumphant weathering of long years of banking, with their economic storms and financial emergencies? Or, is it a new bank that has not had the test of adversity? Is it headed by men who are pillars of strength and leaders of the community? Or, are they merely so-so?

If the bank is in a one-industry town, its loan policy must necessarily be more conservative than in a more diversified community. The same caution applies if the bank is subject to the danger of heavy withdrawals by disproportionately large depositors. And, paradoxically, many small, ill-informed depositors make the bank subject to the dangers of mob psychology with panicky withdrawals.

So, the extent and the nature of the loans extended by a bank depend on its depositors almost as much as on its borrowers. The good banker must keep both in mind.

7. *Relation of loans to the business cycle.* American business activity fluctuates in volume—it never stays long at a particular level. In addition to short-term fluctuations, it has longer, rhythmic upward and downward movements, two succeeding swings of which are termed a business *cycle.* By their very nature, bank loans are closely related to this business cycle.

On the upward swing, loan volume necessarily enlarges to finance the increases in inventories, accounts receivable, expenses, etc. Also, price increases, which often accompany this boom phase of the business cycle, further add to the demand for bank credit. Demand eventually reaches such proportions that the banker has to sell securities to meet the loan requirements of his better customers. Increased selectivity then becomes the order of the day, and only those who have carefully developed the proper credit standing with their banks are able to increase, or even maintain, their volume of borrowing.

In the same fashion, the downward swing of the business cycle causes declining loan volume with insistent demands for repayment, forced liquidation of loans, and many other unpleasant things. The banker does not do this because he enjoys making the business man sweat. Quite the contrary, he is forced to do it, as he sweats first. It must be remembered that he is a member of the banking system and, as a member, he must keep in step.

When other banks require payment of loans, your

banker must do likewise. The reason is quite simple: A portion of the credit used to repay the loans at other banks comes from his bank, but if he is not requiring repayment, he receives no offsets from them for such transfers. The resulting imbalance is settled through the reserve accounts (at the Reserve Bank) of the two banks. This means that any bank which does not reduce its loan volume in line with the other banks gets debits in such volume that its reserve account is quickly wiped out, unless it takes remedial action.

8. *Self-liquidity vs. shiftability.* Traditionally, banks relied on a steady flow of repayments of daily maturities of short-term loans for their liquidity. The theory was that if the bank merely stopped making loans, the steady stream of maturities would provide funds to meet all demands. The theory further held that each loan should be made a self-liquidating one through requiring that the proceeds of the loan be used to acquire or produce assets that would be sold to realize the cash to repay the loan at maturity. This method is very sound as far as it goes, but it doesn't go far enough.

While self-liquidity will protect the individual bank, it cannot protect the banks, as a whole. In fact, the protection it affords the individual bank is at the expense of the other banks. Normally, a borrower pays his banks by using credit extended by other banks. This credit may be extended to him directly, in which event it is called a rotating loan, or, as is more likely, it may be extended to his debtors, who repay their debts to him and, thus, make it possible for him to repay his debt to his bank. The plain fact is that, statistically speaking, loans are paid off at one bank by credit extension at other banks in the system.

A steady stream of maturities of self-liquidating transactions will thus not protect the banking system. As a result, while bankers pay lip service to self-liquidity, they really rely on the shifting of assets for their liquidity. This is called the shiftability theory of banking liquidity.

In essence, it is merely something to shift and a place to shift it. This means marketable securities which can be sold to depositors or sold outside the banking system, or borrowers' notes and other obligations which can be shifted to a central bank (in our case, a Reserve Bank). Most of the borrowers' obligations eligible for such shifting are, as a matter of fact, self-liquidating, but it is the ability to shift them to the central banking system for cash that gives the commercial banking system protection when all the banks are under pressure.

This shift from dependence or self-liquidity, to dependence or shiftability has vitally affected the character of the loans made by banks. Many types of loans, such as consumer instalment loans, for example, that bankers would not have even considered a few short years ago, are eagerly sought today. Relying on the shifting of securities and eligible paper for their needed liquidity, bankers have broadened their loan categories to include almost any kind of loan being made today.

9. *Loans classified as to purpose.* On the basis of purpose, there are four principal types of loans. They are:

(a) *Commercial loans.* These are made to cover the short-term needs of industry, trade and agriculture. (Latterly, agricultural loans are shown separately in some compilations.) They are aggressively sought by the banks as they are in considerable measure self-liquidating; moreover, a substantial proportion meets the requirements for rediscounting at the Reserve Banks, in case of need.

(b) *Capital loans.* These are loans which take the place of capital. Since they are thus more or less permanently tied up in the business, banks do not ordinarily make such loans—at least, knowingly.

But it is often impossible to recognize capital loans in advance. It has been pointedly said that all loans are good loans when made—after all, no bank makes bad loans; they become bad only afterwards. So it is that many a seemingly temporary advance becomes frozen and thus a capital loan, despite the best of intentions all around. Even a perfectly proper inventory loan can freeze with a change in style, or a consequential drop in business activity, or a change in competitive factors in the market.

Then, there are the authentic capital loans, where a loan is contracted by a borrower at one bank to pay off a loan at another bank. (These rotating, or capital, loans were more fully described earlier.)

It also must be admitted that, in recent years, some banks, especially the larger ones, have frankly made a substantial proportion of their loans on the basis of repayment in instalments over a period of years. From the standpoint of banking orthodoxy, these are capital loans, and are, consequently, decried by many bankers. Also, the Federal Reserve authorities caution against the practice being overdone, and point to the dangers involved.

(c) *Security loans.* These loans are made on the pledge of collateral security in the form of stocks, bonds, and other obligations. Contrary to popular impression, the proceeds of these loans are used for every conceivable purpose. In fact, when they are made for the specific purpose of carrying securities, they are subject to the added requirements of Regulations T and U, described later in this text.

(d) *Consumption loans.* More popularly known as consumer loans, these are loans made for the purchase of something which will be consumed by the borrower rather than sold to realize funds to repay the loan. This means that the bank must rely on the borrower's income, upon indorsements or guaranties, or upon collateral security, rather than self-liquidity.

These loans have become the economic "patent medicine" of our times. Everybody —

borrower, lender, producer, and government—
loves consumer loans; and they do most of them
good. An economic outcast only a few short
years ago, they are actively sought today by
nearly all lenders.

Consumer loans are characterized by small
payments on principal, high interest rates, and
high costs of operation of the lenders.

10. *Further classification of loans.* Loans may be classified in several other ways, depending on the view-
point taken. The more important classifications are:

(a) *As to borrowers.* Here the two main categories
are (1) loans to customers (of the bank), and
(2) loans to others.

Loans to customers are those to the regular
depositors of the bank. Immediately after
banking safety, good bankers consider their
main responsibility is to take care of the credit
needs of their depositors. They have the first
call, after provisions have been made for
needed liquidity, on the bank's loanable funds.

Loans to others include bankers acceptances
and commercial paper bought in the open market, participations in loans to customers of other
banks, and loans to brokers and others. It will
be noted that none of these loans carry any
obligation for renewal at maturity. In short, it
is purely impersonal lending.

(b) *As to form.* With respect to form, loans are
either (1) unsecured or (2) secured.

Contrary to general impression, most American loans are unsecured in the sense that they do not carry the pledge of specific security. They rely, instead, to use a term from the bond market, on the "full faith and security" of the borrower. The much greater use of the unsecured loan in this country than in Europe is explained by the fact that our opportunities have always outrun our collateral—or, at least, borrowers and lenders have always thought so!

Secured loans are those that require the further backing of collateral of various kinds, or the indorsement or guaranty of responsible third parties. Security loans have always been important in banks; and mortgage loans on real estate have become one of the most important categories of secured loans in recent years.

(c) *As to maturity.* With respect to maturity, loans are either (1) demand or (2) time.

Demand loans are payable at any time at the option of either the lender or the borrower. In practice, they may run more or less indefinitely. If the loan is a good one and conditions do not change, it usually runs until the borrower pays it off. On the other hand, the term may at times be used to gloss over a slow loan, which the banker puts on a demand basis, since he knows it would be impossible to collect it in the regular manner.

Time loans and discounts, by definition, have a specific maturity. But it is frequently un-

derstood in advance that they will not be paid
when due. Instead, they may be renewed in
whole or in part, or even increased.

Thus, the circumstance, rather than the
name, determines the true character of the loan
in each case.

11. *Protection on interest rates.* The interest rates
which may be charged on the various types of loans are
subject to legal limitations for the protection of borrowers. The laws of the 50 states specify varying maximum rates that may be charged and provide a variety
of penalties for violation of these maximums.

Usury, the contracting for or the taking of something in excess of the amount allowed by law for the
loan of money, makes the lender liable to very severe
penalties in some states. In Arkansas, for example, both
interest and principal are forfeited, and in Colorado,
Minnesota, New York and Rhode Island, the contract
is void and the lender may be subject to a fine.

It should be noted, however, that under federal
law the discount of a bona-fide bill of exchange at not
more than the current rate of exchange for sight drafts,
in addition to the interest, is not usury.

In ancient times, all interest was considered usury
and, therefore, forbidden. On this point, Moses reported the words of the Lord to the people of Israel, as
set forth in the two following verses from Leviticus 25:

36. "Take thou no usury of him, or increase; but fear
thy God; that thy brother may live with thee.

37. "Thou shalt not give him thy money upon usury, nor lend him thy victuals for increase."

In ancient days, the taking of any payment for the use of money was considered reprehensible and contrary to the laws of God and man. It has only been in comparatively recent times that the Church has distinguished between interest, as a fair charge for the use of money, and usury, as an unfair charge. In any event, many people earn a good living by taking interest on money these days; but, if they make the mistake of making a usurious charge for the loan of their money, they are subject to the penalties of the law.

Review

Why is the loan and discount function of *paramount* importance to business men?

What are the four factors which determine the ability of our commercial banks to expand their credit?

Compare the efficacy of self-liquidity and shiftability in protecting a commercial bank.

Discuss the significance of the loan-deposit ratio to the business man.

Explain the term loanable funds.

Why is the relation of loans to the business cycle of special importance to the business man?

Classify loans on the basis of purpose.

What protection, other than competition, does the borrower have on interest rates?

CHAPTER VII

Open Market and Other Short-Term Borrowing

1. *Use of the term "open market."* The term "open market" is used for the borrowing by widely varying methods from, *or through,* a widely varied group of institutions. The only thing that these various methods of financing have in common is that the customary close relation between banker and borrower does not arise. In other words, these are impersonal, *market* types of borrowing.

Such borrowing includes the use of bankers acceptances, trade acceptances, commercial paper and accounts receivable as the method of borrowing. In addition to specialized departments in commercial banks, this field includes the commercial receivable companies, factors and sales finance companies. In some lines of business, such financing is of paramount importance; in fact, it may be the dominant method of financing. Moreover, in recent years, nearly all of the methods of open-market financing have experienced an amazing growth. In view of this, and the further fact that new uses for such financing are constantly being developed, these methods and institutions will be presented in some detail.

2. *Disadvantages of open-market borrowing.* Business men should carefully weigh the disadvantages of open-market borrowing against the advantages. Unfortunately, most of the literature in the field emanates from protagonists. There has been little objective analysis of the desirability of utilizing a particular variety of this non-bank type of financing for a particular business need. In view of this, a business man should not resort to non-bank short-term financing without careful consideration of all the factors and implications, particularly the reaction of his commercial banker.

If such financing would prejudice his relation with his regular banking connection, it should be approached with great reserve. This is because a close, working relationship with a commercial bank is one of the most valuable things any business can have. In fact, it is indispensable because, in times of financial and economic strain, the situation often develops to the point where only the commercial bank can aid, since it alone has the power of credit expansion.

The lack of the power of credit expansion tends to make a considerable part of this open-market credit a "fair weather" proposition. True, the multiplicity of sources and methods makes it very attractive so long as business is good and credit is available. But this very feature may encourage expansion and borrowing which will prove embarrassing, if not worse, later on when credit tightens and availability becomes a paramount problem.

In short, the increased volume of credit which can be secured, in comparison with that available from a commercial bank, may encourage or, at least, permit, unwise expansion of facilities or volume, with inevitably unhappy consequences.

Another disadvantage which may be encountered is the high rates charged by certain agencies in this field. These rates can be quite onerous and should be avoided if alternatives are available.

3. *Advantages of open-market borrowing.* The advantages of open-market borrowing can be summed up in the word, *specialization.*

By concentrating on a particular type of financing, or a particular area of business activity, such credit grantors become very expert in extending the last possible dollar of credit in a given situation. Not only are they able to refine their methods of analysis and evaluation, but they become personally familiar with the more important buyers, sellers and borrowers in the field and are thus able to supplement the conventional credit yardsticks with firsthand knowledge.

This means that able, aggressive beginners can generally secure more credit from such non-bank sources than from banks. This ability to finance increased volume on the same capital, while it has its dangers, may be the difference between success and failure for an enterprise, particularly a young one.

Specialization also permits non-bank lenders to become so familiar with the problems of their field that they are able to give valuable advice and policy assistance to their borrowers. This, too, can be especially valuable for the beginning and the smaller business ventures.

Also, some of this non-bank credit can be secured at very advantageous rates. Bankers acceptances, for example, usually carry the lowest rate of any kind of business borrowing.

4. *Bankers acceptances.* Many banks will lend their name (credit) as well as their funds. When they do so, a bankers acceptance results. This can be very advantageous to the bank as well as the borrower.

Although the Federal Reserve Act authorizes all member banks to accept time drafts, nearly two-thirds of all acceptances are made by ten large banks. In addition, the subsidiaries and agencies of foreign banks, private banks, investment houses and three specialized acceptance banks function in this field.

So far as definition is concerned, a bankers acceptance is simply a draft drawn on a bank and accepted by it. But the standards maintained and the outstanding character of the companies using this method give it extremely favorable implications. In fact, it is not too much to say that financing through bankers acceptances is in a class by itself.

As to procedure, a formal arrangement is made with a bank by means of an instrument known as a commercial letter of credit. This document sets forth the terms and conditions of the bank's *accepting*, such as maximum maturity, maximum liability, purpose of financing and required security. As it is a commitment on the part of the bank, collateral security is usually required, except from large customers with unquestionable credit standing.

While there is an over-all limit of 50 per cent of capital and surplus on the amount of acceptance credit that a member bank may have outstanding at one time, a bank may apply and receive permission to accept an additional 50 per cent for the financing of general trade needs. Also, a further 50 per cent may be accepted for the purpose of creating dollar exchange.

In addition to these over-all limitations, there are specific limitations on the amounts that may be accepted for one borrower. More particularly, a bank cannot accept for one borrower an amount in excess of 10 per cent of its capital and surplus unless the excess is secured by warehouse receipts, shipping documents, or some other collateral giving adequate security. Also, if the acceptances result from domestic financing of goods, they must be accompanied by shipping documents or warehouse receipts at the time of acceptance. And, although bills of exchange arising from foreign-trade transactions need have no specific collateral, they are usually accompanied by documents giving title at the time of acceptance.

Drafts drawn under a commercial letter of credit are "accepted" by the bank if they comply with the terms of credit. This is done by stamping or writing on the face of the draft the word "accepted" followed by the date of acceptance, name of the accepting bank, and signature of an officer. Instead of, or in addition to, the date of acceptance, the bank may specify "due on," followed by the actual date it will be paid. The bank thus "accepts" its designation as primary obligor on the draft and it becomes a "bankers acceptance." For this substitution of its credit for that of the borrower, the bank receives a fee of ⅛ per cent to ¼ per cent.

These acceptances are then sold in the open market; thus, the buyers of the drafts finance the transaction. The buyers are generally other banks, foreign correspondent banks, foreign central banks and, to a limited extent, the Federal Reserve Banks. Banks even buy their own acceptances, but such holdings must be reported as loans.

To avoid an increase in loan ratios, banks may sell such bills to each other. This "swapping" may be done directly between two banks, or the services of one of the dealers in the commercial bill market may be utilized for the purpose. Since most of these bills are eligible for rediscount at the Federal Reserve Banks, and all of them have a bank as the primary obligor and have a further claim on the drawer, they are considered prime earning assets by the commercial banks. As such, they are, ordinarily, eagerly sought and command the lowest rate in the money market other than Treasury bills and brokers loans.

Upon maturity, the acceptance is presented to the

accepting bank which pays it from funds previously received from the drawer. This is possible because one of the conditions of the commercial credit agreement is that the accepting bank is to be put in funds for this purpose at least one day before the acceptance is due.

Many business borrowers, who have transactions that can easily be fitted to this type of financing, use, instead, more costly methods. Sometimes this is due to ignorance on the part of the banker, but more often it is the borrower who, through inertia or ignorance, does not take advantage of such financing. In consequence, it is used far less widely than it should be. In any event, it is beyond question that the prestige, the lower rates and the diversification in borrowing afforded by this method make it especially attractive to alert financial managers.

5. *Trade acceptances.* Another method of short-term financing, widely used abroad but largely used as a collection device in this country, is the trade draft. It is an order to pay drawn by the seller of goods on the buyer. It thus falls within the category of bills of exchange, which are defined in the Uniform Negotiable Instruments Act as "an unconditional order in writing addressed by one person to another, signed by the person giving it, requiring the person to whom it is addressed to pay on demand or at a fixed or determinable future time a sum certain in money to order or to a bearer."

Trade drafts may be demand or time, and secured

or unsecured. Depending upon the terms of sale, the draft may be payable on "sight," on "arrival" of the goods, or a specified number of days after either, or after date. The conditions of the financing may provide that certain documents accompany the bill to be delivered upon payment (a documents-payment, or D/P bill) or upon acceptance (a documents-acceptance, or D/A bill). If acceptance is required, it becomes a *trade acceptance*.

Acceptance consists of writing or stamping on the face of the bill the word "accepted," followed by the date of acceptance and the signature of the drawee. At the end of the credit period, the bill is again presented to the drawee — this time for payment.

The traditional American method of selling on open-book account has prevented any consequential use of trade-acceptance financing. A further handicap to greater financing usage is its wide use as a collection device. By drawing such a draft on a customer, the transaction is forcefully brought to the attention of his bank, as it is presented through the bank. It brings the matter to a head, as the buyer must either perform or repudiate. Moreover, sellers on open-book account frequently demand acceptance of a trade draft as a condition of forebearing to exercise an overdue open-book claim. In this way, the seller gets a negotiable instrument on which he can borrow, or more easily bring suit, at a future date.

Many determined campaigns, especially since the

inception of the Federal Reserve System in 1914, have been mounted to bring the benefits of increased trade-draft usage to American business. But they have uniformly failed. This is to be regretted, since this method of financing would tie the credit extension more closely to the goods; it would bring financing into the open market and thus raise standards; it would furnish a dependable supply of two-name paper for banks and investors; and it would supply credit to business at rates below the over-the-counter rates on loans.

6. *Commercial paper.* One of the oldest methods of borrowing in the open market is the use of commercial paper. This paper consists of promissory notes of large business concerns in denominations of $5,000 or multiples of this amount. Blocks of such notes signed by the appropriate corporate official are either sold directly, as in the case of the larger finance companies, or turned over to a dealer for placement.

These notes are generally single-name, unsecured promissory obligations of the issuer, although occasionally securities or warehouse commodities may be offered as collateral. Maturity is ordinarily 4 to 6 months, although some maturities may be as short as one month and, occasionally, as long as one and one-half years. The number of concerns using this type of financing and the number of active commercial-paper dealers have sharply declined in recent years. Whereas there were 4,400 concerns utilizing the commercial-paper market at its peak in 1920, the number in recent years has fallen below 400. Also, the volume of such paper, other than the sales-finance-company issues which are placed directly, has also declined, but less sharply.

In contrast, the sales-finance companies, which act as their own agent in selling their paper directly to investors, have at times approached as much as $4 billion in their borrowing with such paper. Typically, their volume is four or five times that of the paper placed by dealers for other corporations.

Practically all dealer-offered paper is registered at the National Credit Office as a safeguard against the danger of overissue, a hazard which proved costly on three or four unhappy occasions in the past. In more recent years, the higher standards and larger borrowers have resulted in a payment record that, as a practical matter, is perfect.

Commercial paper is bought by banks, non-financial corporations, and other investors. It thus enables an issuer to tap funds which might otherwise be unavailable for short-term financing. Moreover, the rates are lower than for straight borrowing. Nonetheless, other than finance-company borrowings, this method of borrowing has become relatively unimportant in recent years. And this, despite countless paeans of praise from writers stressing the lower rates and the greater freedom of such open-market financing, as compared with direct bank lending.

7. *Sales-finance companies.* Those engaged in distribution have another very important source of credit,

namely, the sales-finance companies. Ordinarily thought of only in connection with automobile selling, they actually finance all manner of sales. Thus, the entire range of consumer durable goods can be financed not only through the distribution process but during most of the consumption period. And latterly, near-soft goods and even some soft goods are being financed in this fashion.

The sales-finance company is a specialized type of institution that engages primarily in *buying from dealers* consumer instalment contracts and providing wholesale financing for these dealers. Having pioneered the instalment-sales financing business, these companies have the important advantage of long experience and technical knowledge. They offer a fully integrated financial service covering all the stages in the distribution of consumer durable goods from the end of the assembly line at the factory to the last trade-in at the dealer's place of business. Even more important to most borrowers, these companies operate on a risk-capital base which is proportionately much larger than that of the banks, and are thus able to take greater risks in financing their dealers.[1]

The financing of retail sales by the purchase of instalment contracts from dealers needs no special explanation; almost everybody has had experience with

[1] See *Instalment Sales Financing* by Clyde William Phelps. This and other excellent studies on consumer credit and commercial financing can be secured free by writing the Commercial Credit Company, Baltimore, Maryland.

this type of financing. However, the extremes to which these specialized agencies will go in accepting marginal risks is worthy of special comment.

On this important point, sales-finance companies boast, "We never decline a transaction. If an offering is not acceptable the way it is proffered to us by the dealer, instead of rejecting it we tell him under what conditions we will buy it. A home-owning co-signer might make a deal acceptable, or a larger down payment, or accelerating the first five or six instalments, or making the instalments larger . . . there is always a way you can shape a transaction so that you can buy it." [1]

These problems most frequently arise on the trade-ins. Since it is said that three used cars must change hands (in the process of trading down) for each new car sold, the paramount importance of financing such sales, many of which are to marginal risks, in the automobile field is apparent. But it is also important in the distribution of other consumer durable goods, such as refrigerators, television sets, etc., since their percentages of trade-ins to new sales have steadily mounted in recent years.

Sales-finance companies also finance the inventories of dealers. This *wholesale financing* is very important to a dealer, since most consumer durable goods are sold only on a cash basis by the manufacturers. Through a

[1] Fred Mathison, "Credit on Retail Paper Purchased," *Time Sales Financing*.

method known as *floor-planning*, since it involves a continuous physical check by the lender of the serial numbers of the pledged merchandise, the dealer can finance the full factory cost of most consumer durables at reasonable rates. Since this wholesale financing is not very profitable, most lenders will do it only if they are also given the retail financing, which is quite profitable. In any event, by this method a dealer can borrow considerably more, and at reasonable rates, than by traditional methods.

Capital loans for worth-while purposes are also made by sales-finance companies to dealers. For instance, a dealer may wish to improve his facilities by constructing a new building, purchasing larger quarters, or modernizing present quarters. Or, an automobile dealer, for example, may need a working-capital loan to carry an enlarged inventory of parts and accessories to keep pace with expanding operations. Or, he may want to expand or improve his shop facilities by the purchase of new equipment which will pay for itself out of earnings. These and many other capital needs will be financed for alert and progressive dealers.

Such capital loans are made in various forms to good dealers. Thus, an Automotive Equipment Plan loan may be made on the security of machinery and equipment purchased by a dealer; or a Working Capital Loan Plan, under which the advance is unsecured and based only on the ability of the dealer, may be utilized; or, a Real Estate Loan Plan, based on the security of a mortgage on the land and building, may be used for such capital financing.

It should not be thought that these capital loans are extended indiscriminately by the sales-finance companies. Quite to the contrary, considerable care is exercised in making such loans in order to avoid subsidization of unsound practices and uneconomic proliferation of dealerships.

At first hand, the stated rates of interest in this field appear high. The question may well be asked why a dealer borrows from a finance company when he can get the funds at a cheaper rate elsewhere. The answer, as Professor Clyde W. Phelps of the University of Southern California so trenchantly puts it, is that "cheap and economical are not synonymous in dealer financing or in anything else."

Borrowers bent on getting the largest possible profit out of their businesses want the most economical, not the cheapest financing service. They know that, other things being equal, the lower the rate, the more conservative and selective must be the sales and financing policy of the dealer and his finance company. Such a policy precludes many of the marginal risks which must be sold to survive in the keen competition which characterizes the field of consumer durable goods these days.

So, regardless of apparent cost, these agencies must be in line on real net cost, since competition for this business is very keen among several different types of

lenders. It seems beyond cavil that they would not be
growing at the rate they are if they were not fully competitive.

8. *Factors.* Although little known to the general public, factors are among the oldest of the special types of
financial institutions used in financing the marketing
of goods. In fact, their origin is lost in the mists of antiq-
uity. The clay tablets of ancient Babylon, however,
indicate that the Chaldean *shamgalu* acted as agent
for merchants and warranted trade credits, the distinguishing characteristics of the modern-day factor,
more than 4,000 years ago.

Today, factoring is a multi-billion-dollar business.
In fact, some five billion dollars of financing is supplied
to our business firms each year through the factoring of
open accounts receivable. It is truly big business and
it is not only growing in dollar volume, but it is also
spreading into many lines where it was formerly unknown. It thus merits our careful consideration as a
means of financing.

In essence, factoring can be defined as a continuing
formal arrangement under which an institution, known
as a factor, assumes the credit and collection function
for a client and purchases his receivables as they arise,
without recourse to him. These relationships, in turn,
give rise to other auxiliary services of a financial character, such as cashing receivables, lending on inventory, fixed assets, other security or open credit, and
providing advisory services.

Assumption of the credit and collection function distinguishes factoring as a unique institution in the field of business finance. No other method of short-term financing shifts the credit and collection work to the financing institution.

In addition to doing the actual work, the factor assumes the financial responsibility for credit losses. He can safely do this, since he checks all credits before shipment and trade debtors are notified that payments are to be made directly to the factor. It should be emphasized that this purchase of accounts receivable is without recourse for credit losses. In all other methods of financing short-term receivables, the concern being financed assumes the risks of credit losses.

This *purchase* of accounts receivable does not involve any extension of credit by the factor, since proceeds are paid over only after being received. The services involved are credit granting (by the factor on behalf of the seller), accounts-receivable bookkeeping, and collection of the accounts. For these services, the factor charges a commission or fee of 1 to 2 per cent or more of the full *net* face value of the receivables handled by him. The term *net* means that the commission is calculated not on the gross amount of the receivables, but on that amount less discounts, credits for merchandise returns, and other allowances granted customers by the seller.

The exact commission charge is set by negotiation between the factor and the client. It will depend on many factors, such as the normal credit risk in the industry, the annual sales volume of the client, the average size of invoices, the average annual sales volume per customer, the length of the credit terms, the extent of extra services (such as actual billing), and so on. In short, these, and all other factors that affect the credit risk and the amount of detail work required must be covered in the rate the factor charges.

In addition to these basic functions of assumption of full responsibility for credit and collections through purchase of the accounts receivable without recourse, the factor performs the further function of *advancing cash for these receivables* whenever the client needs funds. In other words, he will give immediate cash for the receivables purchased in the amounts and at the times desired by the seller. For this advance of funds, interest is charged at an agreed rate, which is usually 6 per cent per annum. This charge is incurred, however, only if, and to the extent that, the client wants funds before their average due date. He may need such credit only on a seasonal basis for a short period each year. If so, he pays only for the time and extent of actual use and pays nothing for the "stand-by" or ready availability of such credit accommodation. This latter is, of course, a valuable feature for which some lenders make a "stand-by" charge.

The foregoing services comprise the *factoring* of receivables in a basic sense. But these major functions give rise to certain auxiliary or collateral services which

factors typically offer their clients. It should be understood that the specialized factoring organization does
not offer these collateral services to anybody and everybody, but only to those clients whose receivables it is
factoring.

These other services of loans on inventory, fixed
assets, other security and open credit are thus truly
supplementary to their main function of factoring. In
similar fashion, the *advisory service* with respect to financing matters, and also with respect to the broader
aspects of production and marketing problems and
developments in the client's industry, supplements
the basic service of assumption of credit risk.

Factoring offers real advantages to aggressive, growing concerns which can make profitable use of additional cash, and whose management can make profitable use in product development, production and
sales, of the time, effort and worry that would otherwise
have to be devoted to credits and collections. Moreover, as specialists in credit, with superior information
and a key position as large-scale credit grantors, factors can extend more credit safely than can the client.
Sales are thus increased and, even more important,
sales are better maintained in times of economic un-
certainty than would otherwise be the case. Factors
have every incentive to do this, since their compensation is based directly on the volume of credit they
"check."

In weighing the commission paid the factor, allowances should be made for the costs of a separate credit department and the maintenance of accounts receivable and collection facilities that would otherwise be necessary. For many concerns, such costs could actually be greater than the commission charged by the factor. Similarly, the interest charged by the factor on actual advances, plus the advantages of the free stand-by service when credit is not needed, should be weighed against the costs of these *two* services from other sources. When these comparisons are made, it will be seen that factors are competitive and offer definite advantages for many concerns. That is why they have been growing at the rate they have in recent years.

9. *Accounts receivable financing.* In contrast to the factoring, or "notification," method, there is an ordinary, or "non-notification," method of accounts-receivable financing. This, too, is a multi-billion-dollar industry with annual credit extensions in excess of six billion dollars. Basically, this financing is by means of a contract whereby the financing institution purchases the seller's open accounts, or makes an advance secured by the pledge of such accounts, *with recourse to the seller* for credit losses and *without notice to the debtors* on such accounts. It thus differs widely from factoring.

Spelling out the differences: (1) the factor must approve all credits—the commercial receivable lender approves none; (2) the factor assumes all credit risk— the commercial receivable lender assumes none, so far as the purchaser is concerned; (3) the factor performs

accounts receivable bookkeeping and collection services
—the commercial receivable lender renders no such
service; (4) factoring does not necessarily involve an
advance of funds—the other is solely an advance of
funds; (5) factoring involves notification of the debtor
and payment directly to the factor—the commercial
receivable lender has no contact with and, in fact, is
not known to the lender; and, most importantly, (6) factoring may involve as much as 100 per cent advance on
the outstanding accounts receivable—the cash advances of the commercial receivable lender typically are
from 70 to 90 per cent and never exceed 95 per cent
of the outstandings.

The method of charge in this type of financing is a
per diem rate on the average daily face value of the accounts outstanding during the month. This per diem
rate is naturally directly related to the percentage of
advance on the accounts outstanding. Thus, for advances of 75, 80 and 85 per cent, the per diem rate of
charge on average daily outstanding gross receivables
may be $\frac{1}{49}$ of 1 per cent, $\frac{1}{46}$ of 1 per cent, and $\frac{1}{43}$ of 1
per cent, respectively. As these rates indicate, such accounts-receivable borrowers must expect to pay a minimum of some 10 per cent. This rate can mount rapidly
as credit risk increases or as unscrupulous lenders take
advantage of a necessitous business borrower.

Although the standards have risen considerably in
this field in recent years, since better lenders, and more
lenders, have offered greatly increased competition, a

prospective borrower must still be wary. In particular, he should be certain to calculate carefully the actual interest demanded and compare this per annum rate with his costs from alternative sources. If he has no alternatives and can still use the money profitably, or if he must have the funds as the lesser of two evils, he will have to go ahead. But he should satisfy himself as to all the financial factors involved.

Until comparatively recent years, borrowing on accounts receivable was viewed as a certain indication of financial ineptitude. It was derisively called "hocking accounts receivable," and commercial banks, in particular, took a very dim view of the practice. But the Great Depression of the 1930's caused some banks to start making such advances in an effort to secure badly needed loan value. This banking benediction brought accounts-receivable financing from a somewhat clandestine, last-resort type of operation to a respectable method of financing working-capital needs.

Today, many factors have departments for such financing; likewise, many commercial banks. In addition, there are thousands of commercial receivable companies, usually small and local, throughout the country which specialize in such financing. These companies are organized into a trade association of their own, known as the National Commercial Finance Conference (New York), which is doing a splendid job of supplying information, standardizing procedures and raising standards in this field.

Review

Give the basic difference between open-market and bank borrowing.

List the dangers of open-market borrowing.

Evaluate use of the bankers acceptance as a method of borrowing.

Compare the use of trade acceptances in the United States with that of other countries and give the reasons for the difference.

What are the advantages of using factors in financing a growing business?

Explain the charges made by factors and indicate the services rendered for each.

Contrast factoring with accounts-receivable financing from the standpoint of (1) assumption of risk; (2) book-keeping service rendered; (3) credit extended, and (4) costs.

CHAPTER VIII

Bank-Deposit Services

1. *Countless services of banks.* Commercial banks perform a myriad of services for business, for government and (directly) for the public. Some of these services are necessary to the functioning of their primary services of loans and deposits. But most of them are incidental to their main activities and have developed because of special advantage the banks may have for rendering the services or because of the pressure of the keen competition which characterizes American banking.

Many of these services have become standardized and are offered by all banks. But it is important to remember that there are, literally, countless other services which are offered variously by individual banks. It, therefore, behooves the business man to ascertain the particular services rendered by his bank, and how he can best utilize those services for his business.

Many of these services are entirely free; in fact, some of the most valuable ones, such as the clearing of checks and credit information, are free. On most of the others, the banks either lose money or, at best, break even. Moreover, on a few of the services, such as trust operations, for example, although the well-managed banks make money, there are always many banks that render the services at less than cost on a strict cost-accounting basis with proper allocation of overhead.

2. *Bank investments.* Banks make their credit (our modern money) available to the economy through loans and discounts (which have already been discussed) and through investments. When securities are brought on to the balance sheets of the banks, deposits are created. In other words, when a bank purchases securities from a non-bank holder, deposits are *increased*. Thus, bank investments constitute the basis of an important proportion of our money supply.

In addition to this service to the entire economy, the first-hand aid, or the ultimate aid, which the purchase gives the capital-market borrower is obvious. By furnishing both primary and secondary markets for high-grade securities, such as government obligations, government guaranteed issues, state and municipal obligations, and the higher grades of corporate bonds, banks not only finance such borrowers, but they contribute to their own liquidity as lenders and, more importantly, to the liquidity of the economy. In fact, this contribution to liquidity has become so pronounced in recent years that many economists fear that the economy has become too liquid.

3. *Why banks buy securities.* It should be understood that the service rendered the issuer of the securities is secondary, or rather, incidental, to the main aim of the banks in buying securities. They buy securities to be

better able to render their other services *at all times and under all conditions.* Securities which can be shifted to other holders enable them to meet the seasonal and emergency demands of depositors for credit and for cash.

Moreover, the high-grade securities that banks buy are mostly in the so-called non-risk category, which improves the appearance of their balance sheet as well as strengthens their financial position. It is not too much to say that they use securities as their first line of defense whether it be money management, public demands, or governmental supervision. But, regardless of motivation, important services are rendered all along the line when securities are bought by banks.

4. *The deposit services of banks.* Although taken for granted, the value of the deposit services of banks is truly incalculable. It would be impossible, as a practical matter, to conduct modern business without deposit facilities—the physical burden of handling the cash and the cost of providing safekeeping facilities would be staggering, to say nothing of the "lost motion," delays and over-all slowdown occasioned by it. The latter alone would make it unthinkable!

Opening a deposit account is, of course, a privilege and not a right. Banks may refuse to open a deposit account, even for an agency of government. The important reasons for refusal are: (1) the character and reputation of the prospective depositor may not meet the minimum requirements set by the bank for admission to the banking system; (2) the nature of the account might be such that the bank could not service it properly, or profitably; and (3) the prospective account might fail to meet some technical operating requirement of the bank, such as minimum balance, activity (deposits and withdrawals) per dollar of deposit balance, etc.

On the depositor's part, convenient availability is generally the major consideration in selecting a bank, just as it is in selecting a retail store. This is followed closely as a consideration by the bank's reputation for integrity and friendly, efficient service. The past experience of professional and business associates with a particular bank weighs heavily in the selection process, especially when the choice is being made by a newcomer in the community.

Banks usually require a personal introduction as a condition precedent to the opening of a checking account. Such a requirement, however, is rarely found in the case of savings and special checking accounts.

Special checking accounts are those in which the service is strictly limited to the drawing of checks, with a charge of a stipulated amount for each check. Their restricted nature makes them more like a money-order service than a regular checking account.

For immediate credit to deposit accounts, banks accept cash, matured interest coupons and checks. Other obligations, such as time drafts, notes, bankers and trade acceptances, items previously returned unpaid, etc., are accepted for collection and ultimate credit to regular demand deposit accounts.

5. *Checking accounts.* Although immediate credit is given for all "cash" items, which includes checks drawn on other points and coupons as well as currency, banks refuse to pay checks drawn against uncollected funds. In other words, immediate credit and immediate availability are not synonymous.

To avoid the risk and the cash outlay of paying out uncollected funds, banks require minimum balances as a margin of safety. Moreover, they have established schedules of availability based on the number of days which experience has shown it will take for funds to be received from the points indicated. These schedules also have a substantial margin of safety, as the time allowance is the maximum number of days required rather than the typical or even the average number.

A checking account, in effect, permits a depositor to manufacture his own money to order in that the bank will pay any amount within the account to anyone that he directs. This order for the bank to pay, or draft, is called a check. These checks constitute a record of payment. They are far safer than currency, since they are literally beyond theft and hold-up. As compared with currency, their convenience is obvious. Moreover, in special forms, checks can be used to substitute the bank's credit for the depositor's credit where necessary in special situations, such as the transfer of title of land, bids on property, and delivery of securities. For these purposes, certified checks and cashier's, or manager's, checks are widely used.

A *certified check* is a personal check that has been stamped "certified" by an officer of the bank, who signs the certification as legal evidence of the act. At the time of certification, the amount is charged against the account of the drawer and transferred to "Certified Checks Outstanding" account, and thus becomes a direct obligation of the bank. This transfer of responsibility for payment from the drawer to the bank makes it highly important from a legal standpoint, whether the drawer or the payee secures the certification. Thus, if the drawer has the check certified and the drawee bank fails, the creditor can demand other payment, since the means of payment tendered him has proved defective.

On the other hand, if the payee has the check certified and the bank fails, the drawer is discharged of all liability. This is on the sound ground that the payee went to the bank and could have received payment, but elected, instead, to take the obligation of the bank. He is bound by his choice and has no further claim on the drawer of the check. (It should be remembered that the drawer's account is reduced in either event.) The moral is: make the other fellow certify the check.

A *cashier's check* is a bank's own check, signed by one of its officers, usually the cashier, and used by the bank for its own payments and used by customers of the bank in cases where bank funds are required.

A *manager's check* is, in effect, a cashier's check and it is used in the same fashion. Special low-cost forms of such checks are called *registered* checks or *money orders*, and are sold for a very nominal amount above their face value to anyone, bank customer or not.

6. *Service charges.* In recent years, charges known as service charges have been made by most banks on regular checking accounts. These have been variously called measured service charges, metered service charges, or activity charges, to make it clear that the amount paid is based on the service rendered. Also, all of the plans allow an earnings credit on the deposit balance in the account. This is generally calculated on the minimum balance, although it is sometimes based on the average balance.

To save the clerical cost of computation of per item charges, most banks make no charge for the regular activity of deposits and checks paid unless the balance falls below a minimum amount, which depends on the bank and its competitive position in the community. Since the aim is not only to have each account cover its costs, but also contribute its fair share to profits, activity limits are usually placed on the accounts where the bank relies on the collected balance for its compensation. Thus, for a minimum balance of $300, the bank might permit up to ten checks and four deposits a month without further charge; any additional items would have to be covered by additional balance or per item payment.

The point to keep in mind is that deposit-account activity costs the bank money which it must recoup in some way. Even though no charge is made by some banks on deposit accounts, the customers of the bank must bear the burden in some way. It seems much better and certainly it is fairer to tie the charge directly to the activity causing the expense, than to collect it indirectly through a higher charge on some other service of the bank.

Whether a *computed* charge of deposit analysis to determine whether the balance is large enough to carry the activity on a profitable basis, or an actual charge to the account, the itemization would be, typically, somewhat as follows: A *maintenance* charge of 50¢ to $1.00 per month; a per item charge of 5¢ to 7½¢ for each check paid, and 0¢ to 10¢ for each deposit; and widely varying charges for each item returned, each protest, each over-draft, each stop-payment order, etc. Against these, an earnings credit of 10¢ per $100 of average gross balance, or average collected balance, per month is allowed.

As the reader will note, this amounts to a yearly earnings rate of 1.2 per cent on the balance. Since banks can earn such a rate on their average assets only in times of prosperity, they are forced to reduce this credit when business activity does not permit them to maintain it.

Although there is considerable standardization in charges on the main items of deposits and checks paid, there are wide differences in the amounts charged for the miscellaneous services and in the policy of the banks with respect to waiving such charges. For example, one New York City bank waives every miscellaneous charge under $1.00 on the theory that the cost of making the entries and the annoyance to the depositor would more than offset the additional earnings. As an indication of the extent to which such charges are waived, this bank privately estimates that its income would be increased more than $100,000 if it waived only those charges under 50¢.

In view of the wide range of charges—in fact, many country banks make no charge at all—each business man should carefully consider the nature and the extent of the deposit services he requires and measure his requirements against the charge schedules of the banks available to him. In this way, he can not only save money, but he can select the bank whose operations and policies most nearly conform to his needs. This, of course, makes for satisfaction all around.

7. *Savings services.* Until recently, commercial banks in the eastern states were not permitted to use the word "savings" as a designation for their non-checking, savings accounts. As a result, they had a wide range of names, such as Thrift Accounts, Special Interest Accounts, Compound Interest Accounts, and so on, for these deposits. Now that the legal barriers to the use of the name have been removed, some banks use the term "savings," but most still cling to their original

terminology because of public acceptance as well as the differentiation it gives their savings service from that of the other banks.

In addition to the regular savings deposits, which are restricted to individuals and non-profit institutions, banks have other time deposits owned by corporations and governmental bodies as well as by individuals. Moreover, although regular savings deposits owned by individuals account for the great bulk of time deposits, the various other types of time accounts are usually responsible for any rapid changes in the total of time deposits at the commercial banks.

Regular savings deposits of individuals and non-profit institutions are sometimes evidenced by a written receipt or agreement, but more generally by a passbook which is presented at each transaction. Normally, the depositor can withdraw savings upon request without delay; the bank, however, must, under the regulations of the supervisory authorities, reserve the right to re-quire a written notice of withdrawal of not less than thirty days.

Christmas clubs and similar "package" special savings accounts, as well as the holdings of time certifi-cate deposits of individuals are all of the savings type and should be considered as such.

The other time deposits of commercial banks are evidenced by *certificates of deposit and open-account deposits*. Although these two types of accounts may be held by individuals as well as by others, they are used mostly by business corporations because, through them, the banks can tailor the deposit to meet the specific liquidity and cash operating requirements of the business.

The maximum permissible interest rates that may be paid on the different types of time accounts are set by the Federal Reserve Board for member banks, and by the Federal Deposit Insurance Corporation for insured non-member banks. On Apr. 19, 1968, the Board set the maximum rates that member banks are permitted to pay depositors at 5 per cent on all time deposits and certificates of deposit having a maturity of 90 days or more and 4 per cent on those of 30 to 89 days. Previously, the maximum rates payable were 5½ per cent for time deposits and certificates of 30 days or more. The rate payable on pass book savings remained at 4 per cent.

Since interest on regular checking accounts is prohibited by law, the payment of interest on time deposits is closely regulated to prevent any evasion of the spirit, as well as the letter, of that law, which might otherwise be attempted.

Although not money in the sense that demand deposits are, time deposits are the oldest form of "near money." It must be admitted, however, that the distinction between money and near money is tenuous at best, and that time deposits seem sometimes to fit better in the one category and sometimes in the other. In any event, the huge total of time deposits (in commercial banks) of over $160 billion, and the growth of corporate, foreign and state and local time balances, strongly suggest that a sizable portion of these funds have a high degree of "moneyness," and may be converted into demand deposits whenever there is need for such action.

In other words, time deposits in commercial banks consist of true savings balances which fluctuate but little, and other balances which are subject to rapid changes—both up and down. Since commercial banks must keep this in mind in their allocation of assets, they are restricted in their earnings on such deposits in comparison with the mutual savings banks and the savings and loan associations.

8. *Reasons for regulation of interest payments.* Competition for deposits is so keen that experience has shown it is necessary to regulate the interest paid on them. Otherwise, the high expense incurred in this competitive struggle forces the banks to stress yield rather than safety in their investing and lending operations.

In view of this, Section 19 of the Federal Reserve Act, as amended by the Banking Act of 1933 and subsequent legislation, provides that no member of the Federal Reserve System "shall, directly or indirectly, by any device whatsoever, pay any interest on any deposit which is payable on demand." It further provides that "the Board of Governors of the Federal Reserve System shall from time to time limit by regulation the interest which may be paid by member banks [1] on time and savings deposits, and *shall prescribe different rates* for such payment on time and savings deposits having different maturities, or subject to different conditions respecting withdrawal or repayment. . . ."

The prohibition against the payment of interest on demand deposits is based on the following considerations:

(a) Payment is unwarranted because depositors are compensated for the use of their funds by banking services.

(b) Elimination of this competitive burden of interest payment on demand deposits reduces the pressure on the banks to make loans or investments with excessive credit risks to secure the needed higher yield.

(c) Such interest payments reduce net earnings and thus reduce the bank's ability to set up reserves to protect the bank and the depositors.

In the case of time deposits, the regulation of the rates paid by all insured banks is to prevent excessive payments that would weaken the bank. In other words, regulation is intended to prevent rate wars between the commercial banks and other institutions competing for savings, such as the savings and loan associations and the mutual savings banks and, for that matter, among

---

[1] Maximum rates that may be paid by insured non-member banks, as set by the Federal Deposit Insurance Corporation, are the same as those in effect for the member banks.

the commercial banks themselves. Payment of reasonable rates of interest based on the earnings which can be realized on such time deposits is justified by the following considerations:

(a) Time depositors do not receive the services of demand depositors and are, therefore, entitled to some compensation for the use of their funds.
(b) Legal reserve requirements are less than on demand deposits.
(c) Operating reserves against time deposits can be lower than those of demand deposits.
(d) Costs of maintenance are lower because of lesser activity.
(e) Such deposits being less volatile — in fact, most of the savings component of time deposits stays in the banks permanently — can be invested in longer term, higher yielding assets.

And, finally, in respect to interest rates on time deposits, it should be pointed out that most commercial banks pay less than the maximum rates permitted by the Federal Reserve Board. This may be simply the conservative policy of the individual banks or it may be the result of clearing house association regulations, or because of restrictions established by the state supervisory authorities.

9. *Government deposits.* United States Treasury funds in limited amounts are held on deposit in insured banks designated as "General Depositaries," and in insular and foreign depositaries. Accounts are maintained in

these various types of depositaries, in areas at some distance from Federal Reserve Banks or their branches, to provide agents of the federal government with convenient facilities for depositing funds collected and to permit disbursing officers to make payments in local funds.

The Treasury also maintains special deposit accounts at some 11,000 banking institutions designated as "Special Depositaries." Formerly known as "War Loan Deposit Accounts," these accounts are today termed "Treasury Tax and Loan Accounts."

10. *Treasury Tax and Loan Accounts.* Originally designated to serve the exigencies of war finance by permitting specially designated institutions to buy certain issues of government securities through the simple process of a credit on their books, the function of these accounts has been expanded to permit the banks to credit withheld-income taxes, payroll taxes under the old-age insurance program, and certain corporation income and other tax payments to them. Thus, such payments result in an increase, temporary though it is, in the deposits of the bank rather than an immediate reduction in its reserves at the Federal Reserve Bank because of transfers to the Treasury account.

Tax and Loan Accounts are divided into four categories for money market purposes. The smaller Special Depositaries are placed in Class A; the middle-sized ones in Class B; and the largest ones in Class C. In addition, there is another category of such accounts which may be held by a Special Depositary in any of the above classes, although most of them, because of size, are held by Class C banks. These accounts, known as X balances, arise from the deposit by the Treasury of checks of $10,000 or more, or a percentage thereof, in the banks on which such checks are drawn.

As the Treasury needs funds, calls are made on Tax and Loan Accounts by categories. That is, announcement is made in advance of the percentage of the X balances or other deposits to be called for each class of bank. On the effective date, the announced percentages are debited to the reserve accounts of the member banks by their respective Federal Reserve Banks.

By thus "calling" different percentages from the different categories, the Federal Reserve authorities can temporarily rectify an imbalance in reserve holdings of the member banks. For example, if the large city banks have been losing deposits, and consequently reserves, a heavier call can be made on the Class A accounts (the country banks) to retrieve their windfall and relieve the pressure on the reserves of the city banks. In the same fashion, calls on the X account balances can be tailored to the reserve position of the large money market banks, which hold most of these accounts.

It should be understood that payments are not made from these accounts—only transfers to the Treasury Account at the district Federal Reserve Bank from which, with minor exceptions, all Treasury payments are made. Also, it should be emphasized that, to be appointed a Special Depositary, a bank must deposit sufficient government securities (usually those bought with the Tax and Loan Account credit), or other acceptable collateral with its Federal Reserve Bank to cover its liability to the government on such deposits.

Treasury Tax and Loan Accounts perform valuable services for the government whether it be financing war or collecting heavy peacetime taxes. They constitute a valuable tool in carrying out the credit control and money market responsibilities of the Federal Reserve authorities. Furthermore, they render a great service to the commercial banks in cushioning the impact of heavy tax collections, and in enabling them to realize at least some return on government deposits as a partial offset to the many free services performed for the government.

Review

To what extent do the services of various banks vary? Why?

How does the purchase of high-grade securities improve the position of a commercial bank?

How do regular deposit accounts differ from Special Checking accounts?

Justify bank-service charges.

Differentiate the regular savings deposits of individuals and non-profit organizations from the time deposits of corporations.

Explain why time deposits are, more and more, becoming "near money."

Describe the services of Treasury Tax and Loan Accounts to (a) the government, (b) the Federal Reserve authorities, and (c) the commercial banks.

CHAPTER IX

Deposit Protection

1. *Guaranty and insurance of deposits.* The paramount importance of protecting the integrity of bank deposits has long been recognized. And now that demand deposits serve as our money supply, protection is more important than ever before.

Yet, unhappily, our financial history is replete with instances of loss of public confidence with heavy shifting of deposits from one bank to another, followed by panicky withdrawal of funds from the banking system necessitating liquidation of bank assets at very unfavorable times. The resulting distress-calling of loans and forced selling of bank investments have often caused widespread bank suspensions and drastic reductions of our money supply. So, it is not surprising to find that there has always been widespread public demand for protection of bank deposits.

In response to such public demand, many plans to attain deposit safety have been tried down through the years. As early as 1829, New York established the Safety Fund System in an effort to protect deposits and notes. Numerous bank failures soon demonstrated that the Fund was insufficient to cover both types of liabilities, and protection was withdrawn from deposits. During the decade following the panic of 1907, eight states established some plan of deposit guaranty or insurance, and all of them were unsuccessful.

Among the more important reasons for the failure of the state plans, undue concentration of risk, over-expansion of banking facilities with attendant excessive competition, and withdrawal of the stronger banks from the plans, head the list. The failure of the state plans notwithstanding, the closing of some 15,000 banks in the 1920's and early 1930's sparked an irresistible demand for deposit insurance under the sponsorship of the federal government.

In theory, the guaranty of bank deposits is unwise, since it largely removes one of the chief restraining influences on reckless banking, namely, the banker's sense of responsibility to his friends and neighbors who "trusted him." This restraining influence, which proved by no means sufficient to prevent thousands of bank failures in the past, must be replaced by other, and increased safeguards.

In essence, the main task in deposit protection is to protect the small depositors against loss on their deposit accounts in order to remove one of the major causes of instability in our money supply. To do this, far more than a guaranty of deposits is necessary. Among other things, better bank management, better and more complete supervision, and better examinations, especially for the thousands of banks that are not mem-

bers of the Federal Reserve System, are all needed.
2. *Federal deposit insurance.* The system of Federal
deposit insurance which was established in 1933 was
far more than deposit guaranty under a different name.
Its basic concept was the preservation of public confidence through better banking. The aim was to prevent trouble in the first place, and if that failed, to
prevent the trouble from spreading.

The banking situation had deteriorated in 1933 to
the point where this could be accomplished only on a
national basis and only with the backing of the federal
government. This new effort came at the end of a
period in which literally thousands of banks had failed,
billions of dollars of deposits had been lost or frozen,
currency withdrawals had reached panic proportions,
people had become afraid to put their money in banks,
and bankers had become afraid to make loans. This
progressive deterioration culminated in the Banking
Holiday of March 1933, in which all banks were closed
by a Presidential Order.

Emergency legislation and other measures adopted
during, and following, the banking holiday not only
restored, in considerable measure, public confidence
and permitted a gradual reopening of all sound banks,
but they ushered in a new era in American banking.
To name but a few of the steps taken, the Federal
Reserve System was considerably reorganized, hoarding was prohibited, a gold embargo, followed by a
devaluation of practically 50 per cent of the dollar, was

proclaimed, the gold clause in bonds and the gold redemption of currency were abolished and a system of federal-deposit insurance was inaugurated.

3. *The Federal Deposit Insurance Corporation.* The Banking Act of 1933 contained an amendment to the Federal Reserve Act establishing the Federal Deposit Insurance Corporation as an instrumentality of the federal government to administer the insurance of bank deposits. These original legal provisions were later superseded by a separate law, the Federal Deposit Insurance Act of 1950.

The FDIC, as the Corporation is commonly called, although chartered by the federal government, is now privately owned by the banks. Its original capital of $289 million, which consisted of $150 million subscribed by the government and $139 million by the Federal Reserve Banks, was repaid in 1948, so that it has no capital stock today. It does, however, have an earned surplus of some $2.5 billion, to which substantial additions are being made each year. In addition, the Corporation has the legal right to borrow up to $3 billion from the Treasury, if needed.

While these are large totals, they represent a pitifully small percentage of the Corporation's total liabilities which are in the neighborhood of $225 billion. This small ratio of capital to risk accentuates the earlier contention that the FDIC must rely on financial leadership, better banking and public confidence rather than its own assets, for safety of deposits.

4. *Management of the Federal Deposit Insurance Corporation.* Management of the FDIC, and thus of our system of deposit insurance, is entrusted to a board of three directors composed of the Comptroller of the Currency (*ex-officio*) and two men appointed by the President with the advice and consent of the Senate. Of these two appointees, one, who is of the political party of the President, is designated as Chairman and is the chief executive officer of the Corporation. The other appointed director is a member of the political party which is out of power. On at least one occasion, these two directors have merely exchanged offices when there was a change in Presidents.

To assist the directors, the corporation has a staff of experts in Washington and regional offices, manned by some 30 supervisory examiners and a regular examination force of examiners and assistants. These men receive regular reports from all insured banks; they examine all insured banks which are not members of the Federal Reserve System; and, they receive copies of the examinations of all member banks by the national and the state supervisory authorities, as the case may be. Moreover, they may make a special examination of any insured bank to determine the insurance risk, if they think it necessary.

5. *Termination of insurance.* The FDIC may take action to terminate the insurance of any bank for continued unsafe, unsound or illegal banking practices. The insurance can be actually terminated only if, upon

notice and hearing, the bank is found guilty of the charges. In such event, all depositors are notified and, after a period for withdrawal of deposits, all insurance ceases.

This remedy is so drastic that most banks hasten to correct their practices upon informal notification. And most of the remaining ones which require formal notification of intention to terminate their insurance, get busy and remedy the practices criticized, or merge with another institution before the actual termination becomes effective. A very few, of course, suspend operations and the Corporation takes over as receiver. In the entire history of the Corporation, there have been only three or four banks which tried to continue operation after termination of their deposit insurance, and only one or two of those succeeded in doing so.

As all members of the Federal Reserve System are mandatory members of the Federal Deposit Insurance Corporation, they may not terminate their insurance without surrendering their charter, if a national bank, or withdrawing from the Federal Reserve System, if a state institution. But any non-member insured bank may terminate its insured status upon sixty days notice to the Corporation and notice to its depositors by publication, or otherwise.

6. *Method of protecting depositors.* If, despite all efforts, a bank does get into difficulty, the Corporation has two widely different methods it can use to protect depositors. It can let the bank close and pay the de-

positors the amounts for which it is legally liable. This has the disadvantages of adverse publicity, forced liquidation of assets, and failure to realize anything on the good-will value of the deposits. This makes the method costly to the Corporation and destructive of public confidence.

A much better method, and the one which is used if at all possible, is guarantee of the assets of the insolvent bank in favor of a bank which assumes its deposit liabilities. When first used, there was some Congressional criticism of this method on the ground that the Corporation was utilizing its funds to protect not only the insured portion of the deposits, but the entire deposit total. The Corporation countered this charge on the ground that, with this method, they could protect *all the deposits* at less cost than they could protect the *insured deposits* only, under the liquidation method.

The debate was resolved by the Congress through authority in the Federal Deposit Insurance Corporation Act of 1950 for the Corporation to purchase assets from, extend loans to, or make deposits in, any insured bank in danger of closing. This liberalization of powers permits the Corporation to arrange for continued operation of banks in difficulty in "one bank" towns where merger is not feasible.

Although not required to use the merger or financial assistance methods, the Corporation has since 1944 done so in nearly all cases. The FDIC has thereby protected all the deposits of such banks and not just the insured deposits, as they were legally required to do.

7. *Costs of deposit insurance.* Payments to the FDIC by participating banks are assessments rather than insurance premiums. They are not on an actuarial basis, since they do not vary with the risk of failure of the particular bank; nor are they determined by the amount actually insured, since they are based on total deposits, although the insurance covers only the first $15,000 in each account.

The gross charge is an annual assessment of $\frac{1}{12}$ of 1 per cent on total adjusted deposits. Payment, however, is made semi-annually, based on the average of deposits at the end of March and June for the first-half of the year, and September and December for the second-half. The insured banks receive a credit against their next assessment of 60 per cent of the net assessment income of the Corporation.

In other words, after paying all expenses and losses, 60 per cent of the remainder is credited against the coming year's assessment and 40 per cent is credited to the Corporation's earned surplus. In addition, all of the earnings on the Corporation's holdings of some $2.5 billion of government securities are credited to earned surplus. Thus, its capital resources are continuing to grow at a fairly rapid rate, despite the assessment credits.

8. *Relation of the FDIC to the money supply.* The importance of the service of the FDIC as an insurer absorbing deposit losses arising from the financial diffi-

culties of a particular bank should not cause its important services in connection with the money supply to be overlooked. In its supervisory capacity, it has continually fought against deposit insurance being used as an umbrella for poor bankers and lax banking practices which would overexpand the money supply and weaken confidence in it.

On the contraction side, the claim is even made that the FDIC has ended the runs on banks with their reduction of the money supply and strains on public confidence. This, of course, is not true, since large depositors still analyze the banks on a continuous basis and are quick to transfer to a stronger bank when weakness develops. And it is these large transfers which give the *coup de grace* to a bank in difficulties.

While no way has yet been devised to prevent an individual bank with poor management from getting into trouble, the FDIC does maintain public confidence in banks in general, so that deposits can be transferred from banks in difficulty to other banks, rather than being hoarded by individuals, as in pre-FDIC days. In other words, there is little likelihood of a blind, unreasoning scramble to convert bank deposits into cash, such as drained away bank reserves in 1933.

It seems clear that the greatest service of the FDIC has been along the lines of preventing loss of confidence, with consequent actual destruction of the money supply through hoarding, calling of loans, bank failures and other adversities.

9. *Contribution of banking education to deposit protection.* The banking difficulties and the Great Depression of the early 1930's started a revolution in banking, the end of which no man can see. Great as the other changes have been, the changes in educational standards and in the attitude of bankers toward banking education have undoubtedly been the greatest. Before 1933, the typical banker had "all the answers" needed in this, in the words of Voltaire, "best of all possible worlds." He didn't need any outsiders to tell him how to run his business! And as for participating in a banking conference or an economic session with other bankers, that was strictly "for the birds"!

In contrast, the bankers who survived the economic Armageddon of the early thirties were a thoroughtly chastened lot. They had learned the hard way that banking education is a continuing, life-long necessity for which there is no substitute. And in the vein of the maxim, "None is so pious as a converted sinner," they proceeded literally to make a fetish of banking education. As a result, in no business field has there been such a sharp upward surge in professional and educational standards.

As mentioned earlier, the FDIC took the lead on the supervisory side with regular economic and professional conferences for its own staff and, shortly afterwards, with such meetings for all of the supervisory and examining officials—the Comptroller's staff on the national side, the various superintendents of banking

on the state side, and the Federal Reserve examiners
on the money management side. These meetings, and
active cooperation in other respects, standardized procedures, established a common front on mutual problems, and raised, as well as made more effective, standards throughout the field of banking.

It would also be amiss not to mention the research
and educational efforts of the Federal Reserve Board
and the various Federal Reserve Banks. Their continuing studies, in depth, of banking, money management, the government bond market and related phenomena have contributed much to our understanding
and willingness to cope with the problems of banking
and credit management in the modern economy.

10. *Banking schools.* On their own part, bankers have
established executive training schools, professional
schools and technical schools throughout the United
States.

The American Bankers Association has taken the
lead in these efforts with its Stonier Graduate School of
Banking at Rutgers, with more than 1,200 bank officers
for two weeks every summer. Similarly, there are large
regional banking schools—run by bankers for actively
employed bank personnel—at the University of Wis-
consin, University of Louisiana, University of Washington, and Williams College.

In addition, most state banking associations maintain adult schools of their own. Some of these are in
general banking, but most of them are specialized

efforts in agriculture, consumer credit, personnel administration, public relations, and so on.

The American Institute of Banking, familiarly known as the AIB, the regular educational arm of the American Bankers Association, offers organized programs of study covering some three years of regular academic terms to thousands of bank employees each year, throughout the country.

The various banking associations, local groups of banks, and many individual banks also offer a steady stream of hundreds of general and specialized economic *conferences* for bankers and/or customers of the banks.

Correspondent conferences held by the larger city banks for their correspondent banks have become commonplace. One of the better known of these, the Correspondents Conference of the First National Bank of Chicago, is a two-day session for more than 1,200 of their banking friends and customers.

Then, there are the professional and specialized schools, such as those of: (1) The National Association of Bank Auditors and Comptrollers; (2) The Financial Public Relations Association; (3) The National Association of Credit Management; (4) The National Association of Mutual Savings Banks; (5) The Mortgage Bankers Association of America; and (6) The Consumer Bankers Association. As the names of the sponsoring associations indicate, these schools are devoted to only one segment of the broad field of finance, but they also broaden the specialists who attend, since they practically all have basic courses, also. In any event, at a minimum, they increase the knowledge *in* the field and *of* the field.

11. *Banking "commissions."* The American Bankers Association also conducts a vast program of public education through "commissions" established in fields which need illumination or the awakening of public interest. Although these efforts are generally focused on teachers and active bankers, more recently, especially in the field of inflation, they have taken the battle directly to the public through publications and other publicity media, such as addresses given by prominent bankers.

One of the oldest of these commissions is the Bank Management Commission which, as the name indicates, concerns itself with research, dissemination of the results of the research, and promulgation of standards in the field of bank operations and management. Another well-known one is the Economic Policy Commission. In addition, the Association has commissions in many other fields, such as agriculture, consumer credit, credit policy, monetary policy, inflation, etc.

12. *Bank publications.* Many individual banks also make significant contributions to business stability through publication of monthly "letters" dealing with economic and financial developments and the reasons for them. Some also put out special studies on fields in which they have special knowledge or facilities, such as foreign trade, the New York money market, oil, etc.

Each of the twelve Federal Reserve Banks also issues a monthly "Review" covering developments in its district. In addition to a general economic survey of the district, some of these have become outstanding in fields in which the member banks of their district have a special interest. A good example of this would be the authoritative articles on livestock and agricultural production of the Monthly Business Conditions Review of the Federal Reserve Bank of Chicago.

13. *Banking magazines.* Another powerful force for banking and economic education has been the growth and the upgrading of private journalistic efforts. Magazines, in particular, have been greatly improved in this field in recent years. Articles interpreting economic events, analyzing trends and hazarding informed estimates of future developments appear in every issue. Informed opinion and underlying facts are thus constantly available to the banker (and business man) who will but read. There is no longer any excuse for economic illiteracy or factual ineptitude.

Such general monthly financial magazines as *Banking,* published by the American Bankers Association, and *Bankers Monthly,* published by Rand McNally, are veritable mines of current information and financial guidance.

Then, there are the specialized publications, generally issued by a particular trade association but available to others, such as *The Mortgage Banker,* published by the Mortgage Bankers Association of America; *The*

Industrial Banker, published by the American Industrial Bankers Association; *Consumer Finance News,* published by the National Consumer Finance Association; and *Credit & Financial Management,* published by the National Association of Credit Management.

These publications cover the area indicated by their names and enable bankers and business men to secure an inside view on the problems and the thinking in these fields.

14. *Publications of Alexander Hamilton Institute.* As a part of its contribution to better and more adequate economic knowledge, the Editorial Department of the Alexander Hamilton Institute publishes the following newsletters: a *Business Conditions Weekly;* a *Business Progress Section,* monthly; a *Personal Management Section,* monthly; a *Tax Review Section,* monthly; and an *Investment Bulletin,* a weekly analysis of security movements and earnings.

15. *More Knowledge means better banking.* There has been much talk recently about the powerful "automatic stabilizers" in the economy. The Employment Act of 1946 directs that all the agencies of government be utilized to promote greater stability in the economy. The credit and monetary policies of the Federal Reserve authorities are directed to the same goal. And the Federal Deposit Insurance Corporation was designed to prevent crippling instability in the money supply.

All of these are extremely important in the struggle

against instability and the efforts to protect our money supply. But something more basic is required, namely, *public understanding and cooperation.* In view of this, one of the most hopeful auguries for that better future of which we all dream is the ever-widening diffusion of more and better economic knowledge. That a better understanding of the more dangerous pitfalls that beset our free-choice economy will enable us to avoid them, is a reasonable expectation.

While we must anticipate ups and downs in business and finance in the future, we already have the knowledge (and, let us hope, the inclination) to prevent the wild swings, financial losses and human suffering that too often characterized our past history. For this, banking deserves much credit, for it seems a truism that more knowledge means better banking and greater stability.

Review

Why is protection of bank deposits of such basic economic importance?

How was the FDIC established?

How many members are on the board of directors of the FDIC? How are they appointed?

Upon what does the Federal Deposit Insurance Corporation really rely for protection of bank deposits?

Explain why the FDIC is not on an actuarial basis.

What remedies are open to the FDIC when a bank gets into difficulties?

What is the relation between "banking schools" and deposit protection?

What contribution to deposit safety is made by the various ABA "commissions"?

Why does more knowledge mean better banking?

CHAPTER X

Clearing and Collections

1. *Transferring of values.* One of the most important services of banking to business is the clearing and collection of checks and other valuable claims. In the course of each year, some $3 trillion to $5 trillion of such values are transferred from one account to another, often from one part of the country to another, and mostly without charge.

To render this great service to business and to the economy is costly, since it requires a vast amount of cooperation and the maintenance of a wide system of correspondent relationships on the part of the commercial banks. And, while it is true that this service is basic to public acceptance of deposit credit as money, and thus necessary for them as bankers, it is equally true that it is of incalculable value to business men. An understanding of the functioning of this system enables the business man to get maximum usage at minimum cost.

2. *The clearing principle.* When a bank sends a check or other instrument to another bank at which it is payable, and asks for cash or its equivalent, the operation is known as *collection.* On the other hand, when two or

more banks arrange formally to offset credit items against each other, and settle in cash or the equivalent only the difference or balances that remain, the operation is known as *clearance*.

This method of reducing the actual payment to the differences that remain, obviously, offers many advantages. It is more convenient and more economical; it requires less time and effort; and, most importantly, it greatly reduces the amount of funds that have to be moved between the banks. In fact, one of the best measures of the degree of development of a banking system is the extent to which items can be offset (cleared), rather than paid individually.

3. *The clearing house.* The clearing house is one of the most important means by which banks cooperate with one another in serving their customers. Although it serves several purposes, its basic function is to facilitate the exchange and payment of checks drawn on the banks in a town, geographic region or economic area. Physically, it provides a central point at which checks drawn on member banks can be exchanged, and the differences paid or credited.

The London Clearing House, the first important agency of this type, was established in 1773 as an outgrowth of the originally forbidden practice of bank messengers meeting in a convenient coffee house to exchange checks, rather than making trips to each individual bank. Sad to relate, instead of being rewarded for this conservation of energy, for this extremely valuable contribution to the banking process, these banking pioneers were fired "out of hand"! Their sacrifice, however, was not in vain. Eventually, the London banks adopted their method and commemorated their contribution by calling the first of the several daily clearings the "Walks Clearing."

Nearly a hundred years later, in 1853 to be exact, the banks of New York City adopted the idea and organized the New York Clearing House, which has been a tower of strength in peace and war ever since. As might be expected, it was the prototype of American clearing houses which, today, number in the hundreds. Most clearing houses operate in individual cities, but there are many others of a regional character, which operate within a geographical area such as a county, or an economic area such as, for example, the LeSueur Valley in Minnesota.

4. *Method of clearing.* The actual procedure of the clearing house is simplicity itself. In a town with, say, five banks, it would be as follows: A clerk from each bank bearing all the items payable through the clearing house will come to the place of clearing. This clerk will have four packages of checks drawn on the other banks, which will be exchanged for the four packages of checks drawn on his bank brought by the other clerks.

The actual exchanging is a strictly regulated formal procedure under the supervision of a clearing house official. The difference between the total deliveries and receipts of each bank is reported to the clearing house manager, who confirms the accuracy of the clearing by balancing them (See Figure 1).

STATEMENT SHOWING CHECKS BROUGHT TO CLEARING HOUSE BY REPRESENTATIVES OF BANKS

	A	B	C	D	E	Amount due from banks
A brings checks on		$600	$800	$900	$1,000	$3,300
B " " "	$ 600		500	800	900	2,800
C " " "	1,000	200		800	500	2,500
D " " "	200	500	600		1,000	2,300
E " " "	400	200	300	400		1,300
Amount due to banks	$2,200	$1,500	$2,200	$2,900	$3,400	$12,200

STATEMENT SHOWING PAYMENTS MADE BY BANKS TO CLEARING HOUSE AND BY CLEARING HOUSE TO BANKS

	Delivered	Received	Pay to clearing house	Receive from clearing house
A	$ 3,300—	$ 2,200		$1,100
B	2,800—	1,500		1,300
C	2,500—	2,200		300
D	2,300—	2,900	$ 600	
E	1,300—	3,400	2,100	
	$12,200	$12,200	$2,700	$2,700

FIGURE 1—STATEMENTS SHOWING CLEARING-HOUSE PROCEDURE

Since the checks taken from the clearing house must equal those taken to it, failure to balance means that an error has been made. In such event, the hapless clerk is fined, the exact amount depending on the extent of the error. As soon as balance is attained, the clearing house official signs the slips of the clerks and sends a certified statement by messenger or by wire to the Federal Reserve Bank (of that district) giving the amounts by which the accounts of the various clearing house members are to be debited or credited for the balances arising from the clearing, so that all need for the interchange of cash is obviated.

In the larger cities, there are several exchanges of checks at the clearing house each day—they don't wait for them to pile up. The New York Clearing House, for example, has five clearings in which it handles about 2.5 million checks each day, with a value of over $4 billion on peak days. It is open day and night every day of the year including all holidays, and it handles upward of two tons of checks each day. Its final clearing of the business day, covering all the activities of the previous 24 hours, takes place at 10 A.M., after which it starts all over again on a series of clearings for the next business day.

The convenience and economies of clearing are so great that many banks become clearing members only of the clearing house. In other words, they do not assume the full responsibilities and financial burden of regular membership, just as some non-member banks become clearing members of the Federal Reserve System by making an agreed deposit and without assuming all of the obligations stipulated by law and regulation for members.

5. *Other clearing house functions.* While the clearing of checks, notes, drafts and bond coupons constitutes the primary function of the clearing house, most of them have taken on additional tasks in response to local needs. These activities center on presenting a united

front in time of danger and insisting on the traditional "ounce of prevention" in times of tranquility. The clearing house furnishes an effective medium through which the banks can cooperate effectively for their common good and that of the community.

Their tradition as a rallying point in times of financial emergency is a long and honorable one. But it is in their day-to-day maintenance of standards and prevention of cutthroat competition that they render their greatest service, other than clearing. Long ago, it was learned that excessive competition is particularly dangerous in banking because of the many risks involved, as was the further fact that no bank can stand alone.

Moreover, although not a public utility with respect to regulation of rates, banking is invested with an even greater public interest as the creator and custodian of our money supply. Limitation of the rigors of all-out competition, by regulation of the supervisory authorities and self-policing by the banks, has proved not only desirable, but imperative.

6. *City collection.* Even though a member of the clearing house, a bank must maintain a department to present trade drafts for acceptance, to collect non-cash items, and to give special handling to items which require it. This unit is called the City Collection Department. It consists chiefly of messengers who personally present such items.

Some clearing houses have special departments for

collection items that cannot be included in the clearings which are limited to "cash items." The Federal Reserve Banks, likewise, handle such items as a service for the member banks. Despite these alternatives, most banks insist on giving many collections the personal attention and special handling of their own collection department.

It should be remembered that all items handled on a "clearing" basis are "cash" items for which credit has already been given by the bank. They thus differ from "collection" items which are credited to the depositor's account only after payment.

7. *Transit.* All checks drawn on the country (beyond the clearing house area), for which credit has already been given, are handled in a department generally known as the transit department. Since such checks are processed as if they were cash, the records of the various banks through which they pass are kept to a bare minimum. They are all presumed to be good until proven otherwise and the records are set up on that basis. In fact, the records kept are so minimal that considerable additional work is entailed when checks are returned for insufficient funds and other reasons.

Also, as will be realized, the speed with which they must be processed, because of the credit risk and the enormous annual volume of some 12 billion separate checks, most of which must be handled by two or more banks, necessitates skeletonized record-keeping, even though it complicates the handling of returned items.

8. *The Universal Numerical System.* One of the most important aids in speeding the handling of transit items is the Universal Numerical System, adopted by the American Bankers Association in 1911. Most people outside of banks probably have never even noticed the numbers in the upper right-hand corner of each check, but they are of really vital significance to the banks in sorting and forwarding the vast volume of billions of checks a year.

These transit numbers are really routing symbols for the handling of the check throughout the banking system. For example, suppose a check of the Westport Bank and Trust Company, of Westport, Connecticut, is cashed in Pacific Palisades, California. The bank cashing it can either send it to the Federal Reserve Bank of San Francisco for credit to its reserve account, or to its New York City correspondent for credit to its New York account.

In either event, the Westport bank's transit symbol $\frac{51-233}{211}$ conveys the following information: The 51 means Connecticut, and 233 is the individual number of the Westport bank. The 2 in the lower line means that the check must be sent to the Second Federal Reserve District for collection, the next 1 means the first branch in that district and the final digit indicates the state of Connecticut. This final digit below the line indicates the check clearing arrangement and does not indicate how many days of delay.

The basis of this numerical code is interesting. The Reserve cities existing at the time the numbering was adopted in 1911 were assigned numbers from 1 to 49 inclusive, the lowest number being given to the largest cities—for example, the number 1 designates New York City. The location of banks outside of the Reserve cities was indicated by the assignment of the numbers from 50 to 99, on the basis of states; and, as indicated before, within such areas each bank was given a distinctive number of its own.

Thus, as shown earlier in the illustration, the first number in the denominator indicates the Federal Reserve District, the second number, the branch in this district, and the final number indicates the check clearing arrangement (usually one number relates to one state). If there is no denominator the bank is a "nonpar" institution (discussed later).

All of these numbers were permanently assigned at the inception of the Numerical System, except that banks organized thereafter have been assigned their individual number by the Rand McNally Company under the authorization of the American Bankers Association. This company publishes yearly lists of banks with their numbers for the guidance of all concerned.
9. *Automation.* The designers of the numerical code "builded better than they knew." Its numbers are basic to the new automatic check handling systems—automation would be much more involved and expensive otherwise. And with the number of checks written in-

creasing around a billion a year, automation has become a categorical imperative if banks are to tame their "paper tiger."

Regardless of the system of automation used, each check contains a code printed across the bottom in *magnetic* ink. In addition to the numerical code, this magnetic printing will contain the name of the account to which the check is to be charged; and, in the near future, the actual amount of the check will be encoded, enabling even the deposit account entries to be made automatically. (As yet, however, there is no agreement on the most practicable way to code the dollar amounts on checks.)

Electronic scanners "read" these magnetic instructions at rates of up to 72,000 an hour—or 20 per second. This information is fed to a computer which activates the sorting and recording satellite machines. Thus, the checks can be handled with incredible speed subject to the problems of size of the bank and costs of the automation. Obviously, few banks have 72,000 checks an hour to process; and, even more obviously, few banks can afford the $5,000 or more a month that rental of such automation equipment entails.

What the final outcome of the opposing pressures of the paper blizzard (billions of checks) and the efforts to offset it with automation will be, no one can rightly say. But that it will have a basic effect on the structure of banking cannot be questioned. In the meantime, both business and individuals will continue to get the greatest bargain in the world in the clearing and collecting of their checks.

10. *Country collection.* In contrast with the transit (cash) items which are handled on a quantity, or wholesale, basis, there are many items, such as dishonored checks, drafts on business organizations, promissory notes for presentation on due date, etc., which must be given individual attention.

This work is centered in a Country Collection department in the larger banks. Considerable detail work is involved, since a complete individual record must be kept of each collection. Moreover, instructions must be issued to the bank which will make the actual collection, follow-ups are often necessary, and the customer's account must be credited when the proceeds are finally received.

As the reader will recall, collection items differ from the transit items, since they have not been credited to the customer's deposit account. Moreover, a nominal charge can be made by the collecting (not the paying) bank for the service rendered.

11. *Par collection.* Before the organization of the Federal Reserve System in 1914, the deduction of exchange charges by banks on checks which were not presented "over the counter" for payment, was a great burden on banking and on business. It was far more than a financial burden, since the efforts of the banks to avoid, or minimize, such deductions by the paying banks led to long, circuitous routing of checks with

costly delays from the standpoint of credit losses (because of credit deterioration during the delays in collection, and because of the irresistible temptation it offered
business crooks for "kiting," drawing checks on non-
existent accounts, and the like) and interest foregone
on the great volume of items continually in the collection channels.

A word of further explanation of the reasons for
circuitous routings will be of interest. Banks would arrange reciprocal relationships with correspondents
under which each would agree to collect all items free
for the other. The result was that a bank would send
an item not to the nearest bank but to the nearest bank
which would render the service free. These special arrangements became so involved and complicated that a
check might take three weeks and travel 500 miles, or
more, for payment, instead of going direct to a nearby
bank.

To remedy this situation, the Federal Reserve Banks
established the *par collection system*, designed to do for
all American banks what the clearing houses do for
their members—in other words, a nation-wide system
of clearing. Established in July 1916, par collection is a
compulsory clearing system for all member banks based
on their payment at par (without deduction) all checks
drawn on them and *presented through their Federal
Reserve Bank.* Also, non-member banks which agree to
remit at par and maintain adequate balances at the
Federal Reserve Bank of their district are permitted to

become members of the par collection system and secure the privileges of the Federal Reserve's clearance
and collection mechanism.

On its part, each Federal Reserve Bank undertakes
to collect free of charge cash and non-cash (matured
notes, drafts, bills of exchange, bond coupons and
matured securities) items for its members and non-
member clearing banks. It should be understood that
use of this system for its own collections is optional on
the part of the member bank. It can still use its own
correspondent for that purpose, and banks do so ex-
tensively, especially on the larger items and those which
require special attention. It is compulsory, however, for
them to remit at par for all items presented through the
district Federal Reserve Bank.

As the regulations of the Federal Reserve Board do
not permit the Federal Reserve Banks to handle checks
drawn on non-par banks, banks using the par collection
system are provided with the names of all non-par
banks. This is important, since member banks have
been prohibited since 1938 from absorbing any exchange deductions made by another bank. To protect
against such charges, many invoices, especially those
going into parts of the country where there are non-par
banks, provide that they are "payable only in New York
funds," or that they are "payable only at par."

Despite its manifest advantages to banking and
business, par collection has been bitterly opposed from
its very beginning by many country banks, since it

eliminates their earnings from exchange charges. And, for some of them, such earnings constitute a substantial part of their total earnings. Even today, there are still more than 1,500 banks on the non-par list. Fortunately, they hold only some 2 per cent of all bank deposits, so, for all practical purposes, the par collection system can be considered one of the major accomplishments of the Federal Reserve System.

12. *Mechanics of out-of-town collection.* Although the work is quite burdensome, the actual mechanics of out-of-town collections are fairly simple. Thus, the items can be sent directly to a correspondent for collection and credit to the bank's account on the correspondent's books, or they can be turned over to the Federal Reserve Bank of the district, or its branch, for Federal Reserve collection.

By far, the great bulk of such collection items is turned over to the Federal Reserve collection system. As an indication of the volume handled, consider the some 2.2 million items received by the Federal Reserve Bank of New York (at its head office in New York City) on an average day. Even with the latest electronic equipment, this requires more than 600 machine sorters who work in shifts around the clock.

When the depositing bank and the paying bank are both members or clearing members of the same district, the Federal Reserve Bank merely debits the account of one bank and credits the account of the other.

Where the banks are located in different Federal

Reserve districts, however, the collection process is a little more complicated. Although ordinarily sent to the Federal Reserve Bank of one district and forwarded by it to the Federal Reserve Bank of the other district for handling, there are many exceptions, such as "direct sending" by the payee bank to the payor bank where distance or other special circumstances make it possible to give better or quicker service by so doing. In these latter cases, the respective Reserve Banks are notified so that they can make the necessary entries in the accounts of the banks.

But, regardless of location, or method used, the eventual result is an increase of the reserve (or clearing) account of one bank and the reduction of the account of the other bank. This brings us to the question of how the Federal Reserve Banks settle these interdistrict balances.

13. *Interdistrict Settlement Fund.* In addition to the debits and credits arising from the collection process, the Federal Reserve System transfers funds free of charge for member banks over the leased wire system connecting the twelve Reserve Banks with the Board of Governors and the United States Treasury. And transfers of funds for member banks for the account of individuals, business firms, or other banks are made over commercial telegraph facilities for the cost of the telegram.

Whatever their origin, the net debits and credits between the Federal Reserve Banks are settled through the Interdistrict Settlement Fund in Washington. This Fund is managed by the Board of Governors and financed by the twelve banks, which opened it in 1915 with a deposit that must be kept at a minimum of at least $1,000,000 for each bank. (The gold certificates in the Fund are counted as part of the legal reserve required against Federal Reserve note and deposit liabilities.)

At the close of every business day, this Fund is notified by each Federal Reserve Bank and its clearing branches of the amounts due each of the other Federal Reserve Banks. Settlement is made by transferring ownership of gold certificates (actually held by the Treasurer of the United States for the Federal Reserve Banks) on the books of the Fund. Interestingly, the Interdistrict Settlement Fund has only four employees whose job it is to run an electronic computer which shifts balances of some $6 billion from one district (bank) to another on an average day.

14. *Observations on clearing and collections.* The Federal Reserve collection system remedied most of the defects of the earlier methods. By providing orderly and direct routing of collections and by effecting prompt clearance on the books of the Federal Reserve Banks and the Interdistrict Settlement Fund, the present system saves time and money, raises credit standards, and makes checks more freely acceptable as money throughout the country.

The Federal Reserve collection system greatly reduces the volume of interbank balances required for collection purposes, since the bank's legally-required reserve balances can be so used. Also, the present system has eliminated all currency shipments between banks to settle balances and open accounts. All such shipments today are between the member bank and its Federal Reserve Bank, and are made solely to meet the currency needs of depositors.

Since the Federal Reserve makes no charge for the use of its collection facilities and since it transfers funds and currency throughout the country without charge, one of the main arguments for exchange charges (deductions by the paying bank) is removed. These improvements in the handling of currency and collection of checks have thus made a basic contribution to the quality of the deposit currency of our country. Largely as a result of these improvements, checks, even personal checks, are today a means of payment that circulates at par nation-wide, with the exception of a comparatively insignificant amount of checks drawn on small state-chartered non-par banks, located mostly in the south and the west.

Great as have been the accomplishments in this field, however, it cannot be denied that par collection does not cover all the banks. Some 1,700 banks still refuse to remit the face value of their own depositors' checks which are not paid by a credit on their books or in cash over their counter.

For years, the Federal Reserve authorities conducted an extremely vigorous campaign to force all banks into the par collection system. But, as a result of violent opposition from groups of banks, particularly country banks, and hostile legislation (even amendments of state constitutions), as well as adverse court decisions, the Federal Reserve authorities were finally forced to abandon their attempt to compel all banks to join the par collection system. Since that time, in 1923, the only direct pressure has been the refusal to accept for collection any check drawn on a bank on their nonpar list. The ideal of a check currency circulating at par throughout the entire country has thus not been completely realized.

Business men still have to protect themselves from the exchange charges of non-par banks. For most such banks, these charges are around $\frac{1}{10}$ of 1 per cent of the face value of the item, but a few of them make really exorbitant charges for the service rendered. Happily, the number of those gouging in this respect is declining, so this chapter can close with the observation that improvement is taking place even in the practices of the smaller, non-par banks.

Review

Explain why the "transferring of values" is of such great value to the economy.

Specifically, why do banks typically collect checks without charge?

Differentiate between "clearing" and "collection."

Summarize the services of the clearing house.

What is the significance of the Universal Numerical System?

In what respects is the Federal Reserve collection system an improvement over previous arrangements?

How does the Interdistrict Settlement Fund operate?

Why is automation of imperative interest to banks?

CHAPTER XI

Commercial Banking Structure

1. *Licensed and regulated.* In sharp contrast with most other countries, banking is a licensed and highly regulated business in the United States. Although the banks are privately owned, virtually every phase of their organization and operation is subject to governmental regulation, supervision or control. Thus, all banks must be incorporated under either state or federal law.

But even to be permitted to incorporate, they must first comply with a series of regulations and requirements of the supervisory authorities, designed to weed out those who, for reasons of character, capital, experience or ability, should not be allowed to enter the banking business, and to prevent excessive proliferation of banking facilities, which would dangerously weaken all banks.

An idea of the safeguards on establishing a new bank is given by the "Information and Procedure for the Organization of a Commercial Bank under New York State Banking Law" instructions of the New York Banking Department. These "instructions" cover nine pages of legal-size paper on a single-space basis, and consist largely of requests for specific information on more than a hundred points and advice as to how that information is to be presented to the Banking Department. Among many other things, the "instructions" categorically state:

> The organization of a new bank is a 'man-sized' job for incorporators, representatives and the Department. Literally, scores of problems arise — legal, economic and practical — in the course of organization. They require great understanding, patience and co-operation on both sides to bring them to a successful conclusion. The process of organization requires many scores of interviews with the Banking Department and a still larger number of telephone conversations.

It is interesting to note that deposit insurance is a prerequisite to approval of a bank in New York as set forth in provision 11 of the "instructions," as follows:

> . . . The group should understand that the approval, if forthcoming, will be conditional upon favorable action on its application by the FDIC.

Citation of the New York procedure is not to imply that other states have the same safeguards. But even though the safeguards of other states may be less detailed, and vary widely from state to state, they do have safeguards and their requirements must be met by those desiring to start a state-chartered commercial bank.

The organization of a national bank is also hedged

about with elaborate safeguards. These are administered by the Comptroller of the Currency through the bank examiners, each proposed new bank and its sponsors being subjected to detailed investigation.

Here, too, the new bank must be able to secure deposit insurance as a prerequisite to approval, since all national banks must be members of the Federal Reserve System and all such members are required to have the protection of the Federal Deposit Insurance Corporation.

2. *Number of banks.* The great number of individual American banks is one of the wonders of the banking world—likewise, the failure rate! That there is a close connection between these phenomena is beyond question. It is, therefore, not surprising that during recent years, while the number of banks was declining sharply because of liquidation and mergers, actual failures all but disappeared.

Going back a little further, between 1900 and 1920, nearly 20,000 new banks were organized; and between 1920 and 1940 [1] more than 15,000 banks closed, merged, or failed—and by far the most of them failed.

Since 1940, the number of banks (head offices) has declined still further to less than 14,000—but the number of branches has increased from a little more than 3,000 to more than 17,000. And the number of suspen-

---

[1] In the Great Depression period, 1930–33, 9,106 banks with deposits of $6,859,000,000 suspended. Statistical Abstract of the United States.

sions has been under 100. (This number of bank suspensions is no measure of the banking difficulties of the period because of the FDIC policy of merging or otherwise rescuing a bank where possible, to avoid suspension.)

Putting this on a per capita basis, the number of individual banks (not counting branches) dropped from 1 per 3,500 of population in 1920 to around 1 per 14,000 of population in recent years.

A continual source of amazement to foreign students of American banking is the large number of failures which have characterized our financial history, despite our welter of laws, regulations and supervisions. One explanation is that Americans are always willing to take a chance—especially with other people's money.

A better explanation is that, down through the years, competition between the federal and the state governments in chartering new banks has at times permitted more banks to be started than were needed. This, in turn, caused cutthroat competition and dangerous banking practices until economic law, which is inexorable, eliminated the excess institutions.

3. *National vs. state charter.* The decision whether to incorporate under federal or state laws should be solely a matter for the organizers. But it is not as simple as that. They may be able, and very properly, to get a charter from one of the chartering agencies, but not from the other. For example, the Comptroller of the Currency may feel that there are enough *national* banks

in the area, while the State Superintendent of Banking may feel that another state-chartered institution is needed—and so it goes. These agencies, as a matter of courtesy, ordinarily consult each other before granting a charter; but consultation is not mandatory and strained relations often develop, resulting in unilateral action by one, or the other.

Also, it cannot be denied that, at times, charters have been granted on a political basis. While this is unwise and improper, it is a political fact of life which we must recognize as one of the less attractive features of democracy.

As to choice between the two types of charter, national banks in the past have had the advantage of greater prestige. This is still true in some states today. But, in the more important banking states, such as New York, for example, the standards for state institutions are so high that they measure up to the national standards in every way. In fact, in recent years, the somewhat greater freedom from legal restriction and regulation of its state-chartered trust companies has given them an advantage in the public mind.

Beginning with the McFadden-Pepper Act in 1927, there has been considerable federal legislation to redress the competitive balance between the national and the state institutions. In fact, it can be fairly said that membership in the Federal Reserve System and deposit insurance by the Federal Deposit Insurance Corporation added to the advantages of being a state institution in many states, have actually put the national banks in the position of having to fight legislatively and competitively to keep up.

So, whether a state or national charter is secured will depend on the state in which the bank is being organized, on the organizers, and on the supervisory authorities.

4. *The national banks.* The national banks, chartered by the Comptroller of the Currency, comprise slightly more than one-third of all commercial banks, but their steady growth in branches in recent years has brought them within striking distance of a total of one-half of all commercial banking *offices.*

With respect to deposits, the national banks do somewhat better, since they hold approximately 55 per cent of the demand and time deposits of all commercial banks.

5. *The state banks.* There are nearly twice as many state-chartered banking institutions as nationally chartered ones. Statistically, they differ from the national banks in several respects.

First, they have less branches in the aggregate, so that, on the average, they have less than one-half as many branches per bank.

Second, their average deposits *per bank* are less than one-half those of the national banks. Their lesser number of branches, however, reduces this disparity when comparison is made on a per office basis.

Third, many of them are extremely small, as permitted by the laws of some states, so that there is a wide range in size among the state institutions, some of them being among the very largest in the country.

Fourth, many of them are organized as trust companies (discussed in a later chapter) and administer enormous holdings of assets which do not appear on their balance sheets. They are, thus, far more important than balance-sheet totals indicate.

Fifth, some of them, as permitted in many states, are highly specialized institutions in which conventional commercial banking activities are not even carried on, or, at least, are comparatively unimportant in their over-all operations.

6. *Our dual banking system.* In addition to having more than 1,000 times as many banks as England, for example, we have another unique feature in our *dual* banking system. This term refers to the heartening fact that for nearly 100 years—in prosperity and in adversity—we have had the benefits of the healthy rivalry of a national banking system and a state banking system operating side by side. Only in America, with our particular federal form of government, could this have happened.

While it is true that our dual system at times spawned too many banks, and thus set the stage for reckless banking and failures, its contributions far outweigh any adverse effects it may have had. Moreover, excesses in the granting of charters should be blamed on human fallibility, rather than on the dual system.

On the constructive side, the constant striving for competitive advantage contributed immeasurably to banking progress. First, one system would pull ahead in growth because of legislative enactment or supervisory leadership, and then the other system would get busy, redress the balance between them and take the leadership itself. Having two systems encouraged innovation and experimentation, since it was always easy to shift from one system to the other when ill-advised legislation or unwise supervision made a change advisable. The dual banking system thus contributed not only the advantages of increased competition, but the even greater advantages of banking progress.

7. *Unit banking.* The United States commercial banking structure is characterized by diversity. With respect to authority to operate, the banks are either national or state institutions. Far more important, with respect to ownership and control they may be (1) independent unit banks; or (2) branch banks; or (3) group banks.

The single-office, or unit, bank has been predominant in American banking ever since the Civil War. Although branches had been frequently utilized before that time, they were not specifically authorized in the National Bank Act of 1863, with the result that for many years they were virtually non-existent.

Strictly speaking, the unit bank must be absolutely independent. It cannot, by either banking or popular definition, be related to any other institution through either ownership or control. It is the epitome of "localness." It has its roots, and its reason for being, in the local community's agricultural, industrial and business activity. It furnishes a liaison between the local community and the outside world in financial matters, its officers often being the chief source of economic and financial guidance in the community.

The local unit bank is not only a part of the economic fabric of the community, but it is also, through its directors, officers and employees, an important part of the social fabric of the community. Because of this social integration with the local community, it has often been able to secure local approbation beyond its economic due.

Spelling this out, growth has been held back in many one-bank communities because, lacking the spur of competition, the banker has been able to take a "they shall not pass" attitude toward the assumption of reasonable banking risks or, for that matter, toward anything new. Yet, such communities, never having had the benefits of progressive and aggressive modern banking, often do not realize what is holding them back. It is beyond question that such a local banking monopoly can be one of the most cruel and costly, in terms of progress, of all monopolies.

On the other hand, many areas are fortunate enough to have progressive local banks which give a superior service because of intimate knowledge of local conditions and concentration on the problems of the community. Such banks are usually headed by "dedicated" men who put the interests of community ahead of their own interests. This condition arises because many such communities do not have enough banking business properly to compensate for the wide range of abilities such an *independent* banker must have to serve the community properly. Unfortunately, such "dedicated" individuals are getting scarcer and scarcer in every line.

Unit banking, locally controlled, is characteristic of the country's rural and agricultural communities, with the exception of a few states like California and Arizona where branch banking is almost universal. In states where branch banking is absolutely prohibited, such as Illinois, independent banks are found in all areas.

8. *Outlook for independent unit banking.* Economic pressure in recent years has steadily mounted against unit banking. The growing complexity of business, the growing size of the business unit which must be served, the growing pressures of non-bank competition, and the growing ramifications of credit extension, have all pressed, and continue to press, on the independent banker.

The typical independent unit bank located in the agricultural and rural areas has even more troubles. The shifting of rural population to the cities and the broadening of market areas with our modern roads have caused many such banks to lose the cream of their business to the larger centers.

The absorption of local businesses by national organizations and the decentralization of industry have left such banks with local units whose credit needs are arranged by their head office in a distant city. Even if the local bank is invited to serve their credit needs, its loan limits are so small that a profitable relationship usually does not last long. Of course, the large corporation will leave a small balance with the local bank as some compensation for the many local banking services it requires.

Another reason for the persistent decline in the number of independent unit banks in the face of rapid economic growth has been the inability of the commercial banks to raise the prices charged for their services to the extent that most other industries have been able to lift their selling prices to offset the higher costs of the inflation and general prosperity of recent years. Rates of interest, the chief prices charged by banks, are largely determined by Federal Reserve and government policies that are designed to foster economic stability and growth, with little regard for their impact on bank earnings. And keen competition has further limited the ability of banks to raise interest and service charges commensurate with the price increases in other lines.

But the most implacable foe of the small unit bank has been the steady rise in operating costs in recent years. And now that electronic item-handling and bookkeeping are just around the corner, what the independent banker can do to survive this final onslaught remains to be seen. Certainly, the prognosis is not good.

"Win, lose or draw," the independent banker has always had many friends not only in his community, but also in legislative halls and supervisory circles. So, the Independent Bankers Association, their own militant trade association, (although most of them also belong to their state banking association and the American Bankers Association) may be able to secure legislation which will permit them to survive profitably. Certainly, the Association has fought an outstanding delaying action on many fronts.

As for the position of at least one supervisory authority, the Federal Deposit Insurance Corporation, as early as 1944, flatly stated on pages 10 and 11 of its Annual Report:

> The business of lending money is well suited to private initiative and is best performed under competitive conditions. Monopoly in banking is a threat to American traditions, both because it limits the opportunities to engage in the business of banking, and because it provides an opportunity for favoritism in the extension of credit which may foster monopolies in other industries. The growing tendencies toward monopoly in the banking business are serious, and prompt action should be taken to curb them. . . .
>
> A partial monopoly which develops when one bank obtains a disproportionate percentage of the total banking resources of an area may have a serious effect on the economic life of the district. Another

monopolistic tendency which has aroused customer discontent is the agreement among banks, in some areas, to fix charges and limit services. Bankers can do much to improve this situation by making active efforts to fit their services to the needs of the public rather than by relying upon restrictive agreements for profits.

Partial monopolies over large areas may develop both by means of branch banking and through the holding-company device. The Corporation recommends that such branch banking as is permitted by the laws of the respective states be strictly regulated so that no bank will control a disproportionate percentage of the total banking resources or offices of an area. Holding companies not only tend to become monopolistic, but increase the problem of supervision. The ease with which assets may be transferred from one affiliated corporate unit to another, and the possibility of the manipulation of the accounts of these enterprises make adequate examination of affiliated banks and the appraisal of their condition and capital position extremely difficult.

The Corporation recommends that Congress enact legislation which will prohibit the future creation of holding companies and which will require the liquidation of existing holding companies after allowing a reasonable time for orderly distribution to their own stockholders of the bank stock which they now hold. The Corporation believes that such legislation is distinctly preferable to the enactment of further regulatory laws in the bank holding-company field.

9. *Branch banking.*   Branch banking is the operation of more than one banking office under one charter. A branch bank has one board of directors and senior officers at an operating point called the head office, and it has one or more other banking offices run by managers, who may be very junior officers, if the branches are small, or even senior officers, if they are large.

With the exception of the United States, all the important countries of the Free World permit nation-wide branch banking. In Canada, the eleven chartered banks operate more than 3,000 domestic branches, and more than 150 foreign branches. In England, the thirteen large incorporated banks operate more than 8,000 branches. In France, the six large incorporated banks of deposit that operate throughout the country have more than 4,300 branches. In addition, the regional and provincial banks have some branches.

In the United States, despite statutory restrictions, the determined opposition of the Independent Bankers Association and outright hostility on the part of many legislators, the trend toward branch banking in recent years has been little short of phenomenal. Whereas in the last thirty years—a period of wartime inflation and general prosperity—the number of commercial banks (including stock savings banks and non-deposit trust companies) actually *declined* by more than 2,000 through liquidation and merger, the number of branches *increased* by more than 7,000.

The growing demand for banking services in recent years has been largely met by the opening of branches in those parts of the United States where permitted by law and supervisory authorities. Branch banking has, thus, had the key role in meeting the growing demand for banking services, particularly during the more recent period of accelerated decline of the number of unit banks. The divergent trends in the number of unit banks and the number of branch banks has caused public opinion and legislators to become increasingly aware of the need for adapting the banking structure to changing conditions and requirements, so that economic progress, particularly in the newer and faster growing communities, will not be held back by inadequate banking facilities.

10. *Arguments for branch banking.* Trends and economic pressures aside, the proponents of branch banking claim that:

(a) It reduces costs through economies of scale and structure not ordinarily available to unit banks.

(b) It permits full utilization of automation, particularly centralized electronic bookkeeping and handling of items, and other modern marvels.

(c) It provides needed diversification as it is less dependent on a particular industry, a particular type of customer, or a particular area.

(d) It has greater strength and stability because of size, larger capital and better financial connections.

(e) It facilitates the shifting of funds for seasonal, emergency or local reasons.

(f) It raises banking standards because of more competent banking officers, a wide range of staff officers (economists, investment experts, etc.) and an adequate number of various technical experts.

(g) It provides better banking service through better personnel secured by better pay, better training and more adequate promotion incentives.

(h) It offers greater convenience by bringing the bank to the customer and avoiding the costs of traffic congestion and downtown parking facilities.

(i) It enables banks to follow their customers to the suburbs—a vital consideration in view of the great suburbanization of recent years and the many banking services required, since suburbanites are mostly in the middle and higher income brackets.

(j) It brings banking services to the smallest communities where a unit bank could not survive, since branch facilities can be tailored to fit local requirements. (The writer once had a graduate student who, with the assistance of a porter, had been to 5 different branches of a Canadian bank in the north country of Canada.)

(k) It facilitates government regulation and supervision.

11. *Arguments against branch banking.* The principal arguments of the opponents of branch banking may be summarized as follows:

(a) The substitution of a "manager" for the independent banker who knows the needs of the community and the character of its credit applicants on a personal basis will inevitably result in less credit and poorer service.

(b) The senior officers in the "big city" head office, no matter how hard they try, inevitably must fail to meet the credit needs of the smaller communities.

(c) Local funds will be siphoned off to the big cities and money markets, to the detriment of the local community.

(d) Failure of a branch bank system is a far greater financial disaster than the suspension of individual banks; in fact, it could be serious enough to weaken the credit structure of the entire country.

(e) Branch banking is monopolistic—it permits undue concentration of financial power.

The most bitter and the most telling argument of the opponents of branch banking is that it is monopolistic in nature. This argument completely disregards the likelihood that there will be more competition because the branch method permits the profitable establishment of *more* offices. And as for the argument that the branch bank will not meet the credit needs of the small community, it is hardly likely that a banker aggressive enough to establish a branch in the first place would refuse to let it function after its establishment. Certainly, the experience of small communities in California, Arizona and other states with unrestricted branch banking lends no support to such arguments.

Stripped of its verbiage, the real opposition of most unit bankers is based on their fear that they cannot meet the competition of the branch banking system. But, it is not enough to say that if the unit banker cannot compete, society is entitled to have its banking services performed by branch banking. On more than one occasion in the past, society has decided that concentration of financial power is too great a price to pay for increased economic efficiency. For political, social or other reasons, the American people may again decide not to pay such a price.

In any event, the final decision will be up to the fifty states since the Banking Act of 1933 permits national banks to establish branches only in states permitting branch banking, and only to the extent that the state banks are permitted to establish branches.

12. *Holding-company banking.* American ingenuity has evolved a third form of bank organization, the *bank-holding company.* This form, commonly known as group banking, retains valuable features of both unit and branch banking and offers, in addition, de-

sirable characteristics of its own. In particular, group banking enables unit banks, that otherwise might be forced to liquidate or sell out, to continue as part of a holding company system. In this way, they can utilize capital resources and managerial services of the entire group to strengthen themselves and to expand their services.

The Bank-Holding Company Act of 1956, passed by Congress after nearly two decades of consideration and debate, defines a bank-holding company as one which owns or controls 25 per cent or more of the voting shares of two or more banks, or otherwise controls the election of a majority of their directors. It requires all bank-holding companies to register with the Board of Governors of the Federal Reserve System, which is given broad supervisory and regulatory authority over them.

Among other things, the Bank-Holding Company Act provides that:

(a) Prior approval of the Board of Governors must be secured for a registered holding company to acquire more than 5 per cent of the voting stock of any bank, or for a company to become a bank-holding company.

(b) Bank-holding companies must divest themselves of ownership or control of voting stock of companies that engage in any business other than banking, managing banks, or furnishing services to affiliated banks.

(c) Acquisition of stock of a bank outside the state of the principal operation of the holding company is permitted only if the laws of the state in which the bank is located specifically authorize such acquisition.

In essence, the federal legislation provides a blueprint for regulation of holding companies as an integral and permanent element in our commercial banking system.

13. *Importance of holding-company banking.* Since the depression of the 1930's the number of holding-company groups has declined, but they have increased in size and in number of banking offices. Conversions into branches, mergers and liquidations have reduced the number of such groups to less than 50; nonetheless they control some 1,250 banking offices in 33 states of the United States and hold a sizable part (amounting to some 7.5 per cent) of the commercial bank deposits of the country.

Holding-company banking provides most of the advantages of branch banking, especially those of advice, standards, technical assistance and adequacy of capital funds. In addition, it offers a very special advantage of its own, namely, preservation of local autonomy. Banks affiliated with a holding-company system retain their identity. Each affiliate has its own board of directors, composed largely or entirely of people from the community served. As a rule, it has complete freedom in the choice of personnel, although the holding company is generally consulted on the choice of senior officers.

The tendency of recent years has been for the holding company to become largely a staff organization serving the group and leaving actual banking operations to local management. Holding-company banking thus has a high degree of decentralization and can, thereby, closely adapt itself to the communities served.

14. *Summary on banking structure.* As this chapter has shown, each form of bank organization has advantages and disadvantages. If their advantages did not outweigh their disadvantages, they would not be found competing as they are today. In fact, some of the bitterest complaints on particular forms of organization arise from the very vigor of that competition.

In the final analysis, each form of bank organization will rise or fall depending on the extent to which it helps bring adequate, efficient and dependable banking service to American business and the American people.

Review

Comment on the *number* of American commercial banks.

Compare national banks with state banks on the following points: safety, service to depositors; size; and prestige.

Why should our dual banking system be preserved?

Give the present status of unit banking.

List the arguments for branch banking.

List the arguments against branch banking.

What is the justification for the charge that branch banking is by nature monopolistic?

What is the outstanding advantage of holding-company banking?

CHAPTER XII

Savings Banks and Savings and Loan Associations

1. *Financial intermediaries.* An understanding of the financial intermediaries and of their relation to commercial banking and to the economy in general is warranted by their size, and it is necessitated by their close relation to the management of our money supply. This relationship has been the subject of much research and writing in recent years, which have further served to emphasize their importance.

These financial intermediaries may be divided into *saving* intermediaries and *lending* intermediaries. Those usually considered in the saving category are the savings banks, savings and loan associations, savings departments of commercial banks, credit unions, pension funds, the Postal Savings System, and direct holdings of United States Savings Bonds.

On the lending side, in addition to the above institutions and sources of funds, all of which lend directly, specialized institutions have been developed for bringing such institutionalized savings and direct saving to particular segments of users of longer-term funds. Thus:

Investment bankers specialize in raising longer-term funds for corporations.

Mutual funds specialize in bringing savings, particularly of the smaller investor, into the secondary markets for securities. (They do not originate—they function after the original financing.)

Mortgage bankers specialize in securing mortgage loans for home building and other building construction.

Sales finance and *personal loan companies* specialize in raising the medium-term funds used for financing the purchase of consumer durable goods and consumer services.

On the basis of objectives, the following observations may be made. The savings banks are the only institutions whose primary object is to encourage thrift and collect savings. The primary object of a commercial bank is short-term financing of industry and business; of a savings and loan association, mortgage financing of home building; of sales finance and personal loan companies, consumer financing; and of a credit union, emergency and consumer financing of its members.

2. *Nature of savings banking.* Savings banking is quite different from commercial banking, although they have many things in common. With respect to similarity, commercial banks and savings banks are the only *financial institutions which give deposit account credit*. They are thus both banks in the primary sense of the word. Moreover, they have been getting closer and

closer together, although some of the sporadic and noisome controversy nurtured by self-serving individuals might lead the casual observer to think otherwise.

Commercial banks have always accepted savings deposits, albeit somewhat reluctantly until the boom of the late 1950's made most of them eager competitors for such funds. They not only competed with one another and with non-banking organizations, such as savings and loan associations, but many of them aggressively competed with the specialized savings institutions known as *savings banks*. And they do this despite the fact that the savings banks constitute one of the most important groups of their depositors.

Savings banks must maintain checking accounts with commercial banks, since they are not permitted to maintain such accounts themselves. Thus, other than for currency held in the tellers' departments, all savings bank deposits quickly find their way back to the commercial banks—first, in the deposit account of the savings bank, and then, when disbursed for a mortgage loan or securities purchase, in the names of the recipients and those who come after them.

Putting this differently, savings banks, like commercial banks, accept deposits, but all of the deposits in a savings bank must be non-checking, *time* deposits of savings, which can thus be used for long-term capital purposes. There is thus no deposit expansion in a savings bank as in a commercial bank; in other words, savings bank deposits cannot be created by loans and investments. In fact, the only way savings bank deposits can expand is by an increase in personal *saving* or by securing a larger share of current saving.

3. *Economic need for promotion of saving.* Several trends of recent years have vastly increased the desirability of promotion of saving as a primary objective of national economic policy. The need for increased economic growth, for increased armament, for increased mechanization (automation) of industry, for increased housing, and for increased home ownership—all, without inflation—has made saving the key to our future.

Increased economic growth and heavy investment in armament are prerequisite to survival in a troubled world.

Increased mechanization appears to be the only recourse in the face of ever-mounting wage levels.

Increased housing is necessitated by the "population explosion" of recent years.

Increased home *ownership* must be financed, since it is extremely desirable from a social standpoint. (Since the beginning of this century, the proportion of dwelling units occupied by people who own them has increased from 37 per cent to more than 60 per cent; and the proportion of owner-occupied homes that are mortgaged has increased from 32 per cent to nearly 60 per cent.)

The increased demands flowing from these sources, particularly the great expansion of home ownership, have completely reversed the immediate prewar supply-demand relationship in the capital market. As mounting interest rates testify, the supply of savings has proved inadequate. Unless a far greater part of the mortgage offerings and the bond supply are to be monetized through absorption directly or indirectly by the commercial banks, there must be a sustained increase in savings volume.

Such expansion of savings is the only non-inflationary way to finance homes for the great increase in family formation as the war babies reach marriageable age. All indications are that this will cause the demand for housing to reach levels never attained before. So, if home ownership and avoidance of inflation through large-scale monetization of mortgage debt are to remain twin basic objectives of our national economic and social policy, greatly increased saving is imperative.

It cannot be emphasized too strongly that these, and other, capital needs must be financed by saving and not by the artificial creation of monetary purchasing power by the commercial banking system, if inflation is to be avoided. In no other way can the healthy national growth prerequisite to our survival as a great nation vis-a-vis the peril of international communism be achieved.

4. *The savings banks.* Although organized in only eighteen states, there are 507 savings banks which administer some $66 billion of assets for about 23 million depositors.

Savings banks are concentrated in New England

and the Middle Atlantic states, the four most important states in the order of their deposits being New York, Massachusetts, Connecticut and Pennsylvania. In New York State alone, savings banks hold more than $39 billion of assets for some 11.3 million depositors.

The popularity of savings banks as a medium for saving is due to many reasons. Among the more important ones are:

(a) The excellent record for safety established by the savings banks, as compared with other financial institutions, particularly during the difficult days of the Great Depression in the 1930's.

(b) The high quality of personal service provided by the savings banks, since their procedures and quarters are devoted exclusively to serving savings depositors.

(c) The attractive rate of return paid, down through the years, on savings. (In certain stages of the business cycle other institutions outbid them for the funds of savers, but, historically, their record has been on the high side, making allowance for the high degree of safety and the superior availability of funds they offer.)

(d) As the only institution specializing in stimulating and encouraging thrift among all people, the exclusive objectives of savings bank promotion and advertising activities are attracting savings accounts and encouraging greater saving. This concentration naturally brings results.

Savings banks actively encourage and promote thrift for its own sake (not as a means to an end, as in the case of certain other types of organizations). To do this, they undertake not only to safeguard the savings deposited by individuals, but also to invest these funds so as to provide a steady and attractive income to their depositors. And, most importantly, except in time of emergency, savers are assured of the ready availability of their funds when needed. And, even in time of emergency, savers face only the minimum statutory delay which is, in general, thirty days, although it can be longer.

The extent to which some savings banks go in encouraging thrift is demonstrated by the policy of the Bowery Savings Bank of New York with respect to types of savings accounts. They offer no less than 26 different kinds of savings accounts to meet different needs. Is it any wonder that they have been entrusted with more than $1 billion of savings to administer?

Despite the many different types of thrift service rendered by the savings banks, the regular savings account is by far the most important one; in fact, it is more important than all the others combined. There are, however, certain misconceptions about the owners of savings accounts. Surveys indicate that, instead of being an institution exclusively devoted to collecting the savings of the lower-income group, as is commonly thought, the modern savings bank is a favorite thrift vehicle of the middle class as well.

In fact, ownership of savings accounts today appears to be more widespread among spending units earning $5,000 or more than among those with lower incomes. Moreover, it appears that in the professional, clerical and sales groups, a higher percentage of spending units had savings accounts than among wage earners.

5. *Savings bank investments.* In investing the savings entrusted to them by their depositors, savings banks have as a first objective safety of principal, and as a second objective the highest return commensurate with the necessary safety. Most states regulate the investment policies of savings banks. This is done to protect depositors and, in many cases, to favor investment within the state.

By confining the investments of savings banks to a so-called "legal list," or by specifying specific tests which the securities they purchase must meet, a state can confine savings bank demand to a restricted area and create an artificial situation which will drive up the prices and drive down the yield. Of course, the state's own obligations are always high on such a list.

While different states have different standards, some of them quite severe, total savings-bank investments, as a percentage of assets, are approximately as follows: mortgages, close to 66⅔ per cent; United States Government obligations, 15 to 20 per cent; other bonds, notes and debentures, 5 to 10 per cent; cash and due from banks, about 2.5 per cent; corporate stocks, around 2 per cent; and bank premises, slightly more than ½ of 1 per cent.

Although, by law, savings banks must reserve the right to require notice of withdrawal—usually 30 or 60 days—as a general practice, they pay on demand. This means that they must maintain cash or assets that can readily be turned into cash without much, if any, loss to meet such withdrawals. They also need liquidity to take up outstanding mortgage commitments, and to take advantage of attractive investment opportunities. Such primary reserves of 2 to 3 per cent of total assets are ordinarily maintained for these purposes.

The saving banks' record of ordinarily paying withdrawals on demand has penalized them in recent years. They have had to stay more liquid, which adversely affects their earnings, as more and more people treat their savings account as a *demand* account on which they cannot draw checks. In other words, in recent years people have come to rely on their savings account for personal liquidity. Paradoxical though it may be, present-day depositors expect the higher return of long-term investment and the ready availability of near-cash. Thus, "they want to have their cake and eat it, too!"

6. *Efficiency of operation.* The income of savings banks is composed of interest earned on mortgages and securities and a small revenue from various services, such as rental of safe deposit boxes and excess office space.

The major costs of operating a savings bank are

salaries and other compensation. Other expenses include those of maintaining the banking quarters, Federal Deposit Insurance assessments, taxes, advertising, and mortgage servicing.

The nature of their operations lends itself to mechanization and they are largely modernized in this respect. Also, the relative inactivity of their accounts, as compared with the accounts of a commercial bank, directly affects their costs per dollar of deposits. Whereas the accounts in a savings bank turn over about once in four years, the accounts (including checking accounts) in a commercial bank turn over, on the average for the whole country, about 25 times each year. In other words, the accounts in commercial banks are about 100 times as active as those in savings banks.

Savings banks operate at a lower cost than competing types of financial institutions. As might be expected, their operating expenses are lower than those of commercial banks, when measured either as expense per dollar of assets administered or as expense per dollar of income. Also, as might not be expected, their operating expenses are much lower than those of savings and loan associations per dollar of assets or per dollar of income.

Quantitatively, it appears to cost the savings banks about two-thirds of 1 per cent per year for each $1 of assets administered, whereas the costs of the saving and loan associations generally run 50 per cent to 100 per cent higher. In relation to income, operating expenses of the savings banks average around 15 per cent of income, whereas the savings and loan associations require around 20 to 25 per cent of income for this purpose.

7. *Mutual form of organization.* With negligible exceptions, savings banks are organized as *mutual* institutions. The United States Supreme Court has defined a mutual savings bank as:

> An institution in the hands of disinterested persons (i.e. trustees), the profits of which, after deducting the necessary expenses of conducting the business, inure solely to the benefit of depositors, in dividends, or in a reserved surplus for their greater security.

Thus, the mutual savings bank has no capital stock such as other banks. Instead of promoters and stock-selling campaigns, the mutual savings bank is organized by public-spirited citizens who advance its initial funds. This advance is repaid gradually from earnings. In the meantime, the amounts contributed by the incorporators and trustees to the surplus may be credited only with the rate of dividend paid depositors. Moreover, the state statutes usually impose restrictions on withdrawals of such contributions that could make them unavailable indefinitely.

The absence of promoters' profits, the large amounts required to cover the operating expenses of a new institution, the limited rate of return that can be realized by the incorporators, and the possible risks involved have precluded the formation of new savings banks in recent years. In fact, the number of mutual banks has steadily declined from 540 in 1940 to 507 at the most recent count.

8. *Taxation of mutual savings banks.* Their mutual form of organization has given rise to considerable discussion of the tax status of savings banks, particularly by some commercial bank competitors. In view of the public interest involved, a few comments on this will be in order. These are general observations to which there may be exceptions in a particular state so far as state and local taxes are concerned.

In general, mutual savings banks pay all property taxes and assessments that other owners pay. They also, ordinarily, pay a state franchise tax, the same as other financial organizations. This franchise tax, however, in at least one state (New York), is higher for them per dollar of income than for the commercial banks.

It is on the federal corporate income tax that the arguments have risen. The mutual savings banks were wholly exempt from this tax until 1952 when the Revenue Act of 1951 made them subject to it with the proviso that they do not have to pay such tax if their net worth (surplus, undivided profits, general reserves, and bad debt reserves) is less than 12 per cent of total deposits. The savings banks maintain that the growth of deposits has kept this ratio below 12 per cent, so that they have not been required to pay the tax. Their opponents claim that they have paid out dividends at a high rate to prevent this ratio from exceeding 12 per cent, thereby securing a definite advantage in the competition for savings.

Without taking sides in the controversy, it must be noted that this question never rose during the savings-surplus days before the savings-hungry postwar period. Also, savings banks (and savings and loan associations, too) do not have as favorable a federal tax status as other mutual types of organizations. Specifically, the requirement that they must pay regular income tax rates on all undistributed earnings above 12 per cent is discriminatory in comparison with other mutual organizations.

The attacks on them are, thus, attacks on the mutual form of organization which has been permitted and encouraged by public policy for particular, socially desirable purposes since the early days of the Republic. In the case of the mutual savings banks, this encouragement covers a span of more than 150 years of service.

9. *Importance of management.* The absence of stockholders, the lack of direct control by the depositors, and the self-perpetuating character of the board of trustees of the mutual savings banks have occasioned criticism of the "who is minding the store" type. The answer lies in the statutory limitations placed upon trustees and the considerable authority generally given the Superintendent of Banks (or similar official) over the composition and the functioning of the board of trustees.

In particular, trustees are forbidden to have any interest, direct or indirect, in the profits of their bank. They may, however, paraphrasing the New York law, receive reasonable compensation for actual attendance at meetings of the board of trustees, for service in appraising real property for the board, for service as a member of a committee of the board, or for service as an officer that requires and receives "his regular and faithful attendance at the savings bank." Also, attorneys for a savings bank, even though trustees, may receive a reasonable compensation for professional services. Trustees may thus receive reasonable payment for time and effort actually expended for the benefit of the bank, but may receive neither compensation nor profit for merely filling the office of trustee.

The acid test of management is, of course, results. On that basis, savings banks rank high as compared with other financial institutions. Since safety of savings entrusted to them is their primary consideration, their solvency record is the ultimate test. The great depression of the 1930's presented as severe a test, as can be imagined, of the ability of financial institutions to maintain solvency under highly adverse conditions.

Despite the necessity of heavy foreclosures, which in New York State ranged above 10 per cent of total mortgages for *each* year of the five-years of the 1935–1940 period, and were substantial immediately before and immediately thereafter, no mutual savings bank suspended during the depression period, while thousands of commercial banks and building and loan associations (old type of savings and loan associations) were forced to suspend.

In addition to the protection of good management, close state supervision, and substantial reserves, most mutual savings banks have the added protection of either the deposit insurance of the Federal Deposit Insurance Corporation or one of the state plans which operate in certain states. The FDIC protects the bulk of the deposits, however, with over half of the mutual savings banks, holding over three-quarters of all deposits, participating as members of the Corporation.

10. *Savings and loan associations.* The rapid growth of savings and loan associations has been one of the most outstanding phenomena of the period since the end of World War II. After trying difficulties in the 1930's and from a relatively modest base at the end of the war, they have grown by more than $50 billion. They are indeed a type of institution worthy of close consideration.

Numerically, the associations have had a downward trend from their peak of 12,403 in 1925 to slightly more than 6,000 in recent years. However, as indicated in the preceding paragraph, they have far more than made up in size for their decline in numbers.

Originally known as building and loan associations, and still chartered as cooperative banks and otherwise in some states, they acquired their present name of savings and loan associations when the Home Owners

Loan Act of 1933 provided for national charter of Federal Savings and Loan Associations. They generally, however, refer to themselves as savings associations.

Their use of the word "savings" notwithstanding, their original function was, and their primary function today is, the financing of home building.

To secure funds for this purpose, most of them sell various types of shares, which may be classified as follows:

(a) *Optional savings shares,* on which the subscriber can make payments at will.
(b) *Installment thrift shares,* on which the subscriber is required to make uniform periodic payments called "dues."
(c) *Prepaid shares,* on which sufficient cash payment is made for them, with the aid of dividend credits, to become fully paid at maturity some time in the future.
(d) *Income shares,* on which full payment is made in advance so that they can receive dividends in cash when declared.

The word "shares" which appears in each of these plans is the key to savings and loan operation. Association members are *shareholders,* not *creditors* as are depositors in a bank. As creditors, bank depositors ask for the return of their funds; as investors, savings and loan association members must apply for repurchase of their shares by the association.

11. *Liquidity of shares vs. that of deposits.* Although no problem in normal times, the provisions on repurchase of shares could make their repayment record quite different in times of economic difficulty. Whereas if banks do invoke the 30 (or sometimes 60) day delay, as provided in their savings deposit contract, they must pay all withdrawals on demand in the full amount requested upon the expiration of the delay period. If they cannot do this, they are in default and the Federal Deposit Insurance Corporation steps in and makes all insured deposits promptly available.

In contrast, if a savings and loan association is unable to repurchase members' shares within 30 days after demand, they may invoke a "take-your-turn" plan. In the words of the Indiana Bankers Association (commercial bankers), the operation of such a numerical rotation is as follows:

> In such a case, if the value of a member's share is more than $1,000 he may be paid $1,000, if available, when his number is reached, and then his application is renumbered and moved to the bottom of the list. When his number is reached again, the process is repeated. Under these circumstances, however, an Association may pay up to either $100 or $200 (depending on how chartered) to any holder, in any month, for the repurchase of share accounts without regard to numerical order or filing of application. If unable to pay all withdrawal requests within 30 days, Associations must apply a

minimum of either one-third or 80 per cent (depending on how chartered) of their receipts to repurchase of member's shares.

12. *Difference between FDIC and FSLIC (Federal Savings and Loan Insurance Corporation).* Since some 95 per cent of total savings and loan assets are insured up to $15,000 per account by the Federal Savings and Loan Insurance Corporation, an agency of the United States Government, the question may well be asked as to what is the difference in the protection afforded by it and that of the Federal Deposit Insurance Corporation?

First, it should be understood that the wording of the respective applicable federal statutes is identical. It is in the definition—in practice—of the key word "default" that the difference lies. Whereas, when a bank cannot pay depositors it is in default and the FDIC steps in and makes all insured deposits available, a savings and loan association can invoke its charter provisions on numerical rotation of share purchases. If these charter provisions should be invoked, the result would be a waiting period which, conceivably, could be of long duration.

Only after an insured association is declared in default is the FSLIC legally obligated to give the shareholder a new insured account in a solvent institution or to pay in cash. And, unless closed by supervisory authorities for some other reason, an association is not in default so long as it applies one-third or 80 per cent of its cash receipts (depending upon how chartered) to the repurchase of its shares. Thus, the shares in the savings and loan association might not have the same liquidity in an emergency as the deposits in a commercial or savings bank. In normal times, the problem does not arise, as they are redeemed on demand.

13. *The Home Loan Bank System.* In addition to having their own insurance corporation, the savings and loan associations have the benefit of a central banking system which, in the mortgage field, corresponds to the Federal Reserve System in commercial banking.

This system is headed by a Federal Home Loan Bank Board of three members appointed by the President of the United States "with the advice and consent" of the Senate. The Home Loan Bank Board serves also as the board of trustees of the Federal Savings and Loan Insurance Corporation.

This Board supervises the eleven regional Home Loan Banks scattered throughout the country, as well as the members of the System. As in the case of the Federal Reserve System, nationally chartered associations (the word "Federal" must appear in their title) are mandatory members, and state-chartered associations, which meet the standards of the Board, may become members. In addition, a few mutual savings banks and insurance companies are also members, to secure the advantages of access to the loan and other facilities of the Home Loan Banks.

Review

What does *saving* have to do with our national survival?

Discuss the economic need for promotion of saving.

List the more important thrift services of savings banks.

Why do savings banks maintain higher liquidity than savings and loan associations?

Compare the cost of operations of savings banks with that of commercial banks and savings and loan associations.

Outline the reasons for use of the mutual form of organization by savings banks.

What is the basic legal difference between the rights of a bank depositor and a savings and loan shareholder?

Specifically, what is the difference between FDIC and FSLIC protection, as a practical matter?

Describe the Home Loan Bank System.

CHAPTER XIII

The Federal Reserve System

1. *A central banking system.* All modern banking systems must have a central bank to take the responsibility for credit leadership and coordination and to serve as a bank for the banks of the country. In the United States, however, instead of *one* central bank, as in other countries, we have *twelve*, which, under the guidance of a Board of Governors in Washington, function as a central banking system under the name of the Federal Reserve System.

Put in broad terms, the function of the Federal Reserve System is to make possible the maximum flow of money and credit that our economic system can utilize without inflation. Thereby—and only thereby—credit, the great facilitating agency, can contribute its full potential to our economic and social goal of an ever-expanding economy, with an ever higher standard of living for all. History has amply demonstrated that an efficient, responsible monetary credit mechanism is indispensable for the steady, orderly development of a nation's natural and human resources.

The United States has not always had such an orderly development; nor has it always had a maximum contribution from its banking and credit system.

Quite to the contrary, before the signing of the Federal Reserve Act on December 23, 1913 by President Woodrow Wilson, money, credit and banking, far from being a great facilitating agency, was generally a great drag on our progress. Only a country with incalculable natural resources and unbounded human enthusiasm could have made the progress we did with the handicap of the incredibly bad money and banking that characterized most of our history before the organization of the Federal Reserve System.

This is not to imply that the Federal Reserve System is perfect—in fact, far from it. But, despite its many imperfections and shortcomings, particularly the blot of the boom of the late 1920's and the resulting Great Depression of the 1930's, the Federal Reserve System is a giant step forward in our efforts to keep our credit environment a "reasonable facsimile" of economic reality by preventing unbridled optimism or unreasoning pessimism from causing economic excesses with their heavy costs, particularly in human suffering.

2. *The "independence" of the Federal Reserve System.* The establishment of twelve Federal Reserve Banks rather than the one advocated by the proponents of central banking was a deliberate effort of the Congress, spearheaded by the agricultural bloc of those days, to prevent centralization of the money power. They sought, through numerous safeguards in the Act, to prevent either private or political domination of the monetary system. Their intent, reaffirmed on many

subsequent occasions, was that the Federal Reserve should be *independent*.

This does not mean independent of the government —only the Deity can be independent of modern-day government! But it does mean that the System is independent within the over-all framework of government. In other words, it is not dominated by the Treasury, or the military spenders, or the Department of Interior, and so on. In short, it is an independent agency set up by government to perform certain functions. As such, it can be abolished by joint resolution of the two houses of Congress in a matter of minutes any time they might get into the mood to do so.

Every American should understand that the Federal Reserve, as such, is not mentioned in the Constitution or any of its amendments; nor does it have the protection of being a part of the organic law of the land. It is man-made, and its only protection is the influence wielded by an informed, and occasionally aroused, electorate on the Congress.

This places the responsibility for protection on the business man, since he should supply the leadership in economic matters, especially those that mean as much to him as this one. If he abdicates this responsibility and refuses active protection, he must expect the "do-gooders," the "tax and tax, and spend and spend" advocates, and the ever-lower-interest-rate-cheap-money agitators to take over our monetary direction, since, as has been well said, "nature abhors a vacuum."

3. *Board of Governors of the Federal Reserve System.*
The establishment of twelve [1] regional central banks
made it necessary to provide a central mechanism
for coordinating their policies and activities. The
Board of Governors of the Federal Reserve System is
this coordinating and policy-making body. The composition of the Board, the method of appointment of
its members, their term of office, and various aspects of
its authority make the members of the Board trustees
of the public interest, rather than servants of the banks
of the country.

The Board of Governors has seven members appointed for fourteen-year terms (except when appointed for an unexpired portion of a term) by the
President of the United States with the "advice and
consent" of the Senate. As safeguards against political
domination, these terms were: (1) deliberately made
for a long period, which far outspans the typical administration of either political party; (2) staggered so
that one term expires every two years; and (3) not
open for reappointment of any member who has served
a full term of fourteen years.

Moreover, in selecting members, the President is
directed by the Federal Reserve Act to give "due regard to a fair representation of the financial, agricultural, industrial and commercial interests and geographical divisions of the country." In the same vein,

[1] They have twenty-four branches strategically located around the
country where needed to give better service.

not more than one member can be selected from any one of the twelve Federal Reserve districts, nor can a member be a director, officer or stockholder of any banking institution or trust company.

In fact, as might be expected, members of the Board of Governors are not permitted to have any outside business connection—they must devote their full time to their responsibilities at the Board. And, although the Federal Reserve Act provides that a Governor may be removed by the President "for cause," this undoubtedly would be invoked only in the extremely unlikely event of "moral turpitude," and certainly not because of a difference of opinion as to credit policy.

4. *Functions of the Board of Governors.* One of the members of the Board is designated by the President as Chairman and one as Vice-Chairman, each for a term of four years. The Chairman, subject to the general supervision of the Board, is the chief executive officer, and he is also the spokesman for the Board and the System, especially in all relations with Congress and the executive departments of the government.

The more important functions of the Board may be summarized as follows:

(a) It "reviews and determines" discount rates established bi-weekly by the directors of each district Reserve Bank. (This has been construed by the United States Attorney General as authorizing the Board not only to pass on rates proposed by the Federal Reserve Banks, but also to establish discount rates on its own initiative.)

(b) It fixes, with statutory limits, the legal reserves which member banks of the System must maintain at their district Reserve Bank. (The Federal Reserve Act stipulates that such changes are to be made "to prevent injurious credit expansion or contraction.")

(c) Its members are *ex-officio* members of the Federal Open Market Committee, constituting a majority on this very important committee which determines the System's policies on influencing the *availability* of credit through the purchase or sale of government obligations in the open market.

(d) It fixes margin requirements on loans on stock exchange collateral.

(e) It has various supervisory responsibilities with respect to member banks, including examination responsibility on their use of credit.

(f) It administers the Federal Reserve Act, bank holding company, and other financial legislation.

(g) It supervises and annually examines the twelve district Federal Reserve Banks and has special supervisory control over their foreign contacts and operations.

(h) It assembles, maintains and disseminates a vast volume of economic, monetary and financial data.

To carry on these manifold activities, the Board of Governors maintains a large staff housed in a magnificent building in Washington, D. C. Other than nominal amounts received for certain publications, the funds to maintain its activities are obtained by regular assessments on the twelve district Reserve Banks.

5. *Structure of the Federal Reserve System.* In addition to the twelve Federal Reserve Banks, the Board of Governors and the Federal Open Market Committee, the Federal Reserve System includes all national banks (mandatory membership) and state-chartered institutions which meet certain minimum requirements that apply and are accepted for membership. A state member bank may withdraw upon six months' notice; and it may be expelled by the Board for cause.

There are more than three times as many state banks that are not members as there are state bank members. Putting it differently, somewhat less than half of all commercial banks are members of the Federal Reserve System, but they hold around 85 per cent of all demand deposits. Moreover, the banks which are not members of the System gain access to many of its benefits through their large city correspondents, who also directly perform many other central banking services for them.

Prior to 1952, state member banks had to meet the capital requirements of national banks similarly located, but in that year Congress made membership easier by authorizing the same standards as those applied to membership in the Federal Deposit Insurance Corporation.

Each member bank must subscribe 6 per cent of its paid-in capital and surplus to stock in the Federal Bank of its district. Only one-half of this subscription is paid in, the balance being subject to call, but none has ever been called. On this stock, they receive 6 per cent cumulative dividends, which makes it the best investment of the bank.

The principal other privileges of membership are access to the rediscount window of the district Federal Reserve Bank, use of Federal Reserve facilities for collecting checks, settling clearing balances and transferring funds to other cities, shipment of currency when needed, and participation in the election of six of the nine directors of the district Reserve Bank.

The important obligations of membership are:

(a) To comply with the reserve requirements of the Federal Reserve.
(b) To keep such reserves on deposit without interest at its Reserve Bank.
(c) To submit to various requirements of the federal law with respect to holding company regulation, interlocking directorates, certain loan and investment limitations, and other matters.
(d) To remit at par for all items drawn on it.
(e) If chartered by a state, to be subject to general supervision and examination by the Federal Reserve.

6. *The Federal Open Market Committee.* One of the most important components of the Federal Reserve System is the Federal Open Market Committee. This Committee is comprised of the seven members of the Federal Reserve Board (which thus always has a majority) and five presidents (or first vice-presidents) of Reserve Banks elected annually by their respective boards of directors on a rotation basis, except that the president of the Federal Reserve Bank of New York, whose bank, as agent, executes all transactions for System Account, is always a member.

Alternates to these five representatives of the Federal Reserve Banks are required to be chosen in the same way by their boards. In actual practice, representatives of all twelve Federal Reserve Banks attend meetings and participate in the discussions, although only the members of the Committee are permitted to vote.

The Federal Open Market Committee is required by law to meet at least four times a year in Washington, at the call of the Chairman of the Board of Governors or at the request of any three members of the Committee. In recent years, the Committee has met much more frequently—generally, once every three weeks.

The Committee establishes policies on the purchase and sale of government securities in the open market, for the guidance of the Manager of the System Open Market Account, who is also the vice president in charge of the securities function of the New York bank.

The Federal Open Market Committee is a very important one. Its operations create reserves for the member banks when securities are bought; conversely, reserves are destroyed when securities are sold. Thus, by buying or selling securities, the Committee can almost instantaneously create tighter or easier credit conditions as it, from time to time, deems desirable. It should be understood that such transactions are for System Open Market Account, that is for all of the twelve Reserve Banks. An individual Reserve Bank is not permitted either to buy or sell securities, since such transactions might run counter to, or at least interfere with, the credit policy of the Board of Governors.

7. *The Federal Advisory Council.* To permit high-level, official contact with commercial bankers, the Federal Reserve Act established the Federal Advisory Council of twelve members. These members must be commercial bankers and they are elected annually, one from each Federal Reserve district, by the Board of Directors of the Federal Reserve Bank of that district. The Council is required to meet at least four times a year, and those meetings must be in Washington. The place and number of additional meetings, if any, are left to the Council.

The Federal Advisory Council, as its name indicates, functions solely in an advisory capacity to the Board of Governors. More specifically, it is empowered by the Federal Reserve Act to counsel with the Board on general business conditions, to make representations on any developments within the jurisdiction of the Board, to call for information, and to make recommendations on open-market operations, discount rates, reserve conditions in the districts, and similar matters of concern to banking and the economy.

8. *Regulations of the Board of Governors.* To permit adjustment to constantly changing conditions, Congress legislates general principles and policies, and empowers the Board of Governors of the Federal Reserve System to issue all regulations necessary to effectuate those statutory aims. The Board's general authority to issue such regulations is set forth in Section 11 of the Federal Reserve Act, in the following words:

> . . . and said Board shall perform the duties, functions or services specified in this Act and make all rules and regulations necessary to enable said board effectively to perform the same.

Many other acts also give the Board authority to promulgate regulations covering specific matters. The authority to prescribe rules and regulations is of great importance to the Board of Governors, since they constitute the mechanism through which it carries out a large part of its responsibilities.

The importance attached by the Board to these Regulations is clearly indicated by the detailed procedures and safeguards employed in their issuance. Since the extreme lengths to which they go in trying to protect the interests of all parties concerned are not generally known, and since it will give an idea of how the Board functions in respect to Regulations, the procedures involved in establishing a Regulation are quoted below from a highly informative article [1] by Charles B. Dunn, a former General Counsel of the Federal Reserve Bank of Chicago.

> . . . After a thorough study of the legal, technical, and practical problems involved, a tentative draft of a regulation is prepared by the board's staff. Without being acted upon by the Board, copies of this tentative draft are furnished to all twelve Federal Reserve Banks, the Federal Advisory Council, a Committee of the American Bankers Association, the Comptroller of the Currency, the Federal Deposit Insurance Corporation, and any other interested governmental agencies, all of whom are invited to submit criticisms and recommendations in writing.
>
> Each of the Federal Reserve Banks confers with a number of its member banks and the tentative draft of the regulation is made the basis of study and discussion by a committee of the staff of the Federal Reserve Bank, after which their comments, criticisms and suggestions are transmitted to the Board. Likewise, the other agencies submit their comments to the Board for consideration.
>
> After criticisms and suggestions have been received from all of these sources, they are assembled by the Board's staff and thoroughly considered. If

[1] Charles B. Dunn, "The Organization and Functions of the Federal Reserve System," the John Marshall Law Quarterly, December 1941.

the revisions are very extensive, another draft of the regulation may be prepared and the same process repeated until differences of opinion are reduced to a minimum.

After members of the Board have had ample opportunity to study and discuss the final draft of the regulation and the accompanying data submitted, the matter is brought up for consideration at a meeting of the Board. If it is satisfied with the product, the regulation is adopted and promulgated in pamphlet form, copies being furnished promptly to all member banks, and, as far as practicable to every other person or organization affected by it. The effective date of the regulation is usually at least thirty days after the member banks have had time to receive copies. The text is then published promptly in the Federal Register and in the next issue of the Board's monthly bulletin.

The Board is always willing to give adequate consideration to requests from banks and other interested parties that the regulations be amended. They are also amended from time to time on the Board's own motion in the light of changing conditions or in order to effect improvements in the light of experience. From time to time, as circumstances warrant, the regulations are revised and the same process usually is followed in connection with a revision or amendment if it includes any substantial or important changes. When, in the opinion of the Board, a regulation serves no further useful purpose it is rescinded.

Twenty-five regulations with alphabetical designations running from A to Y (inclusive) have been issued, of which two are suspended as of this writing. Space does not permit discussion of these regulations, important though they be. Their titles alone in the following listing, however, will give a good idea of their importance and wide range.

REGULATIONS OF THE BOARD OF GOVERNORS

Regulation A — Advances and Discounts by Federal Reserve Banks.

Regulation B — Open-Market Purchases of Bills of Exchange, Trade Acceptances, and Bankers' Acceptances Under Section 14.

Regulation C — Acceptance by Member Banks of Drafts or Bills of Exchange.

Regulation D — Reserves of Member Banks.

Regulation E — Purchase of Warrants.

Regulation F — Trust Powers of National Banks.

Regulation G — Definition and Rules Regarding Non-Cash Items.

Regulation H — Membership of State Banking Institutions in the Federal Reserve System.

Regulation I — Increase or Decrease of Capital Stock of Federal Reserve Banks and Cancellation of Old and Issue of New Stock Certificates.

Regulation J — Check Clearing and Collection.

Regulation K   Corporations Doing Foreign Banking or Other Foreign Financing Under the Federal Reserve Act.

Regulation L   Interlocking Bank Directorates Under the Clayton Act.

Regulation M   Foreign Branches of National Banks and of Corporations Organized Under the Provisions of Section 25(a) of the Federal Reserve Act.

Regulation N   Relations with Foreign Banks.

Regulation O   Loans to Executive Officers of Member Banks.

Regulation P   Holding Company Affiliates—Voting Permits.

Regulation Q   Payment of Interest on Deposits.

Regulation R   Relations with Dealers in Securities.

Regulation S   Industrial Loans by Federal Reserve Banks.

Regulation T   Credit by Brokers, Dealers and Members of National Securities Exchanges.

Regulation U   Loans by Banks for the Purpose of Purchasing or Carrying Registered Stocks.

Regulation V   Loan Guarantees for Defense Production.

Regulation W   Consumer Credit (regulation suspended).

Regulation X   Real Estate Credit (regulation suspended).

Regulation Y   Bank Holding Companies.

In addition to these Regulations of the Board, many of which are booklets of several pages, the various Federal Reserve Banks issue Operating Circulars giving information and instructions supplementing the Regulations.

A steady stream of rulings and interpretation of the Regulations appears in the monthly Federal Reserve Bulletins and in more permanent book form. They are generally issued in response to written inquiries from those affected by a Regulation, although they may be issued upon the initiative of the Board. Thus, a vast body of administrative precedent is available in addition to the Regulations and Operating Circulars for the guidance of member banks and others concerned.

9. *Supervisory functions of the Federal Reserve.* The Federal Reserve System, established to provide, among other purposes, a "more effective supervision of banking in the United States," has supervisory authority with respect to all of its members. In practice, the System confines its visitorial examination powers to state member banks and, whenever practicable, such examinations are made jointly with state supervisory authorities.

The actual field work of bank examination is delegated to the Reserve Banks. To avoid duplication, the chief national bank examiner for the district furnishes them with copies of examinations of all national banks. And the Reserve Bank examiners cooperate with the state bank examiners, whenever feasible, in joint or alternate examinations of state member banks at least once a year. They thus secure the information needed for them to correct unsatisfactory conditions in, or violations of, banking law by member banks, and take, if necessary, disciplinary action to remove officers and directors for unsafe and unsound banking practices or for continued violation of banking law.

10. *Earning assets and liabilities of the Federal Reserve Banks.* A quick look at the combined statements of the twelve Federal Reserve Banks will give a good idea of their size, method of operation and source of earnings. This is particularly necessary, since the exigencies of war finance, heavy public debt, and the easy-money emphasis which have characterized our national policy from time to time, have necessarily left their marks on the Federal Reserve. In other words, the Federal Reserve System of today is far from what its founders contemplated.

Comments will be made on the basis of the balance-sheet figures as of this writing. Since they are constantly changing, the reader is urged to consult more current figures, which appear weekly in the New York Times and other newspapers, and monthly in the Federal Reserve Bulletin and many other banking publications.

The first thing that strikes the eye is the almost infinitesimal holdings of eligible paper. Although such paper, discounted by the member banks, was designed to be the foolproof, inflation-proof method of access to reserve bank credit, it has usually been, since World

War II, only a fraction of a billion dollars, as contrasted with government security holdings of more than $25 billion and total assets of more than $50 billion.

The next striking thing on the asset side of the balance sheet is the comparatively large holdings of gold certificates. Although down considerably from the fear-induced holdings of the World War II period, they are still sizable; moreover, they yield no earnings whatsoever for the Federal Reserve Banks.

On the liability side, there are two very large and important items. The first is "Federal Reserve notes" which typically fall a little short of $30 billion. The second is "member bank reserves" which typically fall a little short of $20 billion. The overwhelming importance of these two accounts, which approach a $50 billion total, in comparison with all other accounts, is indicated by "Total liabilities" of a little more than $51 billion and "Total liabilities and capital accounts" of a little less than $53 billion.

The chief earning assets of the Federal Reserve Banks are government securities, which supply around 95 per cent of total earnings, and loans and discounts to member banks. The other, and very minor, sources of earnings are interest on the special loans to business firms, on holdings of bankers acceptances, and profits on the sale of securities. (Of course, there can be a loss for the year on the sale of securities, since those operations are dictated by money management rather than market considerations.)

Turning to the expense side, three functions account for four-fifths of the Banks' expenses. Approximately one-third of total expense is incurred in check collection and currency and securities handling. Fiscal agency functions performed for the government account for nearly one-fourth of total expense. Space, equipment and personnel absorbed another one-fourth. This leaves less than one-fourth for the overhead of research, general administration, bank supervision, auditing, etc.

After expenses, other deductions and payment of a 6 per cent dividend on paid-in stock to member banks, approximately 90 per cent of the balance is paid to the Treasury as interest on Federal Reserve notes outstanding not covered by gold certificates. The Federal Reserve Board fixes the interest on such uncovered notes at a rate which will capture approximately 90 per cent of the net earnings and the remaining 10 per cent is transferred to surplus.

11. *Contributions of Federal Reserve System.* The Federal Reserve System renders many services to business, government and the economy. Many of them have been discussed, and others, particularly its money management and its international services, will be considered in subsequent chapters.

It is appropriate, however, to observe at this point that the basic powers and responsibilities of the Federal Reserve System relate to credit and money—that its activities directly affect the availability of banking funds and the willingness of other lenders and investors to supply funds.

The "inelastic currency" and "scattered bank reserves" which characterized our previous banking history were promptly remedied by the Federal Reserve System. For many years, including the periods of two world wars, the volume of currency has expanded and contracted in accordance with the varying needs of the public. In fact, the currency function today is largely a matter of routine, free from uncertainties and administrative difficulties.

As for bank reserves, fifty years of reserve banking experience have demonstrated that the reserve function is much more than just mobilizing scattered reserves and making the surplus reserves of some bank available to other banks in need of funds. Today, the main problem is recognized as that of providing a pool of reserve funds which adjusts to the changing pace of business activity and increases over time as the economy grows. This is so important that it, too, will be specially considered in coming chapters.

Review

Why is a central bank needed by all modern banking systems?

What is really meant by the term "independence" of the Federal Reserve System?

Why do we need a Board of Governors at the head of our banking system?

Enumerate the more important functions of the Board of Governors of the Federal Reserve System.

Describe the structure of the Federal Reserve System.

Differentiate the Federal Advisory Council from the Federal Open Market Committee.

Outline the procedure used by the Board of Governors in formulating a Regulation.

Discuss the Federal Reserve Board Regulations from the standpoint of number, importance and range.

Upon what basis and with what justification does the Treasury take the major portion of the net earnings of the Federal Reserve Banks?

List a representative selection of the contributions of the Federal Reserve System.

CHAPTER XIV

The Money Market

1. *The money market.* Our financial markets are the result of gradual evolution and increasing specialization. In consequence, there is considerable overlapping with respect to instruments traded. There is even more overlapping with respect to agencies doing the trading, most of them being on both sides of the market, frequently simultaneously. Also, there is even overlapping with respect to functions served. And there is more overlapping with respect to the delineation of boundaries, as many credit instruments and some institutions are part in and part out of the various financial markets, particularly the money market.

For the purposes of this text, these various markets and submarkets will be divided into a long-term grouping, or *capital market* (which will not be specifically discussed), and a short-term, highly liquid grouping, or *money market*. Even this very broad characterization leaves much to be desired, since there are frequently heavy shifts from the capital market to the money market, and *vice versa*, depending on the fears and the *time-preference* of individuals and institutional lenders and borrowers (at times we place a much higher value on having our money now, as opposed to the future, than at other times).

The money market is thus, in a sense, a concept of the many forces of demand and supply for liquid and near-liquid funds. The use of such a concept is peculiarly appropriate for the money market since it has no formal organization as a market nor has it any formally constituted trading place. It is, instead, a group of institutions, middlemen and individuals, scattered all over the country, who buy and sell through telephone, telegraph and mail facilities. Since these operations are largely centered in Wall Street, the New York money market is by far the most important of our several money markets. In fact, it is the only one that can fairly be considered a national market, the others being largely local, or regional.

2. *Why Wall Street?* The preeminence of the New York money market is no happenchance of fate. There are many reasons why Wall Street houses a money market which is not only our national money market, but also the chief money market of the entire Free World. In addition to transportation, location and communication advantages, New York is a world center of wealth. The great banks of the Free World either have their head offices in the financial district, or they have agencies or representatives through which they gain access to its operations. The New York Stock Exchange is located there; likewise, our great investment banking houses.

Furthermore, the international operations of the Federal Reserve System are centered in the Federal Reserve Bank of New York, which also acts as agent for many foreign central banks and governments in *their* market transactions. In addition, the New York Reserve Bank acts as agent for the United States Government and the Treasury in a wide range of international and domestic financial transactions. And, most important of all, the Federal Reserve Bank of New York, under the guidance of the Federal Open Market Committee, conducts all of the open market transactions for all twelve of the Federal Reserve Banks in the System.

In the same fashion, most of our great corporations either have their head offices, financial offices, or representatives in New York, and thus have direct access to that money market.

The electronic age notwithstanding, physical facilities must be close together when billions of dollars must be transferred from buyer to seller, from lender to borrower, from depositor to banker and back again, day after day, as is done in the money market. Checks for these huge sums of money must pass from hand to hand along with the evidences of ownership or indebtedness for which the checks are given. So, proximity is of major importance to all central money market participants.

Moreover, those who engage in these huge transactions, as a general rule, have to borrow money to finance their operations. This makes convenient access to adequate commercial banking facilities a categorical imperative. More or less continuous contact with such credit sources is clearly a necessity for most of the agencies in the money market.

For these and many other reasons, the New York market is the central money market through which transactions in the secondary markets are brought together and cleared. By centering highly specialized activities, Wall Street markedly reduces the effort and the cost of money market operations.

3. *Services of the money market.* The money market serves banking and financial institutions, business organizations, government, and the economy as a whole by bridging the gap between lenders and borrowers for the enormous amounts needed for the day-to-day operations of the modern world.

The money market serves the economy by providing a safe and dependable mechanism for transferring money to where it is most needed, as measured by the near-riskless rates bid for the funds, whether the need be in Paris, Washington, or the Congo.

The money market serves as the mechanism through which the Federal Reserve monetary authorities pump new credit into the economy at times and siphon it out at other times in carrying out their money management responsibilities. The efficiency with which the Wall Street money market spreads the effects of these actions throughout the banking system and the entire economy, unequivocally demonstrates that it is an integral and indispensable part of our financial system.

The money market, above all, serves the commercial banks in a vitally important respect—they rely on it in considerable measure for their liquidity. Since their liabilities to the public are largely on a demand basis, they carry a sizable part of their earning assets in the form of "secondary reserves," which fluctuate little in market value and which can be converted into cash within twenty-four hours. Such short-term, highly marketable obligations that can be readily sold in the money market for cash are the first line of defense for most commercial banks.

The money market serves corporations as a source of comparatively riskless investments and as a means for turning their near-money holdings into cash. This has greatly increased in importance in recent years, since corporations have turned more and more to such holdings of near-money to utilize idle bank balances on a profitable basis. Wall Street's money market facilities furnish both supplies and demands for such corporate money, even though it is to be used for only brief periods, sometimes as short as only *one day*.

It should be clearly understood that the New York money market is an *open* market, that is, it is completely impersonal. Neither lender nor borrower feels any obligation whatsoever to a particular counterpart. In short, price considerations prevail over all other relationships, even when the participants are known to one another.

This is a far cry from the close personal relationship which should prevail between the commercial banker and a conventional borrower.

4. *Major institutions in the money market.* Although, as indicated before, no institution is engaged in money market affairs to the exclusion of all other activities, there are several so directly involved in its operations that they may properly be referred to as money market institutions. The institutions which comprise the money market are as follows:

(a) *The money market banks,* including six of the nation's ten largest—each with deposits over $2 billion —and several others that are large by any standard are located within a stone's throw of one another in and around Wall Street. Comprising a pool of more than $20 billion of checkbook money continually available to make payments without previous notice, these large Wall Street banks are the basic institutions in the money market. Without them, and the vast resources and supply and demand they bring together, there would be no money market.

Traditionally, these money market banks were "wholesale" banks concentrating on serving other banks, and on lending to the larger business organizations in New York and other large cities. Today, all except two have gone "retail," that is, they have opened numerous branches and actively seek loans to small business and even consumers, along with their national and international operations.

In fact, these banks have become department stores of credit, divided into departments by area of the world served, by industry, or by both. They are, thus, many banks within a bank, some having staffs larger than a fair-sized town and as many as 150 vice presidents and other important executives. This high degree of specialization makes it possible for these banks to be active on a continuous basis in all segments of the money market.

These Wall Street banks handle not only the great volume of financial transactions originating in New York City and from abroad, but also the *residual reckonings* on the great volume of trade and financial account money payments of the entire country. They do this as bankers' banks, that is, through their position as the center of a vast correspondent network binding them to banks throughout the world.

Such a "correspondent" bank—one has deposits approaching $2 billion from other banks—performs many services, largely free, in exchange for the deposits of out-of-town banks. One of their outstanding services is quick and direct access to the central money market in New York. And the safekeeping aspect alone of the handling of the billions of dollars of negotiable credit instruments involved in such operations is certainly not the least of the services they render other banks, and through them the entire economy. The Wall Street banks are thus not only participants in the money market, they are the bankers for the money market.

(b) *The out-of-town banks,* although linked to the New York banks, as previously set forth, are large enough in many cases to reconcile their various money market forces without having to avail themselves of the final clearing center in New York. Such banks are not only closely linked to New York, but to other banks across the country, particularly those in their own geographic area.

Although the numbers of the institutions which would thus qualify as active money market banks vary from time to time, depending on the money pressures on them, the following totals are illustrative and they are also indicative of the gradual dispersion of money market activity throughout the country: Chicago, five; Eastern Seaboard to Philadelphia, eight; West Coast, five; Midwest (outside Chicago), six; and South and Southwest, six.

(c) *Government securities dealers,* both bank and non-bank, are the next important category of money market institutions. Some five of the major banks— three in New York and two in Chicago—have functioned as government security dealers on a continuing basis. While there are a few other banks located around the country which maintain a limited market in some government securities for customers and other banks in their own banking area, only the foregoing five principal dealer banks have kept regularly in touch with the Trading Desk at the Federal Reserve Bank of New York on a continuous basis.

Active non-bank dealers in government securities are defined by Federal Reserve authorities as those who, among their other government securities operations, are prepared to make markets on a regular basis in Treasury bills (the type of security in which Federal Reserve credit control efforts are generally concentrated). There are approximately a dozen of these dealers who maintain regular contact with the Federal Reserve Trading Desk. In addition to their New York offices, they have some three dozen offices in other financial centers throughout the country.

(d) *The Federal Reserve Bank of New York,* as agent for the other Federal Reserve Banks, for the Treasury, for central foreign banks, and for its member banks, and as keeper of the legal reserves of all member banks and ultimate clearing agent of all commercial banks, is the most important single institution in the money market. Every money market transaction involves it, directly or indirectly, immediately, or ultimately. Its importance is, therefore, quite evident and basic.

(e) *Other major institutions in the money market* are the big insurance companies and other leading financial and non-financial corporations which have large sums to administer and many other activities dependent in varying degrees upon the efficient performance of that market. In addition, there are the investment banking firms, the "over-the-counter" dealers in securities, and the stock brokerage firms.

These firms, although chiefly engaged in furnishing a primary market for capital issues of equities and longer-term debt or a secondary market for such securities after issue, also engage to some extent in money market activities. Such activities include, particularly, the tapping of that market for the large volume of funds needed to carry on their operations from time to time, as well as the lesser amounts used regularly. The same applies to the traders and the trading in the major commodity markets, although the amounts involved are far smaller.

5. *Five markets for money.* The money market is really a collection of markets—five in all. These submarkets are closely related in some respects and quite distinct in others. Their common denominator is that they all deal in the same medium—money. But, after that, the similarity largely gives way to diversity. Moreover, each of these divisions of the over-all money market is important enough from the standpoint of size, service rendered, and impact on the economy, to warrant specific consideration.

Accordingly, this will be done in succeeding sections for: (1) the commercial paper market, in which blocks of promissory notes of the larger business organizations are bought and sold; (2) the bankers acceptance market, in which obligations arising out of the financing of foreign transactions and domestic commodities are traded; (3) the loans to brokers and dealers market, in which the distribution of new securities and secondary markets for outstanding securities are financed; (4) the Federal funds market, in which reserve balances are adjusted and transfers requiring Federal funds are made; and, (5) the short-term government securities market, in which a heavy volume of government borrowing has been carried since World War II. (It is also the market which the money managers use when they want to increase, or decrease, the volume of bank credit.)

Review

Distinguish between the capital market and the money market

Explain: "The money market is . . . a concept of the many forces of demand and supply for liquid and near-liquid funds."

Why is the central money located in Wall Street?

Sketch the services rendered by the New York money market to the economy.

Specifically, how does the New York money market serve the commercial banks?

What makes the money market an "open" market?

How do the money market banks differ from the 14,-000 odd other banks in America?

List the major institutions in the money market.

CHAPTER XV

The Money Market *(Continued)*

1. *The commercial paper market.* The commercial paper market is the oldest of the various divisions of the money market. It is essentially a supplementary borrowing avenue for corporations wanting to increase their short-term financing, or desiring to spread their loans among a large number of lenders rather than to rely entirely on credit from their regular banks.

The debt instruments used are promissory notes, generally unsecured, running from a few days to 18 months, signed by one borrower and ranging from $5,000 to $1,000,000 or more in size. The typical piece of commercial paper, however, is one of a block of such notes with denominations far under a million, and has a maturity of three to six months. They are made payable to bearer, or to "ourselves," and endorsed so that they are negotiable by delivery—in other words, the bill broker and subsequent holders do not have to assume the financial responsibility of endorsement.

The number of organizations utilizing the commercial paper market in recent times has been only some 10 per cent of those borrowing through it in 1920. In fact, commercial paper had practically disappeared (it had dropped to approximately $150 million in outstandings at the end of World War II), until the booms of the 1950's caused sales finance companies to turn to this market in increasing numbers.

Even with the aid of this revival and the pressure of tight money, the notes of only some 90 finance companies and approximately 345 of our leading corporations, all with high credit ratings, were being carried recently in the open market in New York City. Moreover, total outstandings have, in general, been well under $1 billion for the paper placed through dealers. On the other hand, the finance-company paper placed directly by the finance companies has, at times, approached $4 billion.

One of the reasons for its limited size is that not every company which wants to borrow in the commercial paper market can meet the high standards which prevail for such borrowers. Most such paper is listed with an organization known as the National Credit Office which appraises the credit standing of the borrowers. Only the top companies in an industry, with capital of $250 thousand to $10 million, or more, are able to qualify for their listing. Moreover, it is customary for buyers to use options under which they have up to fourteen days to check the credit standing of borrowers and to return the paper, if they are not satisfied.

While most of the sales finance companies market their notes through dealers, there has been a steadily growing tendency for the larger ones, following the long-standing example of General Motors Acceptance

Corporation, to sell directly to investors. In these latter organizations, the finance company itself performs the dealer's functions of locating buyers and arranging purchase terms. In general, this consists of a standing offer to sell their paper (notes) in *any desired denomination,* at various rates of discounts, for any number of days from 5 to 270, and occasionally more. Although less than a dozen large finance companies place their paper directly, they account for nearly four-fifths of all outstanding commercial paper.

Historically, such commercial paper was bought almost exclusively by banks as secondary reserves. But, in more recent years, they have been joined by an increasing number of non-financial corporations which today hold more than half of the total outstandings.

2. *The bankers acceptance market.* Bankers acceptances are a comparatively recent arrival in our money market. Although they were devised by merchant bankers in the City of London in the early nineteenth century, their use in the United States dates roughly from the inauguration of the Federal Reserve System in 1913. Shortly thereafter, World War I gave this method of financing a great impetus, so that it became widely used in the 1920's. After a sharp decline during the Great Depression of the 1930's, the use of such acceptances staged a notable resurgence after World War II, until today the bankers acceptance is again an important borrowing instrument of the short-term market.

Bankers acceptance financing is an ingenious method whereby a bank lends its name rather than its credit. The bankers acceptance itself is a draft drawn on a bank ordering it to pay a specified sum of money at a determinable future time to a third party. It is drawn under a *formal* financial arrangement known as a commercial letter of credit, and when the bank on which it is drawn indicates its acceptance of the draft by writing "accepted" across its face, followed by an authorized signature, it becomes a bankers acceptance. This is readily salable at a favorable rate of discount as the bank is the primary obligor. As for liquidation, one day before due date, the organization for which the bank made the acceptance turns funds over to the bank so the acceptance can be paid on the day it falls due.

Thus, by means of the bankers acceptance, a bank, without having to lay out a dollar of its own, turns the debt of the importer or a merchant into what in effect is a cashier's check, payable at a future date. For this service, the bank charges a fee for the commercial credit, and the purchaser deducts discount on the acceptance at the prevailing market rate. This rate, naturally, will be even nearer the riskless rate of interest than the commercial paper rate mentioned earlier.

Since bankers acceptances are virtually riskless, short-term, negotiable instruments, they are highly liquid and thus are largely purchased by commercial banks as secondary reserves. The Federal Reserve

Banks also buy them from time to time through the Federal Open Market Committee, in connection with their money management activities. Foreign central and commercial banks are also important buyers.

Although they are bought and sold in the open market, most of the buying and selling is by the banks themselves. Fewer than half a dozen firms in New York City, most of them engaged primarily in dealings in government and other securities, act as dealers in bankers acceptances. Moreover, such trading is a minor part of their activities.

Since bankers acceptances largely arise out of foreign trade transactions, New York City, as might be expected, accounts for some 70 per cent of all such financing, and San Francisco is next with some 15 per cent, followed by Dallas with 5 per cent and Boston with 4 per cent.

3. *Loans to brokers and dealers.* Call loans for the purpose of carrying securities formerly constituted an important market for bank funds. Since they were impersonal, being arranged through the money desk on the New York Stock Exchange, and callable at any time after twenty-four hours, they were widely used by the money market banks to adjust their reserve positions. Since the abolition of the money desk at the Exchange in 1946, however, they are comparable to other customer loans, since they are negotiated directly with the banks and are rarely called to adjust a reserve position. Moreover, with the higher margin require-

ments of recent years, they have also declined in volume.

Loans to brokers and dealers today are as likely to be time loans as call loans. Moreover, in times of tight money, they are frequently negotiated with lenders other than the money market banks, oftentimes with out-of-town lenders. So, the brokers loan market no longer has the great significance it had in bygone years when the banks were criticized for permitting credit to be too closely tied to stock market activity.

4. *The Federal funds market.* The Federal funds market started in the 1920's when New York City banks began trading reserves to adjust their reserve position and avoid the penalties of reserve deficiencies. This trading has developed until transfers approaching a billion dollars a day may be made by the some 200 banks which regularly participate in the "buying" and "selling" of these excess reserve balances at the Federal Reserve Bank of their district.

Since the typical trading unit is $1 million, a national bank to participate (because of the 10 per cent limitation on loans to one interest, since such a transaction is in effect a one-day loan for which the borrower pays one day's interest) must have a combined capital and surplus of $10 million, which excludes most banks with deposits of less than $100 million. Furthermore, most smaller banks find that the investment of such excess funds costs more than it is worth to them. They find it more attractive to operate in such Federal funds indirectly through repurchase and similar arrangements involving government securities.

Purchases of Treasury bills with agreement to resell the following day (or with simultaneous sale for repayment tomorrow) are considered loans secured by government securities, and are permissible up to 100 per cent of capital and surplus. This method is also sometimes used by the larger banks, especially when surpluses are large enough to necessitate several separate transactions under the 10 per cent rule.

Federal funds are "purchased" through the buyer giving the seller a regular check drawn on itself, payable through the clearing house the next day, in return for the seller's check drawn on the Federal Reserve Bank, which makes the reserve balance instantly available. The "bank wire" connecting more than 200 commercial banks in 60 large cities and the Federal Reserve leased wire system connecting the twelve Banks, their 24 branches, the Board of Governors in Washington, and the Treasury offices in Washington and Chicago may be used in the same fashion to transfer funds, especially from one Federal Reserve district to another.

The rate for Federal funds varies from day to day, and, at times, from hour to hour, but it is, except for unexpected, sharp squeezes of a temporary character in the money market, always below the discount rate. The charge is calculated on the amount involved at one day's interest at the rate quoted, based on a 360-day year.

There is no centralized market or recognized "dealers" in Federal funds. There are brokers, generally members of the exchanges or security dealers, who bring buyers and sellers together, as a service in connection with handling their security transactions. Many buyers and sellers are also brought together by the New York City banks themselves, who may take trading positions, act as brokers, or act as agents in their dealings with correspondent banks.

The purchase of Federal funds by a bank accomplishes the same purpose as borrowing from the Federal Reserve Bank, but, unlike the latter, it does not increase the volume of bank reserves. It merely permits more intensive use of existing reserves. Both the widely varying availability of such funds and the imperfect nature of the market make Federal funds inadequate as a dependable source of ultimate liquidity for our commercial banking system.

In fact, buyers and sellers of such funds can safely arrange full use of their reserves only because of the assurance that they always have the discount window of the Federal Reserve Bank available for any "last resort" reserve needs in emergencies. In this connection, it should be remembered that use of Federal funds is the most temporary of all forms of borrowing. As one authority has put it, they are "here today, and gone tomorrow."

5. *The short-term government securities market.* With more than $100 billion of Treasury bills, certificates of

indebtedness, and Treasury notes (under 5 years), the short-term government securities market, at this writing, was by far the largest of the several markets comprising the money market. Moreover, treasury bills and certificates of indebtedness, all maturing within one year, amounted to more than $50 billion of the above total.

First used in this country in 1929, Treasury bills now are sold with maturities up to one year and are always issued on a discount basis. They are important from the standpoint of size, since they account for $36 billion of the $100 billion total of all short-term securities. They are thus the most important single money market instrument being used today. This popularity arises from their ability to meet the needs of large financial institutions and business firms for an income-producing investment for temporary funds that can be instantly sold for cash, with a minimum risk of loss on principal.

Treasury bills are important also because they have largely supplanted the certificate of indebtedness as the principal short-term financing device used by the government in its efforts to cushion the impact of its operations on the money market.

Treasury bills are important also because they are the principal medium through which the Federal Reserve injects and withdraws funds into and from the money market.

Although short-term government securities are the most important of the close-to-money substitutes which serve the money market, their very success sometimes affects the usefulness. In recent years, for example, such a large part of them have become virtually impounded in the precautionary reserves of large corporations, foreign central banks and other holders, that the proportion of them marginally available for the traditional needs of the money market in settling interbank reserve differences and reconciling shifts in the liquidity preferences of investors has become smaller and less assured. Thus, whereas in the immediate postwar years (1946–1950 inclusive), combined Federal Reserve commercial bank holdings of short-term governments averaged four-fifths of the total supply, recently, this has been running at less than two-fifths.

6. *Money market rates.* The keystone of the entire money market rate structure is the discount rate of the Federal Reserve Banks. Fluctuating around this, although generally below it, is the rate for Treasury bills established at the weekly auctions. Loosely related to these are the rates on bankers acceptances, and somewhat higher are the rates on commercial paper.

Then would come the "one-year" rates on government securities, followed by the rates on the various other government securities with maturities of less than five years. This would customarily be followed by the bank lending rates on stock exchange collateral, and the considerably more stable (since it is a *posted,* rather than negotiated rate) "prime rate" of the large money market banks.

The most significant rate in determining the spot state of the money market would be the rate for "Federal funds." Probably next in importance, as an indicator of the degree of ease or strain prevailing in the market, would be the dealer loan rate posted by the leading money market banks around 11 o'clock each morning, after appraising the effects of their clearings and all other developments likely to affect their money position that day.

The pattern of these rates, however, changes with the changes in the liquidity preference of investors. Some of these changes in recent years have been striking indeed, but space does not permit further discussion of them.

7. *Relation of the money market to the economy.* Thirteen thousand *independent* banks make the money market as a coordinating, integrating factor much more important in America than in other countries with a few very large banks, each with many branches under the same control. In contrast to such branch banks which merely notify head office that they need more funds, independent banks needing funds must turn to some external source. This means that they must rely on another commercial bank, on the Federal Reserve Bank of their district, or on the money market. There is no other way, as a practical matter, for them to recoup their liquidity.

Since practically all financial and business transactions, most of which are unpredictable, affect a bank's reserve position, the service rendered by the money market in bridging such gaps is easy to see.

In sum, the money market is a series of sub-markets in which the demands for and the supplies of short-term credit meet and are reconciled. It is closely related and partly dependent upon other markets. This is particularly true of the New York money market which is national and international in its scope, largely due to its close relation to our large and well organized markets for securities, commodities and foreign exchange.

And, finally, the money market furnishes the ultimate in dependable liquidity in a world where such assurance is sorely needed.

Review

Sketch the commercial paper market, emphasizing its size, participants, and method of operation.

Sketch the bankers acceptance market, emphasizing its size, participants, and method of operation.

How are loans to brokers and dealers arranged?

Describe the operation of the Federal funds market.

Why is the Federal funds rate of such primary significance?

Explain the importance of the short-term government securities market.

What is the keystone of the money market interest rate structure? Why?

What is the relation between bank reserves and the services rendered by the money market?

CHAPTER XVI

Credit and Money Management

1. *Credit and money management.* The American people take their money for granted. To them, money management or, more properly, credit management, is like the heart, conveniently forgotten until they are confronted with a *fait accompli*. Even many bankers pay too little attention to the slowly maturing process of money management (which will be the term generally used in this chapter, since it is the one with which people are most familiar), until it is too late for them to take the necessary steps to protect their institutions from adverse effects or, at least, too late to reap the rewards of effects favorable to their operations.

Waiting until the harvest of monetary action materializes is a luxury which most banks cannot afford and which well-managed banks *will not* afford. The same, of course, can be said for non-banking business concerns. In fact, the flexible monetary policies of today make anticipation of monetary policies and the trends in money rates and availability of credit of vital importance to any business.

2. *Definition of money management.* In the broad sense, money management means the utilization by a

government of its monetary and fiscal powers for the purpose of influencing domestic business conditions. Thus, money and banking, evolved for the purpose of facilitating the exchange of goods and services, are no longer merely handmaidens of industry and trade, but are now powerful instruments for achieving the economic, fiscal and social policies of the government in power. In this vein, the Employment Act of 1946 directs the federal government "to coordinate and utilize all its plans, functions, and resources . . . to promote maximum employment, production, and purchasing power."

Money management is thus legally constituted as a social and economic weapon with preconceived goals spelled out in categoric terms. Although important aspects of this control of money have been delegated to the Federal Reserve Board and the twelve Federal Reserve Banks with statutory safeguards to their independence, control of the supply of money is becoming increasingly recognized as a government function. It is even an issue, and often a major one, in our national political campaigns.

Another important reason for the great influence of the federal government in this field is our enormous national debt of over $350 billion. Such a large public debt, obviously, must be managed; and its management, just as obviously, is bound to have a powerful effect on money management. This debt, which is the very cornerstone of our financial structure, must be constantly kept in mind in any consideration of money management.

3. *Goals of money management.* The goal of our monetary authorities, in the language of the Federal Reserve Act, is "to furnish an elastic currency" and "to prevent injurious credit expansion or contraction,"— in other words, to keep the economy sound by preventing excesses and, at the same time, *to provide the banks with sufficient reserves to enable them to finance the growth in our economy arising from the increase in population and the rise in our standard of living.*

In providing the reserves for this growth, however, they must be especially careful not to overdo it, since that could only result in inflation which, in turn, would have deflation as an inevitable consequence. When production is near capacity, an increase in the money supply can lead only to higher prices, followed, or accompanied, by higher wages, thus setting in motion a spiral between prices and wages. Under such conditions, an increase in the money supply obviously would not lead to increased production or greater productivity.

Another goal is to lower *real* prices through promoting competition by maintaining stability of the dollar.

Still another aim is to assist the Treasury in financing the great public debt mentioned earlier.

Since 1960, another aim or, rather, responsibility has been to aid in the protection of the international value of our dollar. After long years of a gold surplus, weakness of the dollar in the international markets caused such an outflow of gold in the 1958–60 period that the monetary authorities found it necessary to weigh carefully the effect of their policies on our gold position. While domestic considerations are still the paramount factors motivating their actions, they can no longer be unmindful of foreign reaction to their money management and the government's fiscal policies.

Another objective, although seldom mentioned in the literature of banking, is to maintain the maximum degree of independence from the political and economic pressure groups which continually harass our money managers.

In short, the money managers' basic purpose is to try to avoid the classic boom and bust of the business cycle by "spreading out the good times" and limiting the rate of growth of the economy to a sustainable one.

4. *Determinants of monetary policy.* As might be expected, there can be many determinants of monetary policy. Such policy is not made in a vacuum. On the contrary, it arises from the manifold and multifarious activities of our vast and complex economy. Moreover, at times, certain factors—such as, for example, market support of government securities—determine policy to the virtual exclusion of other factors. In the main, however, the monetary authorities determine their policies on the basis of the following major factors.

Employment is probably the most important determinant of their policy under normal conditions. Since the Federal Reserve Board, and, in fact, the entire System, is a creature of the Congress and could be abolished by a Joint Resolution in a matter of minutes, the money managers cannot be unmindful of the political tides. Since unemployment is "political dynamite" these days, they are very sensitive to any increases above politically tolerable levels.

The *movement of prices* is also high on the list of the factors determining their policies. Sharp price increases or, for that matter, decreases, too, loose a barrage of public criticism of the money managers. So they go to extreme lengths to avoid blame for any sharp or unusual price movements. In other words, they try to establish policies which will prevent such changes and, if not prevented, which will enable them to shift the responsibility to non-monetary factors.

Business activity, particularly the volume of trade, is another basic determinant of Federal Reserve policy. This is particularly important because our government is so largely dependent on the corporate and individual income tax for its revenues that any consequential slackening in business throws the federal budget out of balance, and the Treasury immediately, as a general rule, resorts to deficit financing through the sale of government securities to the commercial banks. As this is definitely inflationary, the Federal Reserve Board, naturally, tries to prevent it from happening by easing credit when business falters.

The needs of the Treasury are another important consideration in policy determination. The central bank cannot turn its back on the needs and the problems of the Treasury with the public debt exceeding $335 billion and annual government expenditures reaching over $135 billion. Although there has been much noble talk of divorcing our monetary authorities from any responsibility for the public debt, the plain fact is that so long as our commercial banks have over $50 billion of government securities on their balance sheets and the Federal Reserve Banks themselves hold additional billions of such securities, the money managers have a direct interest in the prices of government securities which talk cannot gainsay.

International considerations also necessarily weigh heavily, especially at certain times, in the determination of Federal Reserve policies. As indicated earlier, any policy which makes the dollar cheap domestically also makes it cheap internationally and leads to a gold outflow. This must be kept within the bounds of our capabilities and our governmental aims.

5. *Two aspects of monetary policy.* Monetary policy, or credit control, can be either qualitative or quantitative, or both. Most students of banking prefer qualitative controls, such as, for example, the margin requirements on security loans. They reason that specific regulation of a particular field enables the central bank to put the medicine on the "spot that hurts." By localizing the impact of their actions, they do not run the

risk of adversely affecting a field which may already be suffering deflationary pressures or, of course, *vice versa*. Qualitative controls are effective and direct. They can cure an undesirable development almost instantly, without adversely affecting other borrowers or the economy in general.

In sharp contrast to the theoreticians, most commercial bankers and central bankers oppose selective controls on the grounds of interference with the free market. They maintain that any qualitative control limits the ability of the market to allocate resources on the basis of the forces of supply and demand, as reflected by the prevailing rates of interest in the respective fields. Also, they are no doubt influenced in their attitude by their first-hand knowledge of how difficult it is to apply such controls with fairness and public approval. Those who have had experience with such controls, particularly the regulation of consumer credit, feel that the criticism engendered more than outweighs their additional effectiveness, as compared with general credit control.

Opposition of the men who have to administer the qualitative controls notwithstanding, it seems clear that they should be used in fields which do not move in unison with the general economy. Consumer credit is a good example of such a field. Since interest rates in this field are higher than in most other fields, consumer credit is affected but little, if any, by quantitative credit control and a general increase in interest rates.

The commercial banker always finds plenty of money for consumer borrowers, regardless of how tight money may be for other borrowers.

Construction, in general, and housing, in particular, would also seem to be especially suited for qualitative controls, with standards fitted to the special factors obtaining at a given time and under a given outlook. However, such controls, if used, should, in all fairness, and to be effective, embrace all lenders and not merely the member banks of the Federal Reserve System.

It should be kept in mind, however, that there is considerably more qualitative credit control than is generally realized. In the mortgage field, for example, FHA requirements, the policies of the Home Loan Banks, the activities of the Federal National Mortgage Association (Fannie Mae), and the Federal Reserve Banks' attitude on "warehousing" mortgages, all have heavy qualitative aspects. The same may be said of the activities of the Federal Small Business Administration and the other special considerations extended to small business borrowers.

Also, one of the most valid criticisms of general credit control, although it is vigorously disputed by the commercial banks, is that general credit control has an undesirable qualitative effect, since small concerns find it much more difficult to get credit in times of credit restraint than the larger corporations with better credit standing and more powerful banking connections.

Whatever else may be said about it, selective credit

control can prevent a dangerous deterioration in the character and soundness of loans in a particular field, in periods of rising prices and booming sales. Since speculation breeds speculation, "wild blue yonder" situations which endanger the entire economy may develop in particular fields. It is for this reason, for example, that Regulation T and Regulation U controlling security loans have been promulgated by the Federal Reserve Board. The bitter experience of 1929 and the years immediately thereafter taught us the hard lesson that we cannot afford the luxury of the free market for such credit if it permits such unbridled speculation and economic distortion that the entire economy is pulled down.

Likewise, in consumer credit, there is danger that intense competition may force lenders to so liberalize their credit terms that the sales of consumer durable goods are in economic effect little more than rental arrangements. When such "borrowers" do not have any real equity (ownership) in the article "purchased," it is very easy for them to decide to walk away from their obligation upon the appearance of any economic adversity.

The leaders in this field recognize the danger and continually campaign for maintenance of sound credit terms. Clearly, if they are not able to maintain the integrity of their credit by private action, selective credit control will be necessary, since the entire economy should not be made to suffer the adverse consequences of unwise credit extension in a particular segment of the whole.

6. *Techniques of quantitative credit control.* The Federal Reserve Board, which administers our quantitative credit control, has various tools at its disposal. A basic one which is rarely mentioned, since it is embedded in the Federal Reserve Act and in years of administrative rulings and is thus not flexible, is the determination of eligibility for access to the primary credit of the Federal Reserve Banks. In recent years, the almost universal use of government securities for replenishing the reserve accounts of the member banks has made eligibility of relatively minor importance. But it should be kept in mind, since circumstances conceivably could arise where this power to separate the "sheep from the goats" might again become of controlling importance for a particular industry.

Open market operations are by far the most widely used and the most important credit control mechanism of the money managers. Open market operations comprise the buying and selling of government securities and, to a very small extent, bankers acceptances by the Federal Reserve Bank of New York, under the direction of the Federal Open Market Committee, for the account of all twelve of the Federal Reserve Banks. Purchases of government securities are ordinarily confined to the shortest maturities, particularly Treasury bills, to minimize the interference with the *pattern* of interest rates established by the free market. This leaves it up to market forces to translate the easing or tightening of short-term credit to the long-term market.

It should be noted that all such operations must be conducted through the Open Market Committee—no individual Federal Reserve Bank is permitted to buy or sell obligations on its own motion. Otherwise, the different Federal Reserve Banks, like Stephen Leacock's famous horseman, might be going in all directions at once.

As the reader will remember, purchases of assets by the Federal Reserve Banks necessarily supply the member banks with reserve balances, since there must be an offsetting liability (credit to a deposit account, in this case) to the asset increase. Conversely, sale of assets reduces member bank reserve balances, since payment can be made only through a member bank. Non-banking institutions and non-member banks do not have deposit accounts at the Federal Reserve Banks.

Purchases and sales are not only made for the purpose of tightening or easing credit, they are also made to offset the strains of *abnormal* conditions, such as war, and *temporary* conditions, such as the outflow of currency at the Christmas season (which reduces the reserves of the member banks, since all currency must be secured from the Federal Reserve Bank of the district *via* reduction of the deposit account of the bank securing the currency), and such as short-term movements of gold to, and from, our monetary gold stock.

Other temporary influences on member bank reserves, which are offset by open market operations, are heavy transfers of funds from the member banks to or from Treasury account and abnormal changes in "float," i.e., uncollected checks held by the Reserve Banks for which credit has been given to the depositing member banks.

By neutralizing abnormal and temporary influences, the monetary authorities prevent such forces from interfering with their maintenance of the desired degree of ease or of tightness in the money market.

Open market operations are also used to make changes in the discount rate effective. For example, an increase in the discount rate brings no direct pressure on the member banks when they are not borrowing. But open market operations can quickly eliminate excess reserves and bring them to the discount window of their Federal Reserve Bank. Open market operations thus make changes in the discount rate effective particularly on the "up" side. In other words, it is possible (in the more serious recessions in business activity) that the member banks may let the newly-created reserves of credit ease lie idle as *excess* reserves, but they have no such choice when reserves are eliminated under a policy of credit restraint.

Discount rate change is the traditional weapon of the money managers. In fact, open market operations became important only after experience over a considerable period of years indicated their greater efficiency. Evolution based on our experience in money management has now relegated the discount rate to a "stop, look and listen" warning signal. Changes in the discount rate trumpet the views of the money managers with respect to the money market and credit availability. *But,* they may have been putting their views into effect even before the change in the discount rate, since such changes in recent years have generally *followed* rather than *led* the market.

This might be as good a place as any to observe that the frequent charge that the Federal Reserve "likes" high interest rates is not warranted. Like nearly everyone else, they prefer low interest rates, but they also know, as the distinguished central banker, Allan Sproul, the then head of the Federal Reserve Bank of New York, so pointedly put it, "The country cannot afford to keep money cheap at all times and in all circumstances if the counterpart of that action is inflation, rising prices and a progressive deterioration in the purchasing power of the dollar."

Changes in reserve requirements have been another important tool of the monetary authorities since the beginning of World War II. This is another device arising from our actual experience with money management. Changes in reserve requirements are unquestionably very direct and very powerful. They have a sort of "meat ax" finality. This means the Federal Reserve Board must use its power to change requirements with great discretion and, of course, within the limits set by law on reserves. Open market operations are clearly far preferable to changes in reserve percentages, particularly as an instrument for the restriction of credit.

Moral suasion is another tool of monetary policy which is widely used in many other countries, especially where the banking system consists of a mere handful of private banks. But, here in America, where we have such a large number of banks and competition is so keen, not only among the banks, but, also, between them and the many non-bank lending agencies, moral suasion obviously has far less chance of success.

So, although most American bankers are receptive to appeals for cooperation from the monetary authorities, moral suasion is not heavily relied on. In fact, the Federal Reserve authorities do their best to refrain from making such appeals, although circumstances do arise where they feel it incumbent upon them to marshall banking support for a particular policy.

7. *Results achieved by money management.* It is difficult to measure the contributions of money management. The real measure of its success is a comparison of what did happen with what might have happened, and that becomes hypothetical, indeed.

Despite much criticism, especially from the advocates of cheap money, who often cloak their criticism in other guises, money management has many solid successes.

First, and most important, we no longer have currency problems. From the first settlement on these shores, currency plagued us in one way or another. That is all a matter of the past now, thanks to the Federal Reserve System.

Second, extreme fluctuations in interest rates are also now things of the past. Interest rates depend on the supply and demand of credit. The money managers can *increase* or *reduce* the supply at will; and they can *influence* the demand. So, their influence on interest rates is indeed great.

Third, extreme fluctuations in business activity have been prevented since the end of World War II. While many new structural economic stabilizers have contributed to this happy result, more able money management is certainly entitled to some credit for it.

Money management is often blamed in political campaigns as retarding economic growth. Such criticism largely stems from the popular fallacy, endemic in America, that we don't have enough money. People who cannot borrow all the money they would like to have to carry through their plans feel that, as a result, the economy is held back. High interest rates, they maintain, are proof that there is not enough money. On the contrary, high interest rates mean that an economy is undeveloped and has no consequential ability to create capital, or, if not, it is enjoying booming business activity. One thing certain, dead economies do not have high interest rates.

8. *Problems of money management.* Despite its successes, money management still has serious short-

comings. Prices still fluctuate; inflation is an ever-present danger, although it may be temporarily quiescent; business activity still has its ups and downs. Although money management certainly cannot cure these economic problems by itself, it must ever strive to do more in this respect.

Money management faces many problems, the more important of which will be briefly outlined.

First, there is a lag, generally of 6 to 9 months, in the response of the economy to Federal Reserve actions affecting reserves. Moreover, the reaction is not mathematically determinable, so money management is still an art and not a science.

Second, the quantity of money is no longer as important as it was in the past. Today, the quantity of money simply means the extent people desire to hold their savings in the most liquid form. The huge volume of near-money—time deposits, E and H bonds, cash value of life insurance policies, etc.,—greatly complicates the problem of the money managers, since it makes the economy so liquid that their actions can be to a considerable extent circumvented.

Third, the increasing importance of the financial intermediaries—the insurance companies, sales finance companies, small loan companies, etc.,—over whose lending activities the monetary authorities can exercise no direct control, is becoming an increasingly serious problem.

Fourth, it should always be remembered that

money has two dimensions—quantity and rapidity of use, or turnover. The monetary authorities cannot control the turnover, or velocity. As a result, by increasing turnover, the public can go far in offsetting the effects of tight money, and *vice versa*.

Fifth, the problem of the relation of the Treasury, with its huge debt and heavy financial requirements, and the Federal Reserve Board is still very much with us.

9. *Dangers faced by money management.* Money management has always developed fatal shortcomings in the past. There is a very real danger that this may happen again. Pressure groups never give up. Labor, in particular, has been very critical of post-World War II money management. Yet, our Gross National Product and, also, Personal Income After Taxes increased nearly 4 per cent a year in *real dollars.*

There is always the danger that Federal Reserve credit policy (i.e., monetary policy) will become a permanent partisan issue. In such event, our only hope would be an economically informed electorate. With regard to this, Mr. Sproul (who was previously quoted) observed: "Our failure—to the extent that we failed— was a failure to gain sufficient understanding and acceptance for our policies. The influence of a central bank depends a lot on tradition—on the belief that its actions will be wise, timely, and effective."

The gold standard of happy memory left economic affairs to be shaped by economic forces, rather than by governmental intervention. Money management is an effort to cushion those forces and shape them to fit better our social needs. In short, for the mechanical brute force of the gold standard, we have substituted the flexibility of managed money. Whether it succeeds or not depends on us—it cannot succeed alone.

Review

What is meant by the term "money management"?

What are the goals of money management?

List the determinants of monetary policy.

Explain the two dimensions of money.

Contrast quantitative and qualitative credit control.

Explain exactly how quantitative credit control affects business activity.

List the three main instruments of credit control and explain their relative importance under today's conditions.

Compare the shortcomings and the successes of money management in the United States.

In one word, what is the ever-pressing danger faced by money management.

CHAPTER XVII

Meet Your Bank

1. *Importance of a good banking connection.* The importance of a good banking connection can hardly be overemphasized. The word "connection" is used advisedly as it connotes the relationship which should exist between customer and bank. When the business man uses the phrase, "my bank," he should mean exactly that. In no other business field should the relationship be as close as between the bank and its customers.

Unfortunately, this is not always the case. Such a situation may be the result of shortcomings of the bank. If so, the customer should look for another bank —there are plenty of them and competition among them is very keen. On the other hand, the unsatisfactory relationship may be due to the shortcomings of the customer in not knowing what the bank has a right to expect and what he (the customer, corporate or individual) has a right to expect.

This chapter sets forth the typical relationships and points of contact which arise between banker and customer. By studying them, you can easily see what to expect and will be in a position to determine whether you are getting the vitally important banking service to which you are entitled in these days of keen competition.

2. *Selecting a bank.* Most people are very casual in their choice of a bank. They are likely to select it solely on the basis of convenient availability or because of continued (maybe the word should be "incessant") advertising appeal or some other factor, to the comparative neglect of the more important considerations which should govern such an important choice.

The larger corporations are anything but casual in the selection of their banking connections. They usually maintain a group in the Treasurer's Department charged with the responsibility of recommending to top management the banks that should be used, the particular purpose for which each bank should be used, and the "wherewithal" (compensating balance, loans, foreign exchange business, etc.,) that the corporation will have to offer to get that service.

Moreover, this group keeps close watch on the performance of the bank after the account is opened. It even goes so far as to make personal calls on the banks in a continuing effort to make these relationships mutually profitable. And they must be mutually profitable, since the banker cannot take care of his customers in hard times if he has been starved in boom times by their patronizing non-bank lenders.

The first thing in selecting a banking connection is to decide what you need and want from a bank. All banks have much greater familiarity with some lines than with others. For example, you certainly wouldn't go to a money market bank in Wall Street for a crop loan. And, by the same token, you wouldn't go to the Bank of Lost Creek, Kentucky, for a broker's loan.

After you decide the various services you need from a bank, your next job is to find the bank which renders those services in the highest degree, subject always, of course, to the prerequisite that it must be reasonably accessible to you. This does not mean, however, that it necessarily has to be the closest bank. After all, if, as the advertising sloganeers put it, people will "walk a mile" for a cigarette, they ought to be willing to go far enough to get the best banking service, in view of its basic contribution to success in business, or in life, for that matter.

3. *Head office or branch?* There was a time when it was worth-while, especially for the business man, to have an account at the head office rather than a branch, when such alternatives had to be considered. In those days, head office held a tight rein on the branches. Decisions were too greatly centralized. As a result, quicker and better service was available at the head office, if the size of balance warranted keeping the account there rather than in the neighborhood branch. Fortunately, those differences, which were essentially problems of managerial control, have been largely surmounted.

Today, because of the closer contact possible with the limited number of officers in a branch, the more intimate relationship may very well lead to better service than could be had at the head office with its hosts of officers and employees. So, there is no structural reason why you should avoid a branch, if the choice must be made. On the contrary, in states where branch banking prevails, such as California, as a general rule, customers prefer the branches. They seem to be not only satisfied but actually enthusiastic about the service they receive at such branches.

The main thing, of course, especially in the choice of a business banking connection, is to select a *banker* in whom you will have confidence and, even more important, who will have confidence in you. And by banker, we do not mean the president or chairman of the board, or some other distant higher-up. We mean the bank officer—vice president, manager, assistant manager, or who-not—on the firing line with whom you will have to do business. So far as you are concerned, he is the bank. And as you probably know, "the chief difference between banks is the people in them!"

4. *Opening an account.* After considerable study and a process of elimination, the extent of which will be determined by the choices available, you are ready to begin negotiations with the bank you have tentatively selected. This should be done as formally as the circumstances warrant, and in no event should it be rushed. The potential rough spots in the relationship should be ironed out then, rather than later. In short,

there should be utter frankness on both sides, or else the result may be a business *mésalliance* which will not be good for either.

Competition is so keen that many banks do not stand on ceremony where a new account is concerned. But even though they may require only a signature card as the "Open Sesame" to the bank's facilities, it is to the definite advantage of the potential customer to clearly set forth what he expects—and what he offers. After all, it isn't a one-way street, as pointed out before.

Proper procedure in opening an account would involve, first, the presentation of a letter of introduction to the appropriate bank officer, if there is no antecedent account in any bank. On the other hand, if it is merely a transfer from a bank in another part of the country, or from a nearby bank, because of dissatisfaction on the part of either the previous banker or the applicant, a letter of "honorable dismissal" from the other bank should be presented and made a part of the record. (The new bank will find out anyway, so it is best to record frankly why the transfer is being made.)

A new depositor form should then be completed. This will indicate the average balance that will be maintained and the probable number of deposits and checks which will be put through the account each month. It will, in addition, ask for certain descriptive personal data, such as age, nearest relatives, present and former addresses, previous bank accounts, other current bank accounts, business connections, etc.

This completed blank serves as the basis for a very frank discussion with the new account officer as to minimum balance requirements, methods of computing the minimum balance, relation of account activity to the balances maintained, service charges, and the facilities and policies of the bank, in general.

At this point, it is well to make clear the credit accommodation which will be needed. It is even a good idea to talk to the actual loaning officer with whom future dealings will be required. If the bank's policies or the loan officer's policies will preclude the credit accommodation desired, it is better to have the matter out in the open in advance than to wait until the issue actually arises—possibly on an emergency basis.

These negotiations may indicate that the tentative selection is unwise; in such event, the process must be repeated, if there are alternatives. If there are no other banks which will offer better arrangements, obviously, the would-be depositor must rearrange his plans. In other words, he "must cut his cloth to fit," since a good banking connection is absolutely indispensable to success in today's highly competitive world.

If, however, the decision is to go ahead, based on the belief of both the bank and the potential customer that the connection would be a happy, fruitful and profitable one, signature cards are filled out and a deposit account is opened by an actual deposit.

If the depositor is a corporation, a resolution of the board of directors authorizing the opening of the account must, in addition, be filed with the bank. Board authorization for drawing checks on the account must also be given the bank. Since the corporate officer authorized to make the deposits will often not be the one authorized to make withdrawals, separate resolutions are generally required.

5. *Kind of deposit account.* Demand deposits may be in either a special checking account or a regular account.

Special checking accounts have a wide variety of copyright-protected trade names, such as Check Master, Autocheck, Thrifty Check and Check-o-matic, but they all have two things in common regardless of the actual plan—there is no minimum balance requirement, and a *per item* charge is made at the time of the event for each item of activity. Typically, this is 10 cents for each check paid plus a flat charge of 50 cents per month for maintenance of the account. The regular charges of the bank generally apply for any other services rendered. It should be understood that these are actual out-of-pocket deductions and not *computed* charges in deposit analysis.

Special checking accounts in some banks run as high as 50 per cent of the total *number* of demand deposit accounts, but in dollars such accounts vary from 0 (some banks do not offer them) to 10 per cent, with the volume for the entire country well under 5 per cent of the over-all demand deposit total.

Special checking accounts have little to offer a

normal business enterprise. They have still less to offer a young man on his way up in the business world. The reasons for this sweeping statement center around the credit relationship. Such special accounts cannot be used as a basis of credit reference, that is, such depositors cannot offer "bank references." This is of considerable importance in many business relationships, especially in the matters of fidelity bonding and the establishment of financial responsibility.

Nor does the special checking account offer much help in establishing credit standing with the bank itself. As the name clearly states, it is a "special" account and is not viewed as being in the same category as the regular accounts.

The *regular checking* account is the kind of account through which nearly all business is transacted. With it, a depositor is a full-fledged "member of the club." With it, a depositor is in position to develop his credit standing and to enlarge the scale of his banking operations as his business grows in size, and as he grows in his personal financial requirements.

Many a young man maintains a savings account, but no regular demand deposit account, during his early years in business and in school, when he would be better served by transferring a portion of his savings account to a regular checking account or, if he is not able to afford two accounts, by maintaining a regular account only. This is not to say that a savings account is not important; it is, in fact, very important.

But, to a young man on his way up in the business world, nothing can be quite so important as the development of credit standing and financial responsibility through the maintenance in good standing of a regular banking connection over a considerable period of time. Only in this way can the necessary personal relationship and character prerequisites be firmly established for a growing financial standing.

6. *The receiving tellers.* Deposits are received by the mail teller through the mail and by the receiving teller "over the window."

According to form, bank deposits may be *special deposits,* which must be returned in kind, or which must be segregated for a special purpose. The maker of such a deposit occupies a special legal position and does not become a general creditor of the bank.

But, by far, most bank deposits are *general deposits* in which the regular legal relationship of debtor and creditor arises. This distinction is academic, as a practical matter, up to $15,000 in each account, in each different "right and capacity" in all banks insured by the Federal Deposit Insurance Corporation. In other words, a particular individual may be protected for the maximum amount in more than one account, if each account is in a different right and capacity. The distinction, however, could become important to the extent that the deposits are not covered by insurance in either an insured bank (all members of the Federal Reserve System must also be members of the Federal

Deposit Insurance Corporation) or in an uninsured bank.

Demand deposits are ordinarily made by means of a deposit slip, prepared in duplicate, on which is listed the cash and the individual checks (by the banks on which they are drawn) which are being deposited, together with the total of all items. The teller quickly counts the cash, checks the indorsements on the checks to see that they have been properly made, and either manually initials the deposit slip or authenticates it by one of various machine methods so that it can serve as a receipt for the depositor.

This deposit slip is an original entry and is legally binding on the bank after it has been initialed by the teller. For this reason, banks generally require depositors to make out their own deposit slips. False claims of errors in deposits can then be successfully met by producing a deposit slip written or prepared by the depositor.

7. *The paying teller.* Originally, the tellers responsible for the bank's cash and for cashing checks presented over the window were called "paying" tellers. It was their function also to make shipments of currency and to certify checks. But, in recent years, the unit teller system, whereby the same teller is responsible for both receiving and paying, has become well-nigh universal. However, even if performed by the same individual, the functions are distinct and should be so understood.

There are many other "tellers" in the bank with whom the depositor has varying degrees of contact, such as the *note* teller, *collection* teller, etc. Their titles indicate their general responsibilities and duties.

8. *Endorsement.* Title to negotiable instruments, such as checks and notes, is transferred by endorsement and delivery or, if to bearer, by delivery only. Legally, endorsement is the act of signing the indicated name with or without qualifications, to any negotiable instrument, for the purpose of transferring it. Such endorsement is completed by the delivery of the instrument. Endorsement is, of course, always required when the negotiable instrument is a promise or an order to pay a specific payee.

Most endorsements are *in blank*, that is, the endorser merely signs his name and specifies no endorsee. Wider use, especially if the mails are used for the transport of checks for deposit, should be made of the other forms of endorsement because of the added protection they give. Thus:

A *special* endorsement specifies to whom, or to whose order the instrument is to be paid.

A *restricted* endorsement limits the endorsement to the accomplishment of some specifically indicated purpose, such as, "For deposit only in Blank Bank and Trust Company," or "Pay to Raymond Rodgers only." This restriction stops further negotiation of the instrument.

A *conditional* endorsement limits payment to the

realization of some future happening, such as "Payable to my daughter, Dianne, upon the birth of her second son," followed by the signature of the original payee.

A *qualified* endorsement is one which merely transfers title without the assumption of any responsibility for the instrument itself. Such qualification is by means of adding the words "without recourse" to the endorsement. Banks ordinarily refuse to accept such a qualified endorsement from a customer. At the same time, they frequently insist on limiting their own endorsement in this fashion.

Endorsement is of paramount importance to the bank. In fact, a good endorsement is its chief protection. With a strong endorser, the bank can always get its money back if anything goes wrong—and things often do go wrong. So, bank customers should not be unduly vexed when their bank insists on the legible, unqualified endorsement of someone whose signature is personally known to them.

Forgery has, however, unfortunately, reached such a stage that identification, other than fingerprints, may be faulty no matter how much care is exercised. Fingerprinting, of course, would be absolute identification, but it has been so long associated with criminal identification that ordinary citizens will not stand for it. It used to be thought that the messiness of the black ink used in fingerprinting was largely responsible for public hostility, but the advent of powders, which do not dirty the hands and, thus, don't have to be washed off, has improved the public attitude toward finger-printing but little.

It is estimated that American business loses nearly a billion dollars a year from *reported* instances of forgeries and fraudulent checks and other negotiable instruments, to say nothing of the many additional millions of unreported losses where the victim is so chagrined by his own failure to take the necessary precautions that he simply bears the loss in silence.

The writer of this text has seen a desk-drawer full of bad checks in a North Dakota town, on the edge of the Williston Basin oil development. The early stages of activity in that oil development attracted so many high-binders and crooks that the banks in the town, in self-defense, had to adopt a rule that they would under no circumstances cash a check for anyone who was not *personally* known to them.

The thing to keep in mind is that endorsement should be supported by *identification,* especially if money is to be paid out. As indicated before, many business men lose heavily because of faulty identification. In particular, too much reliance is often put on driver's licenses, forgeries of which have been bought for as little as ten dollars in some states. Probably the most extreme case in this respect was the merchant who refused to accept FBI credentials, the most carefully guarded credentials in the country, for identification in cashing a check, but readily accepted a driver's license.

Supermarkets, which are the greatest losers to the bad-check artists, have installed cameras and other identification devices to discourage crooks and to aid in identifying them, if they are not discouraged! While the amounts lost by banks are small compared to those of business men, they are nonetheless substantial; in fact, they would be unbearable if banks did not take the precautions they do.

9. *Certification of checks.* Many business transactions, such as the transfer of title to land and other substantial assets, require delivery of a banker's check, or a certified check.

A *banker's check* may be called a *cashier's check* or a *manager's check.* In any event, it is signed by an authorized employee or officer and is a direct liability of the bank. Banks issue such checks upon request, and payment, for a nominal fee—in fact, in some cases, without charge.

A *certified check* is the customer's own check payable to a specific payee, which the bank has certified. Certification means that the funds have been transferred from the drawer's account to "Certified Checks Outstanding Account," and the check has thus become the liability of the bank—i.e., the bank's promise to pay. As evidence of this, an officer or teller of the bank stamps or writes on the face of the check the word "Certified," "Accepted" or "Good," and affixes his signature. In this way, the bank agrees to honor the check (regardless of what happens to the drawer in the meantime) when properly endorsed and presented for payment.

There are certain features of check certification which should be known by every business man—before it is too late. For example, when a check is certified *at the request of the holder,* the maker is released from all further liability on it; but when certification is *at the request of the maker,* he remains liable to the holder if the bank, for any reason, fails to pay the check.

Also, if the maker (drawer) of a certified check finds that he cannot use it (as in the case of an unsuccessful sealed bid, for example), he should under no circumstances destroy it. Instead, he should endorse it and redeposit it in his account, so that the funds can be transferred back to him. He can do this as long as it is in his possession regardless of who the payee may be.

On the other hand, if a certified check is lost or destroyed, the maker will be required to file an indemnity bond with the bank, usually for twice the amount of the check, before his account will be credited. Otherwise, the "lost" or "destroyed" check might show up in the hands of an innocent holder for value, whom the bank would have to pay out of its own pocket. Banks are thus well within their rights in requiring an idemnity bond against this very real risk under the Negotiable Instruments Act.

It also must be remembered that banks cannot be

compelled to certify checks. They have no legal duty to do so. In fact, some banks will certify only under special circumstances, or only for the maker and never for the payee. Certification is thus a special service of the bank.

10. *Stop-payment orders.* Another point of contact, and frequent friction, is that of stop-payment orders.

No legal reason can be required of the maker for stopping payment of any check he has issued. As a result, such orders are frequently capricious and with little justification. In such event, the bank's only remedy is to close the account of the offending depositor. In the meantime, however, the stop-payment instructions must be strictly followed.

To be legally binding on the bank, the stop-payment order must be in writing and accurately describe the check to which it refers. Upon receiving such a proper stop-payment order, the bank as agent of the depositor must refuse payment, and is responsible to the depositor for failure to comply with his instructions, if the check is subsequently paid.

Since the risk of paying a check against which a "stop" has been placed is very great, because of the enormous volume of checks handled each day, banks usually have a clause in their printed "Stop-Payment" forms which limits, or even exempts, them from liability if they fail to comply with the depositor's instructions. After signing such a form, the depositor, of course, is bound by it, except in some states where such exculpatory clauses are not recognized by the courts.

Although most banks refuse to accept stop-payment instructions other than on their own printed form, in most states, other forms of stop-payment instructions are legally binding. Of course, the best thing from the standpoint of both the bank and the depositor is to avoid the necessity of stop-payments. But, if this cannot be done, and the amount involved warrants it, the depositor should consult legal counsel before signing any form which waives rights that he otherwise would have.

In an effort to reduce the number of stop-payment orders, many banks make a charge for each such order. They may also make arrangements with their heavy-volume customers not to place stops on any lost checks of less than $100, and on any lost, destroyed or stolen checks payable to reliable companies. Moreover, some banks, to reduce clerical expense, accept stop orders, but take no action whatsoever on checks of less than $25 or $50, even though they may make a charge for the stop order. They do this because they find it cheaper to assume any losses that may result than to incur the extra clerical expense and bother of trying to prevent the payment of the limited number which will be presented.

Stop-payments are a real burden to the bank. In addition to the financial risk, the clerical cost of taking the many precautions necessary to prevent accidental payment is substantial. Although the bank is legally required to give this service, it nonetheless should not be abused. If abused, it is an easy matter for the bank to require advance waiving of its liability as a condition to further carrying of the depositor's account.

Since either of these alternatives is patently undesirable, reason for such action should not be permitted to arise. In short, while stop-payment may be used, it should be used sparingly and never abused, since the bank really has the final say regardless of its legal liability to follow the depositor's instructions.

Review

What consideration should control the selection of a banking connection?

Outline the actual procedure in opening a demand deposit account at a bank.

Compare the advantages and disadvantages of a branch as opposed to head-office.

Why is a special checking account inadvisable for a young business man?

List the various kinds of endorsements and indicate where each might properly be used.

Why is *identification* so important?

Indicate the things which should be guarded against in check certification.

Why are stop-payment orders such a problem to bankers, and what can they do about it?

CHAPTER XVIII

How to Get the Most from Your Banking Connection

1. *Banking service.* Banks are anxious to give the best and broadest service possible for them to give, within the framework and limitations of legal requirements, supervisory standards, Federal Reserve regulations, banking customs, operating costs and community needs. Bankers know that high quality, growing service is the key to the future of banking. The general recognition of banking as a growth industry in recent years has added to the pressure for expansion of banking services. An increase in the volume and variety of bank services has also been a natural result of the efforts of the banks to cope with the constantly rising level of operating costs.

But banks cannot render increased service if, through lack of knowledge or just plain inertia, customers do not avail themselves of the facilities offered. Nor can they render such improved and expanded service if customers, through ignorance, are so inept and need so much guidance that the increased service is more trouble than it is worth to both customer and bank. So, another name for this chapter might well be,

"Getting Your Money's Worth," but it should be understood as applying to the bank as well as its customers.

As an indication of how you can help the bank help you, consider the simple and ever-present problem of bad checks, mentioned in the previous chapter. A "come one, come all" policy in cashing checks and laxity in the vital matter of identification by the check cashers will place a disproportionate burden on your bank, and the banking system, in the return of NA (No Account), Ins. F. (Insufficient Funds), and forged signature checks. Overloading our banks with such pointless and profitless activity and the resulting lowering of business standards naturally militate against the superior service they could and would like to provide.

It is sometimes suggested that better service can be obtained by becoming a director or, at least, a stockholder of the local bank. This overlooks the risks that a director runs in dealing with his own bank. Such dealings must be at arm's length, that is, the director must withdraw when his own loans are being considered. Even this, however, may not be sufficient protection if the bank gets into financial difficulties. Moreover, there are many legal and regulatory restrictions on loans to directors. And as for becoming a stockholder for this purpose, if the stock holdings are large enough to affect the decision of the board and the loaning officers, considerable risk is also incurred in case of financial difficulty.

But it certainly doesn't hurt to know a director or

two, and the same, of course, is true with respect to the loan officers.

2. *How to borrow from your bank.* Before you can borrow at a commercial bank, your credit standing and your reasons for borrowing must be developed to such a point, and in such a way, that you have a "bankable" proposition. No banker lends to you just because you need money—after all, who doesn't need money. The banker uses many precautions to place credit only at the disposal of those who can, and will, use it productively. Never, never let him think that you *must* have the loan or you will go under for the last time—that bankruptcy is the alternative. No one, least of all a banker, is interested in "feeding oats to a dead horse."

In short, never ask for a loan as a favor. You are either entitled to it, or not. If not, the banker would certainly be committing an "economic crime," and possibly a statutory crime, by putting unwarranted purchasing power at your disposal. On the other hand, if you are entitled to it, you are doing the banker a favor—he is making a profitable sale. So, don't, as so many business men do, shiver and shake when loan application is being made.

Remember, you are trying to sell your credit to the banker for his money. This means it is incumbent upon you carefully to organize your presentation, document it with facts, and present it with such sincerity and force that the banker is able to share your confidence in the feasibility and profitability of your plans.

There are many things you can do to make your loan more attractive to the banker. Additional security, over and above your own credit standing, which, of course, is prerequisite and paramount, may be offered through the specific pledge of accounts receivable (at many banks, but not all), through a chattel mortgage on inventory, machinery, etc., or through a mortgage on real estate. Securities also may be offered as collateral for such a loan, but before doing that, serious consideration should be given to the alternative of selling the securities and thus eliminating the need for the borrowing.

Still another method which is being more widely used each year is that of *field warehousing*. The prime purpose of field warehousing is the creation of acceptable collateral for bank loans that exceed normal open-credit-line limits. By its use, you can gain access to credit substantially in excess of the amount to which you would be entitled on an unsecured financial statement basis alone. This method of short-term financing is particularly suited to credit needs which arise out of seasonal and other regularly recurring needs for working capital.

The method employed in field warehousing is simplicity itself. First, the field warehouse company and the prospective borrower enter into a storage agreement setting forth the obligations of the two parties, the (storage) rates to be paid, and the term for which the arrangement is made. At the same time, the warehouse company obtains from the prospective borrower a lease on that portion of the premises on which the "warehoused" merchandise is to be stored.

The facilities leased may be a building, a floor in a building, or even a partitioned area of a floor; or they may consist of tanks, or a yard area. But, whatever they are, they must be used exclusively for the storage of the goods or materials pledged to secure the loan. Public notice of the special status of this merchandise is given by notices of the warehouse company placed at the public entrance to the area and near and around the goods involved. This area is then placed in charge of two or more persons employed by the field warehouse company, who keep records on the goods and release them in accordance with instructions of the lender, relayed through the warehouse company.

Control is thus established over the goods by this field warehouse method. There can be no claim by other creditors that they thought the assets were available to support their claims. This establishment of definite *dominion* over the goods is very important legally, since it gives the lender the necessary protection in case of default on the loan. Today, there is hardly an article of commerce from the rawest raw-material to the most finished finished-product that is not being used for collateral purposes somewhere in our financial system, thanks to field warehousing.

Charges for such field warehousing service are based on the value of the goods passing through the "warehouse," the rates ranging from one-half of 1 per cent (in the case of high value, very low cost operations) to 2 per cent, with the most common charge about 1 per cent.

3. *An important advantage of borrowing from your bank.* Although there are many advantages of borrowing from your own bank, the most important one is the fact that your own banker will extend more credit to you than anyone else, if you have developed your credit standing properly. There is also a little mentioned advantage of such borrowing which could prove extremely important if the bank should get into financial difficulties. This is the advantage of the equitable principle of offset, which has long been followed by our courts.

By borrowing at the same institution where you maintain your deposit account, in case of failure, you can "offset" your deposit account against your debt to the bank and, thus, salvage your deposit on a 100 per cent basis to the extent of your note. But, to do this, there must be a *mutuality* of claims—that is, the long established fundamental principle of offset. In view of the potential value of offset, when your deposit account exceeds your deposit insurance by a consequential amount, you should consult your counsel as to the operation of this principle of offset under the laws of your own state. You don't want to be debarred from using it because of a technicality, if you should happen to need it.

4. *How to get maximum credit information from your* bank. Credit information can be secured from the great Dun & Bradstreet, Inc., general credit agency, and it can be secured from the specialized mercantile and trade association agencies. All of these agencies charge an annual, or membership, fee, and most of them make an extra charge for specific credit information, although a few, such as the local credit interchange bureaus, function, in the latter respect, on a reciprocal basis.

Credit information can also be secured—and *free* —from your own banker. The amount and the extent of the credit information you get from your banker depend on the skill with which you handle this relationship. A long succession of suits down through the years, challenging their dissemination of credit information, has made the banks extremely wary in this field.

The liability to which they are subject and their financial responsibility force them to "damn with faint praise." Moreover, they never volunteer information, no matter how derogatory the information they have may be. So, your bank must be asked—and it must be asked in proper fashion, or the credit information you get is likely to be highly innocuous.

Oral inquiry will generally prove more fruitful than a written one. But, even here, the banker will be extremely cautious until you establish to his satisfaction that you understand the confidential nature of the information he conveys to you, and that you can be trusted to hold that confidence inviolate.

In any event, whether oral or written, your inquiry should make clear the purpose for which you seek the information. Also, you should, as a prerequisite, indicate to your banker the nature and extent of your past experience with the subject of your inquiry. In other words, you should not approach the bank empty-handed. The relation should be, at least to the extent possible, in the nature of an interchange of experience and anticipations.

The Robert Morris Associates, the national association of bank loan officers and credit men, in their long years of experience as an organization, have developed a formal procedure and protocol for the collection and dissemination of credit information. Since their Code for credit inquiries clearly indicates the approach of the banker to the whole problem of credit information, it is reproduced *in toto* as Figure 2.

This Code warrants your close study, since strict observance of it will enable you to get the maximum credit information from banking sources. Since such information is highly dependable, especially meaningful (as it is professionally phrased) and, in addition, is free, you should use it to the fullest extent.

5. *How to get faster banking service.* The year 1961 marked a great step forward in the automation of check-handling by the banks. In that year, five Federal Reserve Banks—Boston, New York, Philadelphia,

ROBERT MORRIS ASSOCIATES

The National Association of Bank Loan Officers and Credit Men

Code of Ethics for the Exchange of Information

PREAMBLE

The Robert Morris Associates, recognizing the importance and value of the interchange of credit information in the conduct of business, adopted (1916) the following code of credit ethics and urges its use in order to maintain the exchange of credit information on the confidential and ethical basis that this phase of credit activity warrants and requires.

THE CODE

1. The first and cardinal principle in credit investigation is to respect the confidential nature of the information received.

2. The name of the inquirer, in whose behalf the inquiry is made, should not be disclosed without permission.

3. In answering inquiries, the source of the information should not be disclosed without permission.

4. Any betrayal of confidence stamps the offender unworthy of future consideration.

5. Each letter of inquiry should indicate specifically the object and scope of the inquiry.

6. When more than one inquiry on the same subject is sent simultaneously to banks it should be indicated that information from their own files is sufficient as other checkings are being made.

7. All letters, including form letters, should bear the manual signature of the inquirer to establish responsibility.

8. The recipient of a credit inquiry is negligent in his duty if he does not read carefully each letter of inquiry and answer frankly, to the best of his ability, its specific questions.

9. In answering inquiries, it is advisable to disclose all material facts bearing on the credit standing of the subject, including the basis upon which credit is extended.

10. Indiscriminate revision of files, when there is no real need for information, is wasteful and undesirable.

11. Where periodic revision of file information is made, it may be desirable to give your own experience in the letter of inquiry, in order that duplication and unnecessary correspondence may be kept to a minimum.

12. In soliciting accounts, it is not permissible nor the part of good faith for the soliciting bank to make inquiries from a competitor without frankly disclosing the nature and object of the inquiry.

This code was originally adopted in 1916, revised in 1921, 1948 and again in 1954. Copyright: Free use is permitted with proper credit.

FIGURE 2—CODE OF ETHICS FOR THE EXCHANGE OF INFORMATION
(Adopted by Robert Morris Associates)

Chicago and San Francisco—started installations of high-speed electronic check-processing equipment. This introduction of machines that "read, if written to in their own language," and then take the indicated action, enables the banks to give even better and faster service in the clearing, collection and recording of our check-book money.

The banks can do this, however, only to the extent that they get the cooperation of business in the wide adoption of the new common machine language. This means that the faster banking service possible with these new electronic methods depends on customers as well as banks. In view of this, as well as its own importance, the system will be briefly described.

The dimensions of the problem should first be realized. The number of checks used each year rose from about 3.5 billion before World War II to about 8 billion in 1952, to more than 12 billion in 1959, and will exceed 20 billion in the early 1970's. Staggering as these totals are, they do little more than suggest the amount of work necessary, since 80 per cent of them are drawn on other banks, and each such check must be handled ten to twenty times and by two or more banks. Obviously, something had to be done to tame this "paper tiger."

The Bank of America, which was under great pressure from this increase in checking because of its large number of branches, challenged the Stanford Research Laboratory to try, through the new magnetic encoded tapes and the rapidly expanding field of electronics, to solve the rapidly mounting problem of check-handling and account drudgery. After some ten years of hard work, this resulted in their now well-known ERMA (Electronic Recording Method of Accounting), utilizing a National Cash Register sorter-reader input and ledger-printer output. In between, they used a General Electric computer (the so-called electronic brain!), magnetic tape recording and transfer devices.

In addition to National Cash Register and General Electric, International Business Machine, Burroughs Corporation, National Data Processing, and Pitney-Bowes, Inc. have developed individual and joint systems. A condition precedent, however, to the development of any system was the development of a common machine language. Such a language was developed under the auspices of the American Bankers Association with the cooperation of the equipment manufacturers and the check-printing industry. This language, which has gained the necessary widespread acceptance, is known as MICR (Magnetic Ink Character Recognition). It is based on magnetic ink characters (known as the E-13B characters), as shown in the accompanying illustration of an MICR check (See Figure 3).

While the MICR check looks very much like a conventional check, actually, it must have certain very distinct features. Thus, its length must be at least 6 inches and it cannot exceed 8¾ inches; its width must be between 2¾ and 3⅝ inches. And, most important of

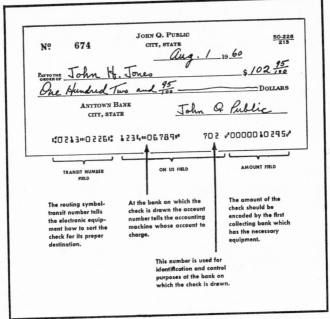

FIGURE 3—ILLUSTRATION OF AN MICR CHECK (Reproduced from *Monthly Review,* Federal Reserve Bank of New York, with Permission)

all, there must be a clear Magic Band of ⅝ inch width extending at least 6 inches along the bottom of the check from the lower right-hand corner, in which no printing other than the prescribed E-13B characters in magnetic ink is permitted.

As indicated in the illustration, the routing symbol-transit number is pre-printed on each check giving it an "electronic address." In addition, banks which have a fully automated deposit-accounting system, pre-print their customer's account number in magnetic ink in the space provided so that their internal bookkeeping also can be done electronically. Since this symbol can only sort the check to the customer's account, the dollar amount has to be coded in the "Amount Field."

Therefore, the final step in making the check fully automatic is the encoding in magnetic ink characters of the dollar and cents amount. This can be done anywhere along the line. Large companies may do it when the check is originally drawn. But, since this operation requires special encoding equipment, most of it will be done by the first bank with such equipment that handles the check. Fortunately, this can be done in most cases as a by-product of proving the deposit.

Electronic handling of checks thus requires some standardization of the check, precision pre-printing of routing and account numbers, and the considerable problem of getting the amounts encoded individually on each check. The reduction in the number of mis-sent items, the more prompt return of unpaid items, and the speedier collection of checks make automatic check-processing of consequential direct value to business. In addition, the MICR symbols permit the drawer of the checks to do his own bookkeeping electronically at considerable saving in expense.

Summarizing, bank customers and, thus, the economy benefit greatly from this increased mechanization, automation, electronization, or whatever it may be called. Banking service is faster, cheaper and more accurate. But, even more important, the improvement has widened the range of banking services to many that were formerly impossible or, at least, impractical. In fact, it *forces* the banks to expand their services, since the increased overhead of mechanization puts a premium on volume.

6. *In-plant banking.* One interesting expansion of banking service is the in-plant banking services now offered by many banks. One of the forces underlying this development was the competitive challenge of the in-plant credit unions. Since such credit unions usually involve subsidies of some sort—office space, equipment, increased bookkeeping, etc.—employers generally encourage in-plant banking service. They feel that a privately operated loan-deposit service ends the moral need for them to give aid and encouragement to the cooperatively owned credit union.

Employers are also not unmindful of the unfavorable consequences of a credit union defalcation or scandal, such as has occurred in some credit unions. Moreover, they realize that the service available from a commercial bank is a broader and more adequate banking service than can be offered by the credit union because of its limited field. Employers, therefore, welcome the development of in-plant banking.

In essence, it means that the pay of employees is credited to an account in their name in a nearby bank. The evolution from the pay envelope to pay check has thus further evolved to deposit credit for many employees. In other words, for them the cashless pay-day has been succeeded by the checkless pay-day.

More specifically, in-plant banking enables office and factory workers to receive credits to their demand deposit accounts and savings accounts, and to arrange consumer loans without even leaving their jobs. This added convenience, the safety of deposits because of Federal Deposit Insurance protection, and the much wider range of services offered make this a significant step forward in taking banking service to the "man in the street." While it certainly is more expensive to take the bank to the customers than *vice versa,* the savings and economic pressures of banking automation, previously discussed, make this a logical development in the evolution of banking service.

7. *Many trust department services.* Banks which have trust departments offer many more services than are realized by the general public. As trustee, as agent, as custodian, and under many other arrangements, they render immensely valuable services to industry and to individuals. For example, they administer more than $50 billion of personal trust assets for widows, orphans, charitable institutions, eleemosynary institutions, communities, etc. Another indication of their great importance is that they also administer more than $25 billion of pension trust funds for the protection of retired workers.

Unfortunately, space does not permit further discussion of the valuable services. But it should be said that an entire book could not do full justice to them because of their wide range, scope and importance.

8. *Advisory service.* One of the most valuable services which any business, or business man, can enjoy is the advice and interest of a competent banker. The banker is in the vanguard. He is in a position to see things before they happen, since credit applications give him direct knowledge of "things to come." And, while under the law as well as banking tradition, he must hold that knowledge confidential, it nonetheless gives him a background for advice and aid to his other customers who come to him with their problems.

The banker has a vital interest in the success of his customers—otherwise, his bank does not grow; moreover, his loans may not be repaid. So, within the limits of his time and his capability, he is glad to work with his customers. This is one of the most valuable unused assets of many a young enterprise and most young business men. If your banker is not interested, or is not capable of helping in this respect, as recommended earlier, look for a banker who will give you this almost indispensable service.

9. *Rules for relations with your bank.* Many years ago, a banker, whose name has long since been lost, listed a set of rules for the guidance of young business men in their relations with their banks. Since these rules are as true today as they were then and since they also admirably summarize the philosophy of this chapter, they are presented here:

Start with your local bank, and start early in life.

Among several safe banks, choose the one whose officers are most progressive and who keep in closest touch with current affairs.

Maintain intimate relations with your bank.

Borrow as necessity arises. It is throwing money away to borrow and let money remain idle.

The amount any bank may loan is limited by law. As your business increases until your money requirements may exceed the lending limit of one bank, take on a new one—usually one in another city may be desirable.

In choosing a second bank, choose one large enough to cover your needs—which means a larger city bank.

Do not have a long string of banks.

Keep a fair-sized deposit, although never an artificially large one.

Do not shop around for rates or try to shade discounts. If you think a bank is not giving you fair rates, go to another one.

Make certain, by frequent personal calls, that your bank knows you and knows what you are doing.

Keep your bank supplied with information about your business and, if possible, with audits prepared by professional auditors.

Get out of the books of the bank at least once a year on your borrowings. Examiners always criticize loans of long standing, because the chances are the borrower is using the money as capital.

Whenever a bank becomes unduly technical or set in its ways, make a change.

Review

What are some of the limitations on banking services?

How do you go about borrowing the maximum amount from your bank?

Indicate some of the ways you can make your loan more attractive to your banker.

Outline the mechanics of field warehousing.

Why should you inform yourself of the operation of the equitable principle of "offset"?

How do you go about getting maximum credit information from your bank?

Describe the automation of check-handling and indicate its impact on banking services.

Why would you welcome "in-plant banking" for your company?

List the more important trust services of banks.

Why is the advisory service of your banker so valuable?

CHAPTER XIX

Financing International Trade

1. *Special problems of international trade.* In recent years, international trade has grown in volume and complexity. The basic division between the Free World, on the one hand, and Russia and her satellites, on the other, presents problems previously unknown. The further division of the Free World itself into the Common Market (officially, the European Economic Community) consisting of France, Germany, Italy, Belgium, Luxembourg and the Netherlands (the "Inner Six"), and the European Free Trade Association, consisting of Great Britain, Denmark, Norway, Sweden, Switzerland, Portugal and Austria (the "Outer Seven"), creates still further problems. But, most serious of all, the tug-of-war by means of trade preferences, subsidies, outright gifts, barter arrangements and even threats, for the uncommitted nations has given international trade characteristics and hazards unknown in former times.

Politically motivated intergovernment loans, the use of money and credit management as conscious instruments of national policy, foreign exchange controls and deliberate interference with the free flow of gold across national boundaries, to say nothing of revolution and civil strife, have made the financing of international trade a special problem of both bankers and business men.

So, let no one tell you that financing international trade is the same as financing domestic trade—or that it is in any way simple. Those who uncritically accept such "sweet talk" may be taking the first step in the "loss of their shirt," or their job. In no field does Pope's injunction, "A little learning is a dangerous thing; Drink deep, or taste not the Pierian spring," apply with greater force than in international trade finance. Moreover, in addition to having a grasp of basic principles and current trends, those operating in this field should keep in close touch with the commercial banker financing their trade, so that they can be warned of the latest developments and forewarned of future threats to their interests.

2. *Differences between domestic and international trade finance.* The more important differences between financing domestic and international trade give rise to the differences in the techniques used. These differences between the two fields will now be briefly sketched:

> *Distance* is the first factor which meets the eye in foreign trade financing. Because of this, control cannot be retained—it must be shifted to someone else. This, in turn, immediately poses the questions of "Who?" and "How?"

Language and trade terms are other points of difference.

Credit standards, too, may vary widely from those which prevail at home.

Credit information on the foreign customer is generally more limited, less dependable, and less up-to-date, than that on domestic customers.

Tariffs and trade barriers, which may be burdensome or even virtually prohibitory, are further points of difference.

Foreign exchange takes the place of domestic currency in the payment of the obligation which arises. This introduces a monetary risk which must be endured or, alternatively, hedged against. Such hedging requires a knowledge of the operations of the foreign exchange market and, of course, constitutes an additional cost.

Payment restrictions established by the foreign government often delay financial consummation of transactions for inordinately long periods of time.

Technical infraction of tax laws, statutory trading requirements, or customs regulations of the foreign government may incur heavy and disproportionate penalties.

Because of the above factors, banks are generally used in financing international trade. Although business is sometimes done on a direct, open-account basis with foreign agents, this is usually unwise. In fact, even in the case of a fully-owned branch or agency, it is generally better to utilize the facilities of the international department of a large bank, in order to get the foreign exchange protection and better financial control which can be secured through such an institution.

3. *Foreign credit information.* It is vitally important for companies engaged in foreign trade to obtain the most complete and the most current credit information they can get on their customers. There are several important sources of such information.

Many domestic mercantile credit agencies, such as Dun & Bradstreet, Inc., for example, can supply credit reports on business concerns anywhere in the world. They secure such information from branches or correspondents located in the leading cities of the world and from trade and financial sources in this country.

The Foreign Credit Interchange Bureau of the National Association of Credit Management is another important source of foreign credit information. This bureau maintains files on more than 400,000 foreign firms. It operates as a non-profit, cooperative association for its members, the leading manufacturers and exporters of the United States, who pool their foreign credit experience through the bureau and secure credit experience reports from it.

The large American banks with departments actively engaged in financing our heavy volume of foreign business are in an exceptionally advantageous position to accumulate information on foreign firms active in the American market. In addition, they receive copies of investigations made by their branches and foreign representatives of firms in their localities.

One of these banks, The First National City Bank of New York, for example, has used this information to develop credit files on more than 200,000 different names. This bank employs some 200 people in the Foreign Section of its Credit Department, "investigating, recording, analyzing, filing, and seeing that customers get their reports with dispatch," to use the bank's own words.

4. *Information and advisory services.* In addition to credit information on specific firms, American companies operating in the foreign field need information of a more general character on economic and trade developments and information in detail on the exchange and foreign trade regulations of specific countries. Banks with international or, as they are sometimes called, overseas, departments furnish a wide variety of such publications to customers and potential customers.

Some of the free booklets which are issued approach 150 pages in size. Moreover, many are published monthly and some annually in completely new editions, to keep them timely and authoritative. Anyone concerned with foreign trade should not fail to take advantage of this wealth of valuable information, which can be had for the asking.

Banks in this field also maintain Business Development Departments or representatives to assist and advise customers considering the establishment of a branch, subsidiary or affiliate overseas. They will also provide names of prospective agents and distributors to American concerns interested in setting up foreign sales organizations. In addition, they are in a position to help their American customers establish original, or additional, sources of supply from foreign countries, etc.

Probably most important of all, the officers of these international divisions have had many years of residence and business experience abroad. Supplementing this basic knowledge, they make periodic trips to the areas of the world with which they are primarily concerned. Their resulting first-hand knowledge of conditions in the countries which are their responsibility enables them to give valuable advice on any situation —actual or potential—involving those areas. Their unique combination of foreign experience and banking training makes their advice unusually prescient and worth-while in a field where guidance is sorely needed.

5. *Financing exports.* Proper procedure in financing exports starts even before acceptance of the order. In addition to securing enough credit information on the would-be customer to determine the financial arrangement to which he is *entitled*, the exporter should make sure that the importer has secured the necessary import, exchange and other permits that may be required by his country. Many American firms avoid the chore of making this decision by demanding cash in advance or, its near equivalent, an irrevocable confirmed letter of credit.

This summary denial of credit accommodation to

those entitled not only to credit but to liberal credit terms, is naturally resented by foreign business men. They are very likely to effectively register their disapproval by purchasing elsewhere, if the goods are available. Moreover, if the goods are not available, they become reluctant, rather than enthusiastic, customers. There is patently no excuse for such loss of business and badly needed good-will through refusal to assume this most elementary responsibility of all trade, namely, to know your customer.

Assuming that the necessary information for making a sound, business-getting decision has been secured, agreement on financing can be reached with the buyer before the sales contract is signed. Basically, four methods of financing are available. The choice between them depends or, at least, should depend, on the credit information previously secured. The remainder of this chapter will be largely devoted to discussion of these methods, which are: (1) cash in advance, (2) open account, (3) trade drafts, and (4) bank financing.

6. *Cash-in-advance financing.* Just as in America, many overseas buyers are not entitled to credit. Also, in many lines, goods have to be made to the special order of the purchaser and, therefore, would have considerably less value to any other purchaser. Moreover, political stability, economic conditions or government restrictions in the foreign country may present such actual, or potential, risks that the seller is not war-

ranted in assuming them on other than a cash basis, which may be either (1) cash when the order is placed or (2) cash at the time of shipment, regardless of the credit standing of the buyer.

In the foregoing cases, and only in such cases, is cash in advance justified. And, when it is so required, the seller, as an earnest of his good intentions and his appreciation of the buyer's assumption of the financing burden, should allow a consequential cash discount or other concession to differentiate this business from the other types of financing with their credit and exchange risks.

Cash in advance is a very attractive arrangement from the seller's standpoint. But it, unfortunately, puts the buyer completely at the mercy of the seller. He not only has to carry the cost burden and the credit burden of financing the distribution of goods, but he has to pay for goods "sight unseen." He, naturally, strongly objects to paying in advance for goods he has had no opportunity to inspect, which will not arrive in his country for months, which may not be sold for months after that, and which may not be paid for until a further long period of time has elapsed.

Therefore, unless there is a world-wide seller's market in the goods, or unless the product enjoys a world monopoly, the seller had better make every effort to use one of the other methods of financing. In other words, while it is reasonable and proper for the American seller to protect himself, it is equally reasonable and proper for the importer to receive terms of payment commensurate with his credit standing–if he doesn't get the treatment to which he is entitled, he'll go elsewhere, and America needs the business.

7. *Open-account financing.* The opposite extreme to cash in advance is open-account financing of foreign sales. It is the same as domestic sales on open account; no documents are involved except the conventional commercial invoice. Payment is made according to the sales agreement and there is no way of enforcing the terms except by lawsuit in a foreign court. Of course, in the unlikely event that assets of the foreign buyer can be located in this country, they can be levied on, but the diverse citizenship of the litigants, etc., makes any remedy expensive, as well as problematical.

Just as cash in advance is unfair to reputable buyers, so open-account financing places the seller, as a practical matter, at the mercy of the buyer. Under this method, the seller carries the entire financing burden and the entire credit risk with very little protection. It is, therefore, and rightly, seldom used. In view of this, any such proposal should be approached with extreme reserve. Certainly, the burden of proof is on the other side, so far as this method is concerned.

8. *Trade-draft financing.* Financing by means of trade drafts is essentially a compromise between the foregoing extremes. It has the further advantage of being an extremely flexible compromise which can be adjusted to a wide variety of situations.

The drafts employed are known as trade bills or bills of exchange. As you know, a draft is simply a written order to pay. The writer of the order is the *drawer,* or *maker;* the one who is directed to pay is the *drawee,* or *payor;* and the one who will receive the payment is the *payee,* or *beneficiary.* Other parties to the draft are the *endorser,* who transfers title by signing on the back and delivering the instrument, and the *endorsee,* to whom the draft is made payable by the endorsement. It should be noted that each endorser guarantees payment of the draft, unless he disavows responsibility by adding "without recourse" to his signature.

Such drafts are ordinarily handled through the collection or discount departments of the international division of an American bank. They are accustomed to handling such drafts in large volume and have developed special facilities which give greater protection to the seller than if they were handled otherwise (through, for example, local agents). Documents giving control of the merchandise can be attached to the draft and the bank can be instructed to deliver such documents only against acceptance (Documents/Acceptance, or D/A, in banking terminology); or they can be instructed to deliver them only against payment (Documents/Payment, or D/P).

Furthermore, presentation can be delayed until the arrival of the goods, or until after examination of the goods by the importer, or until sufficient time has elapsed for the importer to sell and collect for the goods, or until the realization of any other condition stipulated in the sales contract. Necessary protection for both seller and buyer can thus be arranged in advance through the draft method of financing.

In addition to this protection, the trade draft, or bill of exchange, is a formal negotiable instrument which can be discounted (on his own credit) by the seller to raise cash when needed. After acceptance, of course, it becomes the primary obligation of the acceptor, and is even more acceptable as the basis for bank lending. Moreover, acceptance gives the seller the added protection afforded by a formal, negotiable instrument which the buyer has legally committed himself to pay.

Trade drafts, because of their many advantages, are widely used. But there is a further method which presents definite advantages when properly used. This method will now be discussed.

9. *Bank financing of exports.* Although they are not bank *credits,* Authorities to Purchase and Authorities to Pay (A/P) are issued by banks and constitute a method of financing whereby the banks do everything but assume liability for the full credit risk. Used primarily in Far Eastern trade, the two methods are essentially identical except that in the Authority to *Pay,* the drafts are drawn on the bank, and in the Authority to *Purchase,* they are drawn on the buyer.

As clearly stated in the typical Authority to Purchase, which is illustrated by Figure 4, the notifying bank reserves recourse against the seller, who thus remains fully liable until final payment, and the bank can revoke the Authority at any time.

It should be noted that some so-called *Authorities to Purchase* are specifically irrevocable and are *confirmed* by the opening bank. These offer all the security of the outright *Commercial Credit* and should be viewed as such, regardless of the name employed. As this indicates, all Authorities to Purchase or Authorities to Pay must be carefully read to determine your rights and liabilities.

The *Commercial Credit* (commonly called a Letter of Credit because of its form) is a formal financing arrangement which gives definite assurance to the seller (beneficiary) that his drafts will be honored when drawn in accordance with the conditions stipulated in the credit. One important difference between the trade-draft financing previously explained and this method of financing is that under the Commercial Credit, drafts are, with rare exceptions, drawn on a bank, rather than on the customer.

This gives rise to *bank bills* which are easier to sell than trade bills, and which command a lower rate of interest because of the greater security they offer. The *Commercial Credit* thus offers the advantage of the substitution of the bank's credit with its wide acceptability for the importer's credit with its much more limited acceptability.

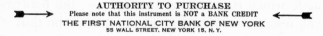

AUTHORITY TO PURCHASE
Please note that this instrument is NOT a BANK CREDIT
THE FIRST NATIONAL CITY BANK OF NEW YORK
55 WALL STREET, NEW YORK 15, N. Y.

DATE_____

_____

Dear Sir(s):

We have been authorized by our Branch in   to purchase,
with right of recourse thereon against you, draft(s) drawn by you at   sight
on
aggregating not more than
for   invoice cost of

shipped from   to
when accompanied by the following shipping documents:

    A. All negotiable copies of "on board" ocean Bills of Lading made to ORDER OF
       THE FIRST NATIONAL CITY BANK OF NEW YORK or to order and blank
       endorsed; freight and insurance to be prepaid and included in invoice;

    B. Invoices (in triplicate) together with Consular invoice in duplicate and sworn certi-
       ficate of origin required (sworn Certificate of origin and Consular invoice may be
       combined in one document), and

    C. All negotiable copies of Marine Insurance Policies or Certificates made to order
       and blank endorsed and, if Bills of Lading contain "both to blame" clause, insurance
       must cover (insurance to include war risks and institute cargo clauses, wartime
       extension, or marine extension clause).

Each draft drawn hereunder shall bear inscriptions reading substantially as follows:

    (i) "Payable at the selling rate of The First National City Bank of New York in the
       place of payment for Telegraphic Transfers or Demand Drafts on New York on
       the date of actual payment, with interest at   % per annum from
       date hereof to approximate date of returns reaching New York", and

    (ii) "DRAWN UNDER THE FIRST NATIONAL CITY BANK OF NEW YORK
       A. P. No.   ".

and the draft shall be presented to us with this Instrument on or before   in order that
the amount of each draft so purchased by us may be endorsed on the reverse side hereof.

The presentation of any draft to us for purchase hereunder shall be deemed an authorization from
you to us:

    1. To place the inscription set forth as "(i)" above on the draft in event it does not
       appear thereon and to insert in the said inscription the interest rate;

    2. To instruct the issuing bank that presentation of drafts may be deferred until the
       arrival of the carrying steamer, and

    3. To waive the noting and/or protest thereof in event of its non-acceptance and/or
       non-payment, unless at the time of such presentation you instruct us in writing to
       the contrary.

In event of dishonor by the drawee and/or acceptor of any such draft(s) purchased by us hereunder, you shall remain liable thereon as drawer for the payment of the principal and interest owing on
such dishonored draft(s) and, in addition thereto, you shall be obligated to pay to us upon demand such
expenses as we may incur in connection therewith.

This Authority to Purchase is NOT a "BANK CREDIT", and we may decline at any time, without
prior notice to you, to negotiate any draft(s) presented to us hereunder. Except as otherwise expressly
stated herein, this Authority to Purchase is subject to the Uniform Customs and Practice for Commercial
Documentary Credits fixed by the Thirteenth Congress of the International Chamber of Commerce.

Very truly yours,

FOS 557 (L) REV. 7-56

....
AUTHORIZED SIGNATURE

FIGURE 4—AUTHORITY TO PURCHASE (Courtesy of The First National
City Bank of New York)

Spelling out the advantages of the Commercial Credit, the seller likes it because payment is guaranteed by one or more banks. Since the two principal, or only, banks are great international banks, the seller has ironclad assurance in place of the problematical credit of a foreign purchaser.

Such a credit offers definite advantages to the importer, advantages which may more than offset the burden of arranging the credit. For example, its virtual elimination of credit risk entitles him to the lowest price and best discounts of the seller. In addition, its expiration date gives him maximum certainty that he will get the goods on time, since the credit cannot be extended or its terms changed in any way without the consent of all the parties to it—the buyer, the buyer's bank, the issuing bank, the confirming bank, and the seller.

Moreover, if it is a *revocable* credit, the importer can cancel it if conditions make it desirable for him to do so. While he would still be liable for damages under the sales contract, it would be very difficult, as pointed out earlier, to secure a judgment against him, and even more difficult to collect any damages that might be awarded.

10. *Mechanics of the Commercial Credit.* There are many kinds of Commercial Credits, so far as details are concerned. Thus, the Credit may be cash or acceptance; documentary or "clean"; assignable or non-assignable; revocable or irrevocable; confirmed or unconfirmed;

and, fixed sum or revolving. Most of these terms are self-explanatory, but those which are not will now be explained by using them in sketching the basic mechanics which apply to all such credits.

When a Commercial Credit is a condition of the sales contract, the purchaser must go to his bank (which, in turn, must go to a large bank with international standing if it is not such a bank itself) and arrange for the opening of such a credit.

Let us assume that the seller is willing to allow 90 days time if the buyer will supply a Confirmed Irrevocable Credit available in the seller's country. In such event, instructions embodying these features are cabled (by means of one code word for the particular form involved), followed by the pertinent data on amount (by means of a test-word which is varied from day to day and serves as a signature), documents required, and expiration date. The banker receiving such a cable (or letter) merely takes the appropriate form, fills it in as instructed, signs and mails it to the *beneficiary*.

Irrevocable means that the seller has until the expiration date to complete the shipment and present the shipping documents and draft drawn on the bank for acceptance. At that time, the issuing bank, as agreed in the credit, inspects the documents, and if everything is in order, endorses and forwards them to the purchaser's bank. It also *accepts* the draft by stamping, or writing, *Accepted,* payable on _____ (giving the maturity date, as authorized by the time specified in the credit) on the front of the draft and returning it to the seller.

This has now become a bankers acceptance which can be either held to maturity or sold in the money market at a low carrying rate, if funds are needed. In either event, it is presented to the accepting bank at maturity and is paid by means of a charge to the account of the buyer's bank. In the meantime, the buyer's bank has delivered the documents giving control of the goods to the buyer, in accordance with the credit arrangements previously made.

The terms *confirmed* and *unconfirmed* arise in this fashion. The *opening* bank (the importer's bank) asks a bank in the seller's country to notify the latter that it (the importer's bank) has opened its credit in favor of the seller. If the bank merely notifies the seller that the credit has been opened and gives the details, that is an *unconfirmed* credit; but, if the notifying bank adds to this the statement, "We *confirm* the credit and thereby undertake to honor each draft drawn and presented as above specified," that is a *confirmed* credit.

A confirmed credit thus rests upon the credit of both banks and could hardly be safer if it is also *irrevocable,* that is, cannot be changed unilaterally (by one party). An illustration of such a credit is shown by Figure 5.

It should be understood that a single bank in the seller's country may perform the functions of opening

The First National City Bank of New York

ESTABLISHED 1812

CABLE ADDRESS "CITIBANK"   *55 Wall Street, New York 15, N.Y.*

CONFIRMED IRREVOCABLE STRAIGHT CREDIT   **DATE**

> ALL DRAFTS DRAWN MUST BE MARKED:
> DRAWN AS PER ADVICE

DEAR SIRS:
    WE ARE INSTRUCTED BY

TO ADVISE YOU THAT IT HAS OPENED ITS IRREVOCABLE CREDIT No.   IN YOUR FAVOR

FOR ACCOUNT OF

FOR A SUM OR SUMS NOT EXCEEDING A TOTAL OF

AVAILABLE BY YOUR DRAFT(S) AT   ON US TO BE ACCOMPANIED BY

EXCEPT AS OTHERWISE EXPRESSLY STATED HEREIN, THIS ADVICE IS SUBJECT TO THE UNIFORM CUSTOMS AND PRACTICE FOR COMMERCIAL DOCUMENTARY CREDITS FIXED BY THE THIRTEENTH CONGRESS OF THE INTERNATIONAL CHAMBER OF COMMERCE.

THE ABOVE-NAMED OPENER OF THE CREDIT ENGAGES WITH YOU THAT EACH DRAFT DRAWN UNDER AND IN COMPLIANCE WITH THE TERMS OF THE CREDIT WILL BE DULY HONORED ON DELIVERY OF DOCUMENTS AS SPECIFIED IF PRESENTED AT THIS OFFICE ON OR BEFORE

WE CONFIRM THE CREDIT AND THEREBY UNDERTAKE TO HONOR EACH DRAFT DRAWN AND PRESENTED AS ABOVE SPECIFIED.

YOURS VERY TRULY,

SPECIMEN   ASSISTANT CASHIER

COM 811(L) 4 PARTS REV. 11-56
ART 808

FIGURE 5—CONFIRMED IRREVOCABLE STRAIGHT CREDIT (Courtesy of The First National City Bank of New York)

the Credit, notifying the seller and negotiating or paying the drafts after the shipment has been made. As a matter of fact, that is the way it is generally done on domestic credits. Because of this over-all flexibility of the Commercial Credit, it is especially adaptable to domestic financing and should be far more widely used for such purposes.

A *revolving* Credit is one for an amount which can be restored through some method. Thus, it might be for a maximum of $100,000 each month and be automatically restored to the full $100,000 on the first of each month unless notice to the contrary is given. Or, it may be "restored" by cable, transaction by transaction, as the goods are received by the buyer. Human ingenuity has contrived an almost infinite variety of such arrangements to protect the buyer and yet give his representative complete freedom within the limitations set.

11. *Traveler's letter of credit.* A *traveler's letter of credit* is one addressed to "Messrs Our Correspondents" wherever they may be authorizing them to buy the named individual's drafts drawn on the issuing bank under the letter of credit. Amounts so drawn are recorded on the credit, which continues good until the full amount has been used.

The *traveler's letter of credit,* through its special method of signature identification, serves as a valuable letter of introduction to correspondent banks throughout the world. It can safely be carried for large amounts. Through advance arrangement, it can be increased by cable when exhausted, if needed. And, finally, it has definite prestige value.

12. *A word about foreign exchange.* The exchange risk in foreign trade financing is a specialized risk which can, at slight cost, be shifted to a bank. Since it can bring together both sales and purchases of the various currencies and their various future positions (30 days, 90 days, etc.), the bank runs no consequential risk unless it takes a position in a particular currency. Taking a position means that it either accumulates holdings in excess of its offsets and its needs or, conversely, that it goes short of the currency by agreeing to make future deliveries and not "covering" (hedging) until some future time.

Since this is highly technical as well as highly specialized, the exporter should rely upon a good bank for guidance, protection and actual operations in all foreign exchange transactions. It is definitely not a "do it yourself" field.

Keep in mind that manufacturing and/or merchandising risk is one thing; foreign exchange risk is quite another thing. The business man has enough risk in his own field without looking for trouble by playing "international banker."

Review

In what basic respects does the financing of international trade differ from that of domestic trade?

Compare foreign credit information with that available on domestic firms.

Outline the information and advisory services available from the international department of a bank.

Under what conditions is cash in advance justified in foreign sales?

Explain why open-account financing is not as widely used in international trade as it is in domestic trade.

Describe trade-draft financing of an export shipment.

Summarize the advantages of Commercial-Credit financing to: (1) the exporter; (2) the importer.

Explain the following terms: confirmed; irrevocable; acceptance credit; Authority to Purchase.

What is a revolving credit?

CHAPTER XX

Canadian Banking

1. *Similarities and dissimilarities.* Canada and America occupy most of one continent and face each other across the longest unfortified border in the world. Since time immemorial, their relations—political, social and economic—might well serve as a model for the world of peace and cooperation of which men dream. It is not surprising, therefore, to find many points of similarity between Canadian banking and American banking.

There are also many important points of dissimilarity—differences which developed in the process of better adapting each system to the special needs and the political realities of each country. Greater freedom in this respect has permitted Canadian banking to evolve in response to economic forces with but little hindrance from political factors. In consequence, Canadian banks down through the years have been able to provide a uniformly high level of banking service. In fact, in some respects, it is far superior to the banking services which have hitherto been available to the people of the United States.

Bank failures, for example, have been all but unknown in Canada. In fact, there has been no failure in

Canada since that of the small Home Bank of Canada in Toronto in 1923. In sharp contrast, more than 10,000 banks (of course, many were very small) failed in the United States during the same period!

Branch banking is another example of the freedom of the Canadian banks to adapt their facilities to the needs of the Canadian economy. Whereas the first Bank of the United States was set up as a national institution with the right to open branches anywhere in the country—a right of which it took quick and full advantage—and the second Bank of the United States likewise had nationwide branches, political controversy doomed all subsequent efforts.

In fact, economic pressures notwithstanding, branch banking today (with one tiny exception) is limited to state boundaries, and certain states still absolutely forbid it in any form. Thus, branch banking, which Canadians have long enjoyed, is still the subject of bitter controversy in the United States.

This chapter will be largely devoted to sketching the important points of difference between banking in the two countries. In other words, it is assumed that the reader is familiar with the principles of banking and with banking in the United States as set forth in previous chapters. As it is important for both Canadian and American readers to understand the common points of origin, and the close relations between Canadian banking and American banking, these factors will be stressed.

2. *The first Canadian bank.* The first bank of deposit and discount established in Canada was the Bank of Montreal (originally named The Montreal Bank) which opened for business on November 3, 1817. The Articles of Association under which nine Montreal merchants organized this bank were, in many of their essential features, based on and, at many points, taken word for word from the charter of the first Bank of the United States. It is one of the ironies of North American history that some of the basic features of this bank, conceived and founded in 1791 by Alexander Hamilton, the first Secretary of the United States Treasury, failed to survive in the American banking system, but did survive, and thrive, in the Canadian system.

The Articles of Association of the Bank of Montreal, like Hamilton's bank, provided for a life of twenty years, as did its first Royal Charter obtained in 1822. Also, there were no restrictions on the establishment of branches. The charters of later Canadian banks, and the federal Bank Act, which has been the common charter of all Canadian banks since 1871, retained many of the features of these original Articles of Association.

3. *Branch banking.* Harking back to this first bank charter, branch banking continues as an outstanding characteristic of Canadian banking. It will seem strange to most readers that in all of Canada, with its vast expanses of territory and great distances, there are only nine banks, whereas, in the United States, there are

some 14,000 banks. But this does not mean that Canada is not well supplied with banking facilities. On the contrary, since these nine banks have some 5,000 branches and sub-agencies in Canada alone, there is a banking office for every 3,600 or so Canadians, whereas the comparable figure in the United States is 7,500.

Long experience with branch banking has enabled Canadian bankers to develop a type of bank which is at once both a local and a national institution. This is very important as Canada is a country of very diverse regions, diverse resources, diverse problems and diverse opportunities. Through its network of branches, the Canadian chartered bank pools the wide range of banking resources and needs of these diversities. In so doing, it also pools the attendant risks. The Canadian chartered bank is thus an extremely diversified institution compared to the typical American bank.

It should be understood that the branch is the point of contact between the public and a Canadian bank. It is to a branch that a customer goes to deposit, borrow and secure the wide range of services available from the modern bank. Even in the large city where the head office is located, there is a main branch, usually in the same building, that is operated as a separate unit and functions just like any other branch. The head office is thus an administrative, policy unit, rather than a direct operating one.

Branch banking probably more than anything else has made the Canadian banking system the outstanding success it has been and is, today. No other method could have so well served a country so vast and as thinly populated as Canada.

4. *The urge to merge.* Large though they are, the Canadian banks have not been entirely immune to the economic pressures for increased size, which have been so marked in the United States in recent years. Sharply increased costs with income held down by low interest rates and government debt-management policies have forced banks in both countries to offer new services and to seek the economies of increased size.

Automation of operations, the speedier communication of the plane, the closer managerial control afforded by leased wires (teletype, etc.), and improved management and personnel methods have all pressed in the direction of ever greater size.

This pressure was reflected in the February 1, 1955 merger, the first since 1931, of The Bank of Toronto and The Dominion Bank. The Minister of Finance approved the union of these two banks under the name of The Toronto-Dominion Bank, on the grounds that although each was in strong financial position, the merged institution, through wider expansion of branch facilities, would be able to render more efficient and more competitive banking service to its customers.

Exactly one year later, The Imperial Bank of Canada and Barclays Bank (Canada) united under the name of the Imperial Bank of Canada. This gave the Imperial Bank of Canada, which had no foreign branches, a closer relationship with the some 3,000 branches in 42 countries of the Barclays banking group, and it gave Barclays Bank (Canada), with only 6 branches, direct access to the 250 Canadian branches of the Imperial Bank.

Under the lash of economic pressure, continuous growth must be expected in the size of banks, unless the public is willing to pay the higher prices of un-economic operation forced by arbitrary statutory interference with this evolution.

5. *Legal requirements.* There are many legal requirements which apply to the organization and operation of a Canadian bank. The Bank Act, as revised in 1954, for example, contains no less than 161 separate sections.

Of these many requirements, probably none has had a more basic effect on Canadian banking than those relating to capital. Judged by capital minimums in the United States, the Canadian requirements have always been extraordinarily high. Nonetheless, the July 1, 1954 revision of the Bank Act increased the minimum requirements further, as follows:

> Authorized capital and subscribed capital, from $500,000 to $1,000,000.
>
> Paid-up capital, from $250,000 to $500,000.
>
> Capital to be paid to the Minister of Finance before issuance of certificate permitting commencement of business, $250,000 to $500,000.

The Bank Act provides that a board of not less than five directors shall manage the affairs of a chartered bank. Each director must own qualifying shares on which not less than $3,000 to $5,000, depending on the paid-up capital of the bank, has been paid in. In an effort to secure a broader representation on the boards of directors, this requirement is reduced by one-half, however, for not more than one-quarter of the total number of directors. The majority of the directors must be subjects of Her Majesty, ordinarily resident in Canada.

The powers, liabilities and delegations of authority by the board of directors to operating officers are very similar to those in the United States, so further discussion is unnecessary.

One of the most unusual features of Canadian banking is the long-standing practice of decennial revisions of the Bank Act. At that time, the charters of all banks automatically expire and must be renewed in new legislation. Paradoxically, the banks themselves favor this arrangement. For example, in 1900 when the government offered to make their charters perpetual, the banks, after full discussion, requested that their charters be renewed for ten years only, since they felt that it was in the public interest to have the whole question of banking discussed and carefully considered by the government and the banks at least once every ten years.

6. *Deposits.* The note-issue banking of the early days in Canada slowly evolved into the deposit banking of today, just as it did in the United States. In fact, the earliest bank, The Bank of Montreal, was in operation

more than forty years before its deposits exceeded its outstanding notes.

The earliest deposits took the form of deposit receipts on which no interest was paid. Later, competition caused the banks to inaugurate the payment of interest on such deposits. Still later came the book deposit, the check money which constitutes the most active and by far the major part of the total money supply. And, comparatively recently, the note issue function was taken over entirely by the central bank, the Bank of Canada. Any note of a chartered bank which may still be in public hands is now the liability of the central bank.

Branch banking has played an important part in the ability of the chartered banks to furnish an adequate supply of this deposit money. By means of their branch systems, they can shift such funds as required by seasonal, geographic and industry variations, since it is rare indeed when the loans of a particular branch match its deposits.

While there are various other savings institutions in Canada, the bulk of savings deposits are held by the chartered banks. More specifically, they hold over three-quarters of total savings deposits as compared with holdings of less than one-half by the United States commercial banks. In other words, they dominate the savings field, holding vast amounts of funds which would be held in the United States by savings and loan associations and mutual savings banks. This is clearly indicated by their total of more than $7 billion of personal savings deposits, as compared with only some $5 billion of *Canadian* deposits in all other forms. (In addition, however, they hold more than $2¼ billion of deposits payable in currencies other than Canadian.)

Since the beginning of this century, Canadians have enjoyed a privilege unknown in the United States: *They can write checks (cheques) on their savings accounts.* Although the banks reserve the right to demand notice of withdrawal through the printing of such a qualification on the flyleaf of each passbook, this restriction has virtually never been enforced. This checking privilege gave the chartered banks with their branch networks such a definite advantage that in time they took over most of the local savings institutions.

7. *Loans.* The loan function is highly developed in the Canadian banks. They lend for, literally, countless purposes to merchants, industry, agriculture, housing, government and individuals. Roughly, one-half of their loan total of some $8 billion consists of loans to industrial and business borrowers; one-third, loans to individuals, farmers and mortgage loans (under the National Housing Act); one-tenth, loans to financial firms; and the small remaining balance, loans to provinces, municipalities and institutions.

Their basic loan policy is the orthodox one of short-term loans for current operations to borrowers who can offer tangible assurance of repayment through salable goods, collectible debts, marketable securities or assured personal income. The great majority of loans are unsecured, but when security is necessary, it may be by means of an assignment under Section 88 of the Bank Act; by endorsement; and, since the 1954 revision of the Bank Act, by chattel mortgage. Loans now can even be made on the security of oil and gas still in the ground.

The Farm Improvement Loans Act of 1944 authorizes intermediate-term credit for farmers. It is widely used, especially in the Prairie Provinces, to finance the purchase of machinery.

The National Housing Act of 1954 authorizes loans on prospective home and rental properties when guaranteed to the extent of 98 per cent by the Central Mortgage and Housing Corporation, a government agency similar to the Federal Housing Administration (FHA) in the United States. This lending, even though against insured and rediscounted mortgages, was a considerable step forward, as the ineligibility of conventional mortgages as primary security for bank loans has always been a feature of Canadian bank law.

Personal loans of small amounts, generally under $1,000, are made to wage earners and salaried employees of good reputation, for a wide variety of purposes, just as in the United States. Most of these loans are unsecured, although an endorser may be required if the amount is above a certain limit, or if the borrower is not well-known to the bank. Repayment is practically always on an equal monthly instalment basis, spread over a period of six months to two years, depending on government regulations on consumer credit and the loaning policies recommended by the Bank of Canada, as well as the bank's own policy.

The branch manager has a key role in all lending. It is to him that the prospective borrower applies, and it is his responsibility to see that the loan application receives proper consideration. If the application is for an amount in excess of the manager's loaning authority, he must refer it with his recommendation to his district supervisor (or superintendent) who, in turn, must similarly refer applications in excess of his authority to the head office, with his recommendation added to that of the branch manager.

8. *Investments.* As compared with banks in the United States, the proportion of Canadian bank assets invested in securities today is considerably smaller. In fact, including the treasury bills they are required to keep for liquidity, the chartered banks' holdings of Canadian securities is only around $4 billion.

In addition to these Canadian holdings, however, they have approximately $1 billion of foreign securities and a further amount of around $1 billion of mortgages and hypothecs insured under the National Housing Act of 1954. Since banks do not buy securities (except to meet their liquidity requirements) when they can make loans, their smaller holdings indicate that the Canadian banks have been more successful in keeping their earning assets in the form of loans.

Most chartered banks maintain an investment department to manage the bank's own investments, and a securities or bond department which buys and sells bonds and maintains an active trading position in government securities.

9. *Clearing and collections.* Bank deposits are continually on the move. In handling this moving money safely and efficiently, the banks render a wide range of services to individuals, to business, and to government. The physical task alone of moving some 3,000,000 items daily from the points at which they are deposited to the points on which they are drawn, in a country as vast, and as sparsely populated in many areas, as Canada, is a staggering one.

Their branch system or organization greatly facilitates this task. The clearing houses maintained in 52 cities by the Canadian Bankers Association through member banks further facilitate the task, since items can thereby be offset and only the balances paid. In places where there is no clearing house, items drawn on or payable through another bank in the town are deposited in that bank each morning. At stipulated intervals, and when balances exceed a prearranged amount, settlement of differences is made by draft payable through the nearest clearing house.

Final settlement of balances for all of the central clearing points of the country is through the Bank of Canada. Instructions as to the amount to debit or credit each bank are given by the clearing house manager to the local agency of the Bank of Canada. On the basis of previous written authorization by the member banks, this information is sent by wire or telephone to the Bank of Canada in Ottawa where the actual transfers from account to account are made. Final settlement is thus made the same day that the exchanges take place.

10. *Bank personnel.* Nearly fifty per cent more women than men are employed in the Canadian banks, which have a total employment in excess of 60,-000. Also, the proportion of executive to clerical personnel is relatively high because of the branch method of operation.

The chartered banks have always had to devote special attention to personnel because of the far-flung nature of their activities. As a result, they established banking as a profession long before it achieved that status in the United States.

They have, from the earliest times, taken full advantage of their unique facilities for training and developing bankers by shifting those who get on the managerial ladder from branch to branch throughout their entire system. They thus can learn different areas, different industries and different responsibilities. And as they grow in experience and seasoning, they can be safely moved to higher managerial levels.

Truly, banking in Canada is a career, and not a fortuitous happenchance.

11. *Banking supervision.* Contrary to popular opinion, the chartered banks are subject to a great deal of

supervision and regulation. For example, they are subject to internal examinations by their own auditors, to shareholders' examinations by outside auditors, and to government examination by officials who report to the Inspector General of Banks, who, in turn, reports to the Minister of Finance.

In addition to many internal standards, they have such informal but, nonetheless, binding ones such as the Bank of Canada's request that they maintain, in addition to the statutory requirement of 8 to 12 per cent, a further amount sufficient to bring up to a minimum of 15 per cent the ratio of liquid assets (cash, day-to-day loans, and treasury bills) to deposits, on a monthly average basis.

They are also subject to the many provisions of the 161 section Bank Act. Not the least of these provisions is the setting of a 6 per cent maximum interest rate with stiff penalties for the failure of any chartered bank to observe it.

12. *The Bank of Canada.* Beginning operations in March 1935, the Bank of Canada is the youngest important central bank. Its objectives, as spelled out in the Bank of Canada Act (1934) are:

. . . to regulate credit and currency in the best interests of the economic life of the nation, to control and protect the external value of the monetary unit and to mitigate by its influence fluctuations in the general level of production, trade, prices and employment. . . .

In contrast to the privately owned Federal Reserve Banks in the United States, the Bank of Canada is owned by the government. In addition to a monopoly of the note issue, its more important powers are:

(a) To "fix" the discount rate on loans to the chartered banks. (In a basic change of policy in November 1956, this was made automatic by providing that the rate shall at all times be ¼ of 1 per cent above the weekly average tender rate on 91-day treasury bills.)

(b) To engage in open market security and *foreign exchange* operations.

(c) To hold the reserves and vary the minimum requirements for chartered bank reserves between 8 and 12 per cent of deposit liabilities in Canadian currency. (In addition to its deposits at the Bank of Canada, the chartered bank can include in this percentage the notes of that bank, that is, the actual cash on hand can be counted as part of its reserves, as can now be done in the United States.)

As the foregoing indicates, the Bank of Canada has the traditional central bank instruments of credit control. In actual practice, however, the chartered banks rarely rediscount; moreover, no firm relationship has been established in Canada's relatively undeveloped money market between the discount rate and other institutional rates. So, the impact of a discount rate change is almost entirely the indirect one flowing from reactions to the Bank's view as to the interest rate and credit policies appropriate to prevailing monetary and economic conditions and its intentions to implement those views with open-market operations.

Since the power to change reserve requirements is viewed as an emergency one, to be used only in case of necessity, the Bank of Canada is left with, as a practical matter, only the weapon of open-market operations. In general, these operations are confined to the buying and selling of government securities. Through such transactions, the Bank can increase or reduce the reserves of the chartered banks, as credit policy requires.

The Bank of Canada has one further tool, *moral suasion*. This does not flow from the statute. Its effectiveness is based on the demonstrated leadership of the Bank, the willingness of the chartered banks to cooperate, and the fact that the small number of banks in Canada makes such an informal, voluntary method practicable. With only nine chartered banks, it is a simple matter for the Governor of the Bank of Canada to influence policies through private discussions with their chief executives.

Under the Currency, Mint and Exchange Fund Act of 1952, the Bank of Canada is not required (unless so ordered by the Governor in Council) to maintain a minimum or fixed reserve ratio of gold or foreign exchange to its liabilities. It thus has full flexibility with respect to gold holdings.

Two collateral functions of the Bank should also be

mentioned: (1) Through a wholly-owned subsidiary, the Industrial Development Bank, it extends intermediate and longer-term credit to small and medium-sized business; and (2) it has the responsibility for management of the public debt and acts as fiscal agent for the Canadian Government.

13. *Money management in Canada.* Conscious monetary management as an instrument of national policy dates from the establishment of the Bank of Canada in 1935. In fact, it was the lack of such a monetary policy in the face of the sharp economic contraction and suffering of the early 1930's that gave birth to the Bank of Canada. Moreover, until 1950, determined use of monetary policy as an anti-inflationary weapon was deliberately rejected. There were two reasons for this. First, reliance was placed on fiscal policy along the lines being attempted by the United States and the United Kingdom. Second, there was a conspicuous lack of faith in the efficacy of money management under the then prevailing conditions.

Since then, there has been a growing recognition of the central position and steadily increasing importance of money management in achieving the statutory goal of the best interests of the Canadian people. Fiscal policy and techniques have not been abandoned as economic weapons, but they have been supplanted by traditional money management as the chief instrument of national economic policy.

Money and credit management in Canada has several special problems. For one thing, Canada does not have a broad, well-developed money market, with established rate patterns, as in the United Kingdom and the United States. Important steps, however, have been taken, particularly by the Bank of Canada, in the direction of developing such a market. Also, the chartered banks (beginning in 1954) make available to dealers in government securities eligible for the rediscount facilities of the Bank of Canada, a new category of call loans, known as day-to-day loans, based on such collateral, with very small margins required.

These loans, on a strictly day-to-day and completely impersonal basis, are at the convenience of the banks, which grant, or call, them entirely on the basis of the surplus or deficiency in their cash reserves. The availability of such loans to investment dealers and the extremely liquid form of assets they provide the banks fill a real need in the short-term financial market.

Another, and basic, problem of Canadian money management is the close economic and financial ties with the United States. This close relationship makes it very difficult for them to chart a completely independent course.

Another problem of Canadian money management is that many sources of credit other than the chartered banks are available to Canadian borrowers. Finance companies, other corporate lenders, individuals, and long-established channels of foreign borrowing, all make credit control especially difficult in Canada.

In addition to these special problems, they have the usual problems of timing, psychology, political expediency, etc., which bedevil the money managers in all countries.

14. *Conclusions.* Of the many conclusions warranted by Canadian banking and its special features, four deserve particularization.

The first is the wide range of services offered over such vast areas, large parts of which are so sparsely populated.

The second is that although the individual chartered bank may be very large, it is, as a practical matter, composed of many local units which, through managerial foresight and consciously designed operating methods, have a local point of view.

The third is that, despite the limited number of banks, competition is very keen.

The fourth is that little study of the history of Canadian banking is needed to demonstrate that it is based on the firm foundation of historical experience, and has grown with the nation and adapted its methods and policies to the needs of the nation. In the words of Mr. G. Arnold Hart, President, Bank of Montreal, "It is a business whose features people would wish, I am sure, to see carefully safeguarded."

Review

Give the most outstanding points of dissimilarity between Canadian and American banking.

Comment on the capital requirements established by law for Canadian banks.

Enumerate the unusual features of savings deposits in Canada.

How are loans in excess of the loan authority of the local branch manager handled?

Explain the method of clearing used by the Canadian banks.

Specifically, how do the chartered banks develop banking and managerial ability?

To what extent are the chartered banks subject to supervision and regulation?

Of the traditional instruments of central bank credit control, which is used by the Bank of Canada? Why?

What is the present position of money management in Canada?

What are the *special* problems of money management in Canada?

Index

A

Acceptances (*See* Bankers acceptances and Trade acceptances)

Accounts receivable financing:
difference between factoring and, 122–124
growth of, 124
impersonal type of borrowing, 104
method of charge, 123

Advisory service of banks, 317

Alexander Hamilton Institute publications, 159

American Bankers Association:
common machine language developed by, 312
in field of banking education, 155–157
Universal Numerical System adopted by, 168, 169

American banking system:
Civil War "greenbacks," 47–48
defects prior to 1913, 50–51
dual banking system, 186–187
Federal Reserve Act of 1913, 52
Free Banking system of New York, 43–44
independent banking, a characterization of, 38–39
Independent Treasury System, 44–47
National Bank Act, reasons for, 48–50
Safety Fund System, 41–42, 44
Suffolk System, 41–42, 44
three types of, 36–37
trial and error of, 19–34

American Institute of Banking, 155

Articles of Association, features of (Canada), 342

Assets:
Federal Reserve Banks earning, 238–239
relation of capital to, 77–78
risk, 91

Assignats, 15

Associations sponsoring schools in field of financing, 156

Authorities to Pay (A/P):
difference between Authorities to Purchase and, 330
method of export financing, 330, 331

Authorities to Purchase (A/P)
Commercial Credit and, 331
illustration of, 332
irrevocable, 331

Automation in clearing and collection of checks, 169–171, 309, 311–315

B

Balance sheet of Federal Reserve Banks, 238–240

Bank account (*See* Deposit account)

Bank Act of Canada, 345–346, 349

Bank bills, 331

Bankers acceptances:
advantages of, 107, 110
buying and selling of, 258
definition of, 107, 257
growth of, 256
impersonal type of loan, 100, 104

Bankers acceptances (*continued*)
 important buyers of, 257–258
 limitations on amounts, 108
 liquidity of, 257
 lowest rate of business borrowing, 107, 110, 257
 markets for money, 252, 256–258
 open-market borrowing, 100, 107–110, 258
 procedure followed, 107–110, 257
Bank funds, sources of, 70–85
 (*See also* Capital)
Bank-Holding Company Act of 1956, 198–199
Banking Act of 1933, 137–138, 147, 197
Banking "commissions," public education program through, 156–157
Banking connection (*See* Bank, your)
Banking credit and other credit, differences, 54–55 (*See also* Credit)
Banking, early:
 civilization's contributions to, 1
 contributions of the past, 16–17
 early banks, 5–16
 Grecian priests, 3
 in the dark ages, 4–5
 origin of, 2–3
 private bankers, emergence of, 3
 temple, 2–3
 under Roman rule, 3–4, 4–5
Banking schools, 155–156
Bank investments:
 Canadian, 350
 government, 88, 261–264, 275–276
 increases deposits, 127
 of savings banks, 209–210
 reasons banks buy securities, 127–128
Bank Management Commission, 157
"Bank money," 7, 10

Bank notes:
 early form of, 8
 unlimited, 32–33
Bank of Amsterdam, 6–8
Bank of Barcelona, 6
Bank of Commercial Discount, 14–15
Bank of Canada:
 Bank of Canada Act (1934), 353
 central bank of Canada, 353
 change reserve requirements, tool of, 354, 355
 collateral functions of, 355–356
 credit controls, 354–355
 Currency Mint and Exchange Fund Act of 1952, 355
 discount rate change, power of, 354–355
 fiscal agent of government, 356
 gold holdings, full flexibility of, 355
 government owned, 354
 money management of, 356–358
 moral suasion, tool of, 355
 note issue function of, 347, 354
 powers of, 354
Bank of England:
 Bank of Venice forerunner of, 6
 beginning of, 16
 Patterson, founder of, 9
Bank of France, 15
Bank of Montreal, 342, 346–347
Bank of North America, 21
Bank of St. George, 6
Bank of the United States, first, 22–23, 342
Bank of the United States, second:
 establishment of, 23–25
 lessons learned from failure of, 29–30
 unsound and scandalous practices of, 25–26
 war with President Jackson, 27–29
Bank of Venice, 5–6

Banks:
  deposit services of, 126–140
  early, 5–16
  governmental regulation of,
    180–182
  loan services of, 87–102
  must be incorporated, 180
  national vs. state charter, 183–
    185
  number of, 182–183
  reasons for large number of
    failures, 183
  safeguards on establishing
    new, 180–182
  sources of funds, 70–85 (*See
    also* Capital)
  structure of, 187–200
Bank stocks, difficulty of selling
  new, 82–83
Bank tellers:
  other, 294
  paying, 293–294
  receiving, 292–293
Bank, your:
  advantage of borrowing from,
    307
  advisory service, 317
  bank tellers, functions of, 292–
    294
  choice of head office or branch,
    286–287
  endorsement, kinds and im-
    portance of good, 294–296
  form of bank deposits, 292–
    293
  how to borrow from, 304–307
  how to get faster service from,
    309–315
  how to get maximum credit in-
    formation from, 308–309
  importance of good connec-
    tion, 284–285
  in-plant banking services of-
    fered by, 315–316
  kind of deposit accounts of,
    290–292
  procedure in opening a deposit
    account, 287–290
  rules for relations with, 317–
    319
  selecting, 285–286

Bank, your (*continued*)
  services, customers' full use
    of, 302–304
  trust department service, 316–
    317
  ways to make your loan at-
    tractive to, 305–307
Barclays Bank (Canada), 344–
  345
Biddle, 27–29
Bills of credit, 20
Bills of exchange, 6, 24, 108,
  110, 329, 330
Board of Governors of the Federal Reserve System:
  administers quantitative credit
    control, 275–279
  approval of membership to,
    225
  determinants of money poli-
    cies of, 269–271
  determines discount rates,
    136, 226–227
  determines eligibility for ac-
    cess to primary credit of
    Reserve Banks, 275
  fixes legal reserves of member
    banks, 227
  fixes marginal requirements,
    227
  functions of the, 226–228
  management of money and
    credit, 266–283
  membership, 225
  regulations of the, 232–237
  research and educational ef-
    forts of, 154–155
  safeguards against political
    domination, 225, 267
  selection of members, 225–
    226
  supervises and examines the
    12 Federal Reserve Banks,
    227
  term of office, 225
Bookkeeping:
  commercial banks, 53–54
  double entry or T accounts,
    use of in banking, 63
  illustrations of T accounts in
    banking, 64–66

Borrowing by banks, 85

Branch banking:
arguments against, 196–197
arguments for, 194–196
definition of, 193
growth of, 193–194
in Canada, 193, 342–344
meeting growing demand for bank services, 194
monopolistic in nature, 196–197
operation of, 193

Brokers loan market, 258–259

Business activity, a determinant of money management, 270

Business cycle and bank loans, 95–96

C

Call loans, 258

Canadian Bankers Association, 351

Canadian banking:
a profession, 352
Bank Act, 345–346, 349, 353
Bank of Canada (*See* Bank of Canada)
board of directors, requirements of, 345–346
basic loan policy, 348–349
branch banking, 342–344, 347
branch manager's role in lending, 350
capital requirements, 345
chartered banks, 342
checking privilege, 348
clearing and collections, 351–352
clearing houses, 351
credit controls, 354–355
decennial revisions of the Bank Act, 346
deposit banking, 347–348
first bank of deposit and discount, 342
greater freedom of, 340–341
home mortgage loans, 349
interest rate supervision, 353
investments of, 350–351
loan functions, 348–350

Canadian banking (*continued*)
loans to farmers, 349
mergers in, 344–345
money and credit management, problems of, 356–358
number of banks, 342–343
personal loans, 349–350
personnel, 352
ratio of liquid assets to deposits, 353
savings deposits held by, 347–348
similarities and dissimilarities with American banking, 340–341
special features of, 358
supervision of, 352–353

Capital:
accounts of today, 72–75
amount needed, 75–76
assets, relation of, to, 77–78
deposits, relation of, to, 76–77
difficulty of selling additional stock for new, 82–83
economic growth, relation of, to, 81–82
Federal Reserve Banks create, 84–85
functions of bank, 70–72
loans, 98–99, 116–117
market, long-term grouping, 243
primary deposits, a source of, 83–84
primary function of, 71
profits, relation of, to, 80–81
responsibility for adequate, 78–80
sources of bank, 70–85

Cashier's check, 131–132, 297

Cash-in-advance financing of exports, 326–328

"Cash notes," 8–9

Central banking:
current system, 36–37, 222
(*See also* Federal Reserve System)
first bank of issue, 22–23
in Canada, 353–354
second bank of issue, 23–25

Central Mortgage and Housing Corporation (Canada), 349
Certificates of deposit, 135
Certified check, 131, 297–298
Charters, bank, 183–185
Chase, Secretary of the Treasury, 48, 49
Checking accounts, use of, 129–134, 136, 290–292
Checks:
　cashier's, or banker's, 297
　certification of, 297–299
　certified, 297–298
　early form of, 9
　electronic handling of, 312–314
　endorsements, kinds of, 294–297
　features of certification of, 298
　forgeries, problem of, 295–297, 303
　meaning of, 130
　special forms of, 130–132, 297–298
　stop-payment orders, 299–301
Cheves, Langdon, 26
Christmas clubs, 135
City Collection Department, 166
Clay, Henry, 28
Clearing and collections:
　automation in, 169–171, 309, 311–315
　circuitous routings, reasons for, 172
　clearing principle, 161
　collection items, special departments for, 166–167
　country collection, 171
　difference between, 161–162
　Federal Reserve collection system, 171–178
　in Canada, 351–352
　Interdistrict Settlement Fund, 175–176
　method of clearing, 163–165 (*See also* Clearing house)
　non-par banks, 174, 177–178
　out-of-town collections, mechanics of, 174–175

Clearing and collections (*continued*)
　par collection system, 172
　service of banking, 161
　transit department, 167
　transit items and collection items, difference between, 167, 171
Clearing house:
　basic function of, 162
　first, 162–163
　functions of the, 163–166
　illustration of statements showing procedure of, 164
　in Canada, 351
　New York Clearing House, 163
　procedure of the, 163–165
　special departments for collection items, 166–167
　statements showing procedure of, 164
Code of Ethics for the Exchange of Information, 309, 310
Colonies:
　early "banks," 20–21
　first real bank in, 21–22
Commercial banks:
　a bookkeeping mechanism, 53–54
　bankers acceptances purchased by, 257
　buying securities, 127–128
　compared with savings banks, 203–205, 211
　credit extended by, 54–56
　deposit services of, 128–134
　deposits insured by the FDIC, 152
　diversity of, 187
　double entry bookkeeping of, 63–66
　factors determining ability of banks to extend credit, 89–91
　functions of, 56–67
　licensed and regulation of, 180–182
　loanable funds, 93
　loan services of, 87–103, 304
　money market serves, 247
　national or state, 183–184, **187**

Commercial banks (*continued*)
power of credit expansion, 105
primary object of, 203
recognition of right to credit, a basic function of, 56–59
savings department of, 202
savings services, 134–137
services offered other than loan and deposits, 126–127
services of Treasury Tax and Loan Account to, 142
structure of, 180–200
substituting bank's credit for borrower's credit, 59–60
time deposits in, 137
transferring of values, 60

Commercial Credit:
advantages of, 331, 333
confirmed and unconfirmed, 335
definition of, 331
difference between trade-draft financing and, 331
illustration of confirmed irrevocable straight credit, 336
irrevocable credit, meaning of, 334–335
mechanics of the, 333–337
revocable credit, 333
revolving credit, 337

Commercial loans, 98

Commercial paper:
as secondary reserves, 256
decline in dealers of, 112–113
endorsement of, 254
impersonal type of loan, 100, 104
importance of, 113
limited size of market, reasons for, 255
market, a money market instrument, 252
maturity of, 112, 254
method of short-term borrowing, 112
promissory notes, 112, 254
purchasers of, 113, 254–256
sales finance companies, 255

Compagnie d'Occident, 11
Compagnie des Indes, 11

Comptroller of the Currency:
authority over bank capital's adequacy, 79
national banks chartered by, 181–182, 185

Conditional endorsement, 294–295

Confirmed credit, type of Commercial Credit, 333, 335, 336

Consumer credit:
consumption or, a loan classification, 99–100
qualitative credit control of, 272–274

Controls, credit (*See* Credit controls)

Correspondents Conference of the First National Bank of Chicago, 156

Country Collection department, 171

Credit:
banking and other, difference between, 54–55
Commercial (*See* Commercial Credit)
establishing the right to, 58–59
monetary, a social product, 54, 55–56
recognition of the right to, 56–58
substituting bank's for borrower's, 59–60

Credit controls, 271–279 (*See also* Money management)

Credit management (*See* Money management)

Credit unions:
a savings intermediary, 202
in-plant, vs. in-plant banking, 315
primary object of, 203

Currency, Mint and Exchange Fund Act of 1952 (Canada), 355

D

Dark ages, 4–5
Demand deposits, 93–94, 136, 137–138, 290–291, 293
Demand loans, 101
Deposit account:
  kinds of, 290–292
  opening a bank, 287–290
  reasons for bank's refusal to open, 128–129
  regular checking, 130, 291–292
  special checking, 129–130, 290–291
Depositors:
  demand deposits, how made, 292–293
  loans to, 100
  selection of bank, reasons for, 129, 285–286
Deposit protection:
  before 1933, 153–154
  contributions of banking education to, 153–155
  failure of state plans, reasons for, 145
  Federal deposit insurance, reasons for, 146–147 (*See also* Federal Deposit Insurance Corporation)
  main task of, 145
  New York State Safety Fund System, 144–145
Deposits:
  demand, 93–94, 136, 137–138, 290–291, 293
  derivative, 61–63
  general, 292
  government, 139–140
  primary, 61, 83–84
  protection of, 144–159
  regulations of interest payments on, 137–138
  relation of capital to, 76–77
  relation of loans to character of, 93–94
  savings, regular, 135
  secondary, 61–62
  special, 292
  time, 93, 135, 136–137, 138–139, 204

Desha, 23
Discount rate, changes in, a weapon of money managers, 277–278
Documents/Acceptance (D/A), 329
Documents/Payment (D/P), 329
Dual banking system, 186–187
Dun & Bradstreet, Inc., credit information from, 308, 323

E

Economic Policy Commission, 157
Educational contributions to banking, 153–159
Elasticity:
  of Free Banking system notes, 44
  of Safety Fund system notes, 44
Electronic Recording Method of Accounting (ERMA), 312
Employment Act of 1946, 267
Employment, a determinant of monetary policy, 269–270
Endorsement:
  definition of, 294
  forms of, 294–295
  importance to bank, 295
  of negotiable instruments, 294
  supported by identification, 296
English banking, 8–9, 16
Excess reserves, 277
Exports, financing of:
  bank financing, 330–338
  cash-in-advance financing, 326–328
  credit information secured first, 325–326
  methods of financing, 326
  open-account financing, 328
  trade-draft financing, 328–330

F

Factors:
  advantages of, 121–122
  commission charged, 119–120, 121–122

Factors (*continued*)
definition of, 118
differences between accounts receivable financing and, 122–124
functions of, 119–121
method of short-term financing, 104, 119
risks assumed, 119
services offered, 120–122

Farm Improvement Loans Act of 1944 (Canada), 349

Federal Advisory Council, 231–232

Federal corporate income tax of mutual savings banks, 213–214

Federal Deposit Insurance Corporation:
Annual Report on Monopoly in Banking, 191–193
costs of deposit insurance, 151
deposits covered by, 151–152
difference between Federal Savings and Loan Insurance Corporation and, 219–220
earned surplus of, 147
establishment of, 147
interest rates on time accounts for insured non-member banks set by, 136
management of, 148
methods used to protect depositors, 149–151
national banks, 182
ownership of, 147
power over adequacy of bank's capital, 80
raised standards of banking field, 154
relation to the money supply, 152–153
savings banks, protection of, 216
termination of insurance, 148–149
total liabilities of, 147

Federal Deposit Insurance Corporation Act of 1950, 147, 150

Federal funds market:
a money market instrument, 253
brokers of, 261
buyers and sellers, 259–261
development of, 259
method used, 260
most temporary form of borrowing, 261
rates, importance of, 264
trading unit, 259

Federal Open Market Committee:
agent of, 230, 245
buying and selling government securities, 275–276
component of the Federal Reserve System, 227, 228
meetings of, 230
members of, 230
operations of, 230–231

Federal Reserve Act:
established FDIC, 147
established Federal Advisory Council, 231–232
established Federal Reserve System, 223, 225
regulation of interest paid on deposits, 137–138

Federal Reserve Bank of New York, 251, 275

Federal Reserve Banks:
bankers acceptances, 258
changes in reserve requirements, 278–279
collection system, improvement over earlier methods, 176–178
credit policies of, 267–279
discount rates, 263
earning assets of, 238–239, 276
interdistrict balances, settlement of, 175–176
liabilities of, 239–240
open-market operations of, 275–277
out-of-town collections, 174–175
par collection system, 172–174
publications of, 157

Federal Reserve Banks (*continued*)
  research and educational efforts of, 154–155
  reserves created by the, 84–85
  services of Treasury Tax and Loan Accounts to, 142
  source of bank funds, 83–85
Federal Reserve System:
  a central banking system, 222–223
  bank-holding companies, 198
  banks who are members of, 228
  Board of Governors of the, 225–228
  contributions of, 240–241
  independence of the, 223–224
  membership subscription, 229
  members must belong to the FDIC, 149
  national banks must be members, 182
  obligations of membership, 229
  privileges of membership to, 229
  state banks and, 38
  structure of the, 228
  supervisory functions of, 237–238
  Treasury bills, importance of, 262
  withdrawal of membership, 228
Federal Savings and Loan Insurance Corporation (FSLIC) and FDIC, difference between, 219–220
"Fiat" money, 15, 20
Field warehousing:
  a short-term financing method, 305
  charges for service of, 306–307
  method employed in, 305–306
  purpose of, 305
Financial intermediaries, 202–203

Financing international trade (*See* International trade finance)
First National City Bank of New York, The, credit files of, 324
Foreign credit information, sources of, 323–324
Foreign Credit Interchange Bureau, 323
Foreign exchange transactions, 338
France, early banking in, 10–15
Free Banking Act of 1838, 43
Free banking system, 36, 37
Free Banking system of New York, 43–44, 49
French Revolution, 15

G

Gallatin, 24
General Bank, 10–11
"General Depositaries," 139–140
General deposits, 292
General Motors Acceptance Corporation, 255–256
Goldsmiths of London, 8–9
Government:
  control of supply of money, a function of, 267–268
  deposits of, 139–140
  principal short-term financing device, 262
  Treasury Tax and Loan Accounts, services to, 142
Government securities dealers, 250–251
Greek banking, early, 2–3, 5
Greenbacks, 47–48
Group banking (*See* Holding-company banking)
Guaranty of deposits, 145 (*See also* Deposit protection)

H

Hamilton, Alexander, 22, 342
Holding-company banking:
  advantages of, 197–198, 199
  Bank-Holding Company Act, 198–199

Holding-company banking (*continued*)
  decentralization, 200
  definition of, 198
  growth of, 199–200
  importance of, 199
Home Loan Bank System, 220, 273
Home Owners Loan Act of 1933, 216–217

I

Imperial Bank of Canada, 344–345
Income shares, 217
Independent Bankers Association, 38, 191, 193
Independent charter system, 36, 37, 38–39
Independent Treasury System:
  effect on banking and note issue, 44–45
  failure of, 46–47
  reasons for, 45–46
Independent unit banking:
  growth of, 188–189
  independence of, 187–188
  outlook for, 189–193
  reasons for decline, 189–190
  when needing funds, 264
India Company, 11–14
Indiana Bankers Association, 218–219
Industrial Development Bank (Canada), 356
"Information and Procedure for the Organization of a Commercial Bank under New York State Banking Law," 180–181
Ingham, Samuel, 28
In-plant banking:
  advantages of, 316
  credit union vs., 315
  development of, 315
  operations of, 315–316
"Instructions of the Comptroller of the Currency Relative to the Organization and Powers of National Banks," 181–182

Insurance of deposits, importance of, 144–145 (*See also* Deposit protection)
Interdistrict Settlement Fund, 175–176
Interest rates:
  on demand deposits, regulation of and reasons for prohibition against, 137–139
  on time deposits, regulations of and justification of, 136–139
  subject to legal limitations, 102–103
International trade finance:
  advisory services, 324–325
  differences between domestic and, 321–322
  exports, financing of, 325–338
  foreign exchange guidance, 338
  publications on foreign trade regulations, 324
  special problems of, 320–321
  sources of foreign credit information, 323–324
  use of international department of bank, 322–323, 329
Inverse elasticity, 44, 49
Investment bankers, 203
Investments (*See* Bank investments)
Irrevocable credit, 333, 334–335, 336

J

Jackson, President, 27–28, 30, 38, 45

K

"Kiting" of checks, 172

L

Law, John:
  failure of "system," 12–14
  France and, 10–14
  General Bank, 10–11
  his "System," 11–12
  Scots and, 9
"Legal list" for investments of savings banks, 209
Legal Tender Act, 47

Letter of Credit (*See* Commercial Credit)
Liabilities in balance sheet of Federal Reserve Banks, 239, 240
Loanable funds, concept of, 92–93
Loans:
  classification of, 98–102
  create money, 60–62
  interest rates, protection on, 102–103
  ratio to deposits, 91–92
  relation to business cycle, 95–96
  relation to character of deposits, 93–94
  rotating, 96, 98–99
  self-liquidity vs. shiftability of, 96–97
Loans and discounts:
  covers nearly all human activities, 88
  revival of, 88–89
Loan services of banks, 87–88 (*See also* Loans)
Loans to brokers and dealers market:
  a money market instrument, 252–253
  call loans, 258–259
  decline of, 259
  rates, importance of, 264
  time loans, 259
Locofocos, 43
London Clearing House, 162–163

M

Madison, President, 24
Magnetic Ink Character Recognition (MICR):
  check, illustration, 313
  common machine language, 312
  features of MICR checks, 312–314
Magazines, banking, 158
Manager's check, 132, 297
Marshall, Chief Justice, 27
McCulloch, Hugh, 49

McFadden-Pepper Act in 1927, 184
"Mississippi Bubble," 11
Mississippi Company, 11–13
Monetary credit:
  a social product, 55–56
  meaning of, 54
Monetary policy:
  determinants of, 269–271
  qualitative and quantitative credit control, use of, 271–279
  (*See also* Money Management)
Money management:
  basic purpose, 269
  business activity determines policy of, 270–271
  changes in reserve requirements, a tool of, 278–279
  credit control mechanisms of, 275–279
  dangers faced by, 282–283
  definition of, 266–267
  discount rate change weapon of, 277–278
  employment, a policy determinant, 269–270
  factors determining policies of, 269–271
  goals of, 268–269
  government influence, 267–268
  importance of, 266
  in Canada, 354–355, 356–358
  moral suasion, 279, 355
  open-market operations of, 275–277
  price movements, consideration of, 270
  problems of, 280–282
  qualitative credit control, use of, 271–275
  quantitative credit control, techniques of, 275–279
  results achieved by, 279–280
  Treasury needs must be considered, 271
Money market:
  banks, 248–249
  concept of, 244

Money market (*continued*)
  five sub-markets of the, 252–263, 265
  interest rate structure of, 263–264
  major institutions in the, 248–252
  New York, 244, 247, 265
  reasons why in Wall Street, 244–246
  relation to the economy, 264–265
  services of, 246–248
  short-term grouping, 243, 244
Money orders, 132
Money-plus, 60
Money process, defense of our, 67–68
Money supply:
  decreases, 63–67
  loans and investments increases or decreases, 63–67
  prices determine quantity of, 62–63
  relation of the FDIC to the, 152–153
Montreal Bank, The (*See* Bank of Canada and Canadian banking)
Moral suasion, 279, 355
Morris, Robert, 21
Mortgage bankers, 203
Mutual funds, specialization of, 203
Mutual savings bank:
  definition of, 212
  growth of, 212–213
  how organized, 212
  management, importance of, 214–216
  protection of FDIC, 216
  taxation of, 213–214
  (*See also* Savings banks)

N

National Association of Credit Management, 323
National Bank Act, reasons for, 48–50

National banking system:
  reasons for organization of, 48–49
  weaknesses of, 50–51
National banks:
  growth of, 185
  members of Federal Reserve System, 182
  safeguards for organization of new, 181–182
  vs. state charter, 183–185
National Commercial Finance Conference (New York), 124
National Credit Office, 113, 255
National Housing Act of 1954 (Canada), 349, 350
Negotiable instruments, 294, 330
Negotiable Instruments Act, 298
New England banks, 39–41
New York banks:
  deposit insurance prerequisite to approval of, 181
  free banking system of, 43–44
  safeguards on establishing new, 180–181
  "safety fund" method, 42, 144
  savings banks, 215–216
  state, standards of, 184
New York Clearing House, 163, 165
New York money market, 244–246, 247, 251
Non-bank credit (*See* Open market)
North American Trust and Banking Company, 31

O

Open-account deposits, 135
Open market:
  advantages of borrowing in, 105–106
  borrowing and bank borrowing, difference between, 104
  disadvantage of borrowing in, 106–107
  methods of borrowing, 104–124, 305
  operations of money managers, 275–277

Open market (*continued*)
purpose of operations, 276–277
Open Market Committee (*See* Federal Open Market Committee)
Optional savings shares, 217
Out-of-town banks, a money market institution, 250

P

"Paper tiger," 170, 311
Par collection system, 172–174
Paying teller, 293–294
Pension funds, 202
Personal loan companies, primary object of, 203
Postal Savings System, a savings intermediary, 202
"Post notes," 34
Prepaid shares, 217
Price movements determine monetary policies, 270
"Prime rate" of large money market banks, 263
Private banks, emergence of, 3
Profits, relation of capital to, 80–81
Promissory notes:
commercial paper, 112, 254
goldsmiths notes, 8
Protection of deposits (*See* Deposit protection)
Publications of banks, 157
Pyramiding of bank reserves, a weakness of the National Banking System, 50–51

Q

Qualified endorsement, 295
Qualitative credit controls:
effectiveness of, 271–272
example of, 271
fields suited for, 272–273
need for, 273–274
opposition to, 272–273
Quantitative credit controls:
changes in reserve requirements, 278–279

Quantitative credit controls (*continued*)
discount rate change, 277–278
Federal Reserve Board administers, 275
moral suasion, 279
open market operations, 275–277
tools used, 275–279

R

Rand McNally Company, 169
Ratio of loans to deposits, 91–92
Receiving tellers, 292–293
Registered checks, 132
Regular checking accounts, 130–134, 136, 291–292
Reserves, 84, 90, 227, 278–279
Restricted endorsement, 294
Revocable credit, 333
Revolving Credit, 337
Revenue Act of 1951, 213
"Right to credit," establishment of, 58–59
Robert Morris Associates, Code for credit inquiries, 309, 310
Roman *Argentarii*, 3–4, 5
Royal Bank, 11–12

S

Safety Fund Act of 1829, 42
Safety Fund System, 41–42, 44, 144
Sales-finance companies:
all consumer durable goods financed by, 113–114
capital loans to dealers, 116–117
commercial paper market, 255–256
financing inventories of dealers, 115–116
method of short-term financing, 104
primary object of, 203
retail sales financing of, 114–115
Savings and Loan Associations:
federal tax status of, 214
growth of, 216
insured by FSLIC, 219–220

Savings and Loan Associations
(*continued*)
  liquidity of shares vs. that of
    deposits, 218
  members are shareholders, 217
  members of the Home Loan
    Bank System, 220
  original name of, 216
  primary function of, 203, 217
  savings banks compared with,
    211–212
  shares sold by, classification of,
    217
Savings banks:
  compared with commercial
    banks, 203–205
  concentration of, 207
  deposit expansion of, 204–205
  economic need for promotion
    of, 205–206
  encourage and promote thrift,
    208
  FDIC protection, 216
  higher liquidity necessary,
    210, 218
  income of, 210
  investments of, 209–210
  management, importance of,
    214–216
  mutual form of, 212–213
  nature of, 203–205
  operating expenses of, 210–
    211
  primary object of, 203
  reasons for popularity as a me-
    dium for savings, 207
  taxation of, 213–214
  types of thrift service, 208
  who saves, 209
Savings deposits:
  in commercial banks, 134–135
  other, 135–137
  regular, 135
Savings, expansion of an eco-
    nomic need, 205–206
Schools on banking, 155–156
Secondary reserves, 247, 256,
    257
Secured loans, 100–101
Securities (*See* Bank invest-
    ments)

Security loans, 99, 271
Self-liquidity vs. shiftability of
    loans, 96–97
Service charges on regular check-
    ing accounts, 132–134
Shamgalu, 118
Shares, liquidity of, for savings
    and loan associations vs.
    bank deposits, 218
Short-term borrowing (*See* Open
    market)
Short-term government securi-
    ties:
  importance of, 262–263
  largest money market instru-
    ment, 253, 262
Society of Tammany in New
    York, 30
Special checking accounts, 129,
    290–291
"Special Depositaries," 140–142
Special Deposits, 292
Special endorsement, 294
Specialization, advantages of
    open-market borrow-
    ing, 106–107
Specie, 24, 25–26, 45
Sproul, Allan, former head of the
    Federal Reserve Bank of
    New York, 278, 282
State chartered banks:
  early, 23, 26, 30–34
  Jackson's "pets," 28, 45
  safeguards for new, 180–181
  statistical difference from na-
    tional banks, 185–186
  vs. national banks, 183–185
  war with second U.S. Bank,
    27–29
State franchise tax of mutual sav-
    ings banks, 213
Stop-payment of checks, 299–
    301
Suffolk Bank, 39–41
Suffolk System:
  advantages of, 41
  basic feature of, 40
  maintained quality of note is-
    sue, 39–41
  reasons for, 39
Superintendent of Banks, 214

T

Tax and Loan Accounts (*See* Treasury Tax and Loan Accounts)

Taxes of mutual savings banks, 213–214

Temple banking, 2–3

Time deposits, 93, 135, 136–137, 138–139, 204

Time loans, 101–102

Toronto-Dominion Bank, The, 344

Trade acceptances:
impersonal type of borrowing, 104
kinds of, 111
method of short-term financing, 104, 110–112
reasons for lack of greater usage of, 111–112

Trade bills, 329, 330

Trade-draft financing of exports:
advantages of, 328
drafts employed, 329
how handled, 329
parties to the draft, 329
protection to parties, 330
use of, 330

Transferring of values, a great service to business, 161 (*See* also Clearing and collections)

Transit department, 167

Traveler's letter of credit, 337–338

Treasury bills:
importance of, 262
rates of, 263

Treasury Tax and Loan Accounts:

Treasury Tax and Loan Accounts (*continued*)
categories of, 140–141
function of, 140
services rendered, 142
uses of, 141–142

Treasury of the United States:
deposit accounts of, 139–140
needs of, an important determinant of monetary policy, 271

Trust department services of banks, 316–317

U

Unconfirmed Credit, 333, 335

Uniform Negotiable Instruments Act, 110

Unit banking (*See* Independent unit banking)

United States Savings Bonds, a savings intermediary, 202

Universal Numerical System:
basis of, 169
illustration of, 168
importance of, 168

Unsecured loans, 100–101

Usury, meaning and penalties of, 102–103

W

"Walks Clearing," 163

Wall Street:
banks, 248–249
money market center, 244–246

Warehouse receipts, 108

Wholesale banks, 248

Wholesale financing, 115–116

"Wildcat" banks, 31

Wolcott, Jesse P., 82